ROUTLEDGE LIBRARY EDITIONS:
HINDUISM

Volume 1

CHRISTIAN AND HINDU ETHICS

CHRISTIAN AND HINDU ETHICS

SHIVESH CHANDRA THAKUR

Routledge
Taylor & Francis Group
LONDON AND NEW YORK

First published in 1969 by George Allen & Unwin Ltd.

This edition first published in 2019
by Routledge
2 Park Square, Milton Park, Abingdon, Oxon OX14 4RN

and by Routledge
52 Vanderbilt Avenue, New York, NY 10017

Routledge is an imprint of the Taylor & Francis Group, an informa business

British Library Cataloguing in Publication Data
A catalogue record for this book is available from the British Library

ISBN: 978-0-367-14300-8 (Set)
ISBN: 978-0-429-05711-3 (Set) (ebk)
ISBN: 978-0-367-14361-9 (Volume 1) (hbk)
ISBN: 978-0-367-14366-4 (Volume 1) (pbk)
ISBN: 978-0-429-03154-0 (Volume 1) (ebk)

Publisher's Note
The publisher has gone to great lengths to ensure the quality of this reprint but points out that some imperfections in the original copies may be apparent.

Disclaimer
The publisher has made every effort to trace copyright holders and would welcome correspondence from those they have been unable to trace.

CHRISTIAN AND HINDU ETHICS

BY

SHIVESH CHANDRA THAKUR

London
GEORGE ALLEN AND UNWIN LTD
RUSKIN HOUSE · MUSEUM STREET

FIRST PUBLISHED IN 1969

SBN 04 170022 8

PRINTED IN GREAT BRITAIN
in 11 *on* 12 *point Old Style type*
BY UNWIN BROTHERS LIMITED
WOKING AND LONDON
2605B

FOREWORD

The Christian and Hindu religions are in closer contact today than ever before in their long histories, but this nearness leads often to curiously variant attitudes on the part of the exponents of the two faiths. It is assumed either that these religions are so utterly different from each other as to be quite incomparable and to have no common means of communication, or else on the contrary they are said to be so alike and virtually identical that each can be expounded in terms of the other.

Comparisons of the two religions have generally centred on theological and philosophical questions, and Dr Thakur says rightly that studies of their attitudes to moral problems have been fewer and essays in comparative ethics scanty. Concentration on Hindu religion and philosophy has led too easily to the assumption in the West that Hinduism is other-worldly and only concerned with escape from this world to some heaven or Nirvana. But if this were fully true it would be almost impossible to explain how this world-denying religion could have produced countless great monuments of culture, often emphasizing the sensuous, such as have abounded at many periods of Indian history. Clearly the popular religion, at least, must have been more world-affirming than the ascetic philosophies, and the underlying ethical principles are worthy of study.

Differently from some of his contemporaries, Dr Thakur admits that diversities of belief are often found between Indian and Christian traditions. The Hindu view of the nature of man, he says, is strikingly different from the Christian in many details, there is an obvious contrast in their views of evil, there is diverse stress on the role of conscience, the ethical model of a historical person is clearer in Christianity, and its acceptability to Hindus today depends on the introduction of a new theme of impassivity. Yet despite these and other differences Dr Thakur maintains that Christian and Hindu teachings on virtues and duties are strikingly similar, and the essential core of their ethics does not appear to be so very different. How far he is successful in supporting these claims readers must judge for themselves, but it is refreshing to see some old ground covered in new ways and other fields revealed that have been little cultivated in comparative studies. It is to be hoped that this work will help to bring a juster appreciation of the moral teachings of these great faiths.

GEOFFREY PARRINDER

King's College, London

ACKNOWLEDGEMENT

For assistance rendered at various stages in the writing and publication of this book the author hereby expresses his deep and sincere gratitude to: Mr A. Basu, Dr D. G. Bretherton, Professor C. K. Grant, Professor T. W. Thacker—all of Durham University; Dr E. G. Parrinder of King's College, London; Mr R. Harré and Miss Eleanor Selfridge of Linacre College, Oxford; and the Commonwealth Scholarship Commission in UK, the Secretary and members of the Spalding Trust, and George Allen and Unwin Ltd, the publishers.

S.C.T.

CONTENTS

I.	Introduction	page 13
II.	Nature of Christian and Hindu Ethics	31
III.	The Nature and Destiny of Man	75
IV.	The Moral Law, Its Authority and Sources	105
V.	The Content of the Moral Law: Virtues and Duties	131
VI.	Moral Effort and Human Freedom	157
VII.	Moral Failure and Responsibility	177
VIII.	Conclusion	197
	Bibliography	209
	Index	214

CHAPTER I

INTRODUCTION

Christianity and Hinduism are two of the world's greatest living religions, and it is of the utmost importance that they should be compared in every possible detail so that through such comparisons Christians and Hindus may understand better each other's, and their own, heritage. This would by no means be insufficient reason for undertaking studies of the sort we are intending to pursue in the following pages. But what makes such efforts especially desirable, even imperative, is the fact not only that Christians and Hindus have in the past made inadequate efforts to understand the best in each other's tradition, but that they have in fact allowed considerable misunderstanding to exist in this area of their knowledge. It is not at all difficult to find sound reasons for this unfortunate state of affairs. Misleading but catchy phrases (which have a power of their own) about 'the East' and 'the West' and the various kinds of political and social strains and conflicts have given rise to strong prejudice—that age-old enemy of man's knowledge and insight!

Owing to the circumstances of the past few centuries, the Christian 'colonial' West and (largely) Hindu India have until recently regarded each other with distrust, fear and hatred. Naturally neither of them can, on the whole, be credited with the best of motives in approaching each other's ethical, religious or spiritual heritage. Almost total ignorance, punctuated by rare individual efforts to understand each other's way of life, has by and large prevailed among Christians as well as Hindus. This may sound paradoxical in a way. For one would expect that the centuries of contact between the Christian and Hindu worlds that was brought about by the colonization of India should have made mutual understanding near perfect. But this is far from true. This contact was not the coming together of equals anxious to understand each other, but rather the unfortunate clash of two cultures, or at best the uneasy co-existence of two religious systems—one that of the victor, the other that of the vanquished. The logic of the situation itself could not have permitted more than the essential minimum of understanding that did keep life in India going.

This is not to deny the immense value of the work of those few Western scholars who had a genuine admiration for the fundamental spirituality and lofty character of the Hindu view of life. Max Müller, Sir William Jones, Schopenhauer, Deussen, and Rudolf Otto are just some of the names in this category. Some of these scholars did indeed spend lifetimes studying, interpreting and translating the Sanskrit scriptures of the Hindus, and are often justly credited with making many Indians themselves aware of their rich cultural and spiritual heritage.

But it must be admitted that these men were exceptions. The general attitude of Christians to Hinduism has been either one of hasty dismissal of it as incomprehensible or else one of benevolent indifference. It is true that the ruling Christian community in India was to an extent obliged to learn about some of the customs of the Hindus, even if for no other reason than to promote the smooth running of the administration. But such learning was generally kept confined to that of superficial but widely prevalent customs so as to avoid giving unnecessary offence to the uneducated but deeply religious masses. In other words, the minimum of tolerance of Hindu practices from purely pragmatic considerations was all that was considered necessary. Not many were particularly anxious to penetrate beneath the thick crust of superstitious practices and beliefs that had enveloped the essential ethical and spiritual substance of Hinduism during and after the Western colonization of India. Western Christianity caught India during its darkest days of decadence and was appalled by some of the shocking practices prevalent then. Only the exceptional person among the ruling Christians tried patiently to discover the inner and essential spirit of Hinduism; the rest identified it with what they saw and dismissed it as a crude, primitive and queer faith.

This, however, is only one side of the story. Hindus, for their part, have generally been no less unsympathetic to the merits of Christianity. Deprived of political power, they clung tenaciously to their faith, and, burying their heads in the sand, refused to face the winds of change and reform coming from outside sources. This resulted in the prevention or at least delay of the much needed purge in the body politic of Hinduism. The fact of political domination by the Christian West aroused in Hindu minds a deep suspicion of Christianity as an instrument of exploitation. The spectacle of the immense resources at the disposal of Christian missionaries engaged in winning more followers for the Christian way of life, though admired in other ways, aggravated the feeling of suspicion. The idea took root that the mild-mannered and soft-spoken missionary was doing in a subtle way the same job that the colonizers were doing in their more officious way: depriving the natives of everything they had, including their faith. To cut a long argument short, the conditions in which the Hindu and Christian worlds came into contact in the recent past have been far from conducive to mutual understanding and genuine appreciation of each other's point of view.

With the change in circumstances during the last three decades, and with much of the cause for mutual suspicion, distrust and apathy gone, it seems to be time to start a dialogue between these two religions. Once this is conceded, there can be hardly any question why it must be ethics and morality, rather than any other aspect of these religions, that should receive attention first. It is not only because ethical and moral issues are treated as extremely important in these systems, but also because it is in the field of morals that the atmosphere of mutual recrimination rather than appreciation seems to be most marked. It is the failure to read periodic moral aberrations as nothing more than aberrations that is primarily responsible for the distorted perspectives of Hindus and Christians regarding the proper worth of each other's faith. If some Christians, for example, maliciously refer to the abhorrent rite of 'Sattee' practised in some parts of Hindu society in its days of decadence and to the practice of untouchability, some Hindus in their turn never fail to remind the Christians of the witch-hunt rampant in the Christian world during the sixteenth and seventeenth centuries and the Crusades which involved so much bloodshed and cruelty. Both parties in this mutual recrimination, however, are guilty of trying to estimate the worth of a religion by exaggerating the importance of the few moments of insanity that have occurred in the course of their long histories.

Since a balanced and objective perspective has been lacking, reactions to the factual content of each other's religion or morals have seldom been free from prejudice. These reactions have either been those of total derision or of unmixed admiration, depending on whether the prejudice has been for or against. To substantiate what we have just said, let us take two examples of the estimation by Christian writers of Hindu ethics or aspects of Hindu ethics. The examples both relate to the ethical implications of the absolute monism enunciated in some of the Upaniṣads and forcefully championed in later days by thinkers like Shamkara. While Deussen finds in this philosophy a complete explanation of the ethics of love, Mackenzie finds no room for ethics at all in this system. The words of Deussen are:

> 'Thou shalt love thy neighbour as thyself' is the requirement of the Bible. But on what grounds is this demand to be based, since feeling is in myself alone and not in another? 'Because,' the Veda here adds in explanation, 'thy neighbour is in truth thy very self, and what separates you from him is mere illusion. . . .'[1]

But commenting on this very system, Mackenzie comes to this conclusion: 'Let the case be stated bluntly. Those ideas which bulk so largely in the Vedanta, and which find expression in other systems of philosophy, when logically applied, leave no room for ethics.'[2] How is one to reconcile these two equally extreme views on the same system? Numerous such illustrations of extreme reactions to Hinduism and Hindu ethical ideas could be quoted. But we shall let these two examples suffice to vindicate our point.

Understandably, there are few works by Hindus on Christianity or Christian ethics. But the pattern of argument or reaction does not seem to be much different from that of

[1] Paul Deussen, *The Philosophy of the Upanishads*, authorized English translation by the Rev. A. S. Geden, T. and T. Clark, Edinburgh, 1906, p. 49.

[2] John Mackenzie, *Hindu Ethics*, Humphrey Milford, Oxford University Press, 1922, pp. 206 *f*.

Christian writers on Hindu ethics. There have been those Hindus who have had a genuine admiration for some of the Christian moral and religious ideas. Foremost among these comes the name of Raja Ram Mohan Roy, who was definitely influenced by Christianity and who founded the Brahmo Samaj with an explicit statement of his indebtedness to Christian scriptures. His deeply pro-Christian sentiments find expression in passages like this one, for example:

'The consequence of long and uninterrupted researches into religious truth has been that I have found the doctrines of Christ more conducive to moral principles and more adapted to the use of rational beings than any others which have come to my knowledge.'[1]

Gandhi more than once acknowledged his admiration of the person of Christ and of Christ's ethics of non-violence and forgiveness as enunciated in his Sermon on the Mount. But these men, again, are exceptions. The large majority of Hindus have either been completely indifferent, or have dismissed Christianity too lightly.

The most helpful thing that can be done under the circumstances seems to be to present comparative accounts of the main ethical ideas of the two systems. Hindus and Christians, who more often than not have a fairly good notion of the ethical ideas in their own tradition, will thus find it easier to understand the other's point of view by placing it against their own. No systematic or detailed comparative study of Hindu and Christian ethics seems to have been attempted. Many writers on Hinduism, Christianity and Comparative Religion have made casual remarks drawing parallels between some feature or other of one of these ethical systems and some corresponding features of the other. But such comparisons usually do not prove very enlightening, for they abstract these features from their total context, and thereby quite often distort the significance of these features themselves. A proper appreciation of the basic facts of the two ethical systems can only be had from a more detailed and systematic comparison of the two.

[1] Quoted by William Paton in *Jesus Christ and the World's Religions*, The Cargate Press, London, 1928, p. 49.

One reason for undertaking this comparative study of the ethics rather than of any other aspect of Hinduism and Christianity is, as we suggested earlier, that it is in the field of ethics that the misunderstanding has been most acute. But this is certainly not the only reason. It seems that if there is any field in which these two religions do have a common ground, it is undoubtedly that of ethics. In matters of metaphysical and theological beliefs, in forms of worship and prayer, the two are vastly different, but when it comes to the ethical implications of these metaphysical beliefs the gap becomes considerably narrower. Though the systems start from different premises, the pictures of the good life that emerge are by and large similar. The most important reason, however, is the intimate relation between ethics and religion itself. But since there are differences of opinion among philosophers as to the precise relationship between ethics and religion, it may be desirable to make some remarks on this issue in order to make our own stand clear.

ETHICS AND RELIGION

The problem of the relationship between ethics and religion, or between morals and religion, has occupied for some time an important place in the discourses of philosophers. Though the problem is on the whole quite complicated and has many aspects, the main question is: Does morality have an essential dependence on one or the other form of religious belief—not merely as a contingent fact of history but logically? On this question, as on many others, philosophers, as usual, are divided. The controversy has gone on for quite some time, and shows no signs of being settled one way or the other.

Whatever the logical position regarding the relationship of ethics and religion in general, the intimate relationship between these two, as contingent facts of history, has never been, and can never be, denied. It may be possible to lay down a system of ethics without any reference to religion or religious belief, but the converse would hardly be tenable. A religion worth the name must incorporate some system of morality for the guidance of its followers. This is an inescapable fact. Professor Lewis states the correct position in this respect in these words:

'Although ethical truths require no direct support from religion, except in so far as we have some specifically religious duties like acts of worship in mind, there can be no adequate presentation of religious principles that does not make a very fundamental use of ethical objectivity.'[1]

This then appears to be the minimum of common ground among the various sides in this controversy. There may be a morality without religion, but there has not been a religion without morality. This becomes all too clear when we examine the contents of the great living religions like Hinduism and Christianity which surely have made a 'very fundamental use of ethical objectivity'. Professor Hare, in his article 'Religion and Morals', quotes a passage from St James to show how intimately morality has been linked with historical Christianity:

'If any man thinketh himself to be religious, while he bridleth not his tongue but deceiveth his heart, this man's religion is vain. Pure religion and undefiled before our God and Father is this, to visit the fatherless and widows in their affliction, and to keep himself unspotted from the world.'[2]

This passage makes it clear that one cannot be said to accept Christianity, unless, as Professor Hare says, 'one accepts and at least tries to act on its moral precepts'. The Upaniṣads anticipate St James when they proclaim: 'No one who has not ceased from immoral conduct, who is restless, who is not self-determined, whose mind is not tranquil, can realize this Self.'[3]

Morality, then, is an indispensable part of these religions, and is presupposed by and incorporated into the latter. Thus irrespective of the purely logical position regarding the relationship of ethics to religion, in historical Hinduism and Christianity, as in other important historical religions, the two are inextricably intertwined. Starting off from this premise, it is easy to see why it is not only meaningful but extremely important to study the ethics of the two religions in order to get an insight into the true significance of the religions themselves.

[1] H. D. Lewis, *Morals and the New Theology*, Victor Gollancz, London, 1947 p. 26.

[2] R. M. Hare, *Faith and Logic*, ed. Basil Mitchell, George Allen and Unwin, London, 1958, p. 180.

[3] Kaṭha Upaniṣad, I, 2, 24.

But we have not yet asked ourselves the most important question: what is meant by 'Christian ethics', 'Hindu ethics', or 'ethics' itself? Let us define our basic terms—'Christian', 'Hindu' and 'ethics'. We shall start with the last first.

THE MEANINGS OF 'ETHICS', 'CHRISTIAN' AND 'HINDU'

Anyone who has read a textbook on ethics would be familiar with the observation, invariably made in such books, that the terms 'ethics' and 'morality' are derived from words meaning 'custom' or 'behaviour'. How they came to mean what they do is rather interesting. The word 'ethics' is derived from the Greek root 'ethos' which originally meant 'dwelling' or 'stall'.[1] The Latin translation given to this word was 'mos', from which the word 'morality' is derived. Paul Lehman records that this term was 'first applied not to human beings but to animals'. He elaborates:

'It was obvious to men that animals needed to be put somewhere for shelter and protection. Thus the germinal idea in the word *τὸ ἦθος* is the stability and security provided by a "stall" or "dwelling" for animals. The verb root *εἴωθα* means "to be accustomed to" or "to be wont to". Hence the relationship between stability and custom was a kind of elemental datum of experience. It was really the primary office of custom to do in the human area what the stall did for animals: to provide security and stability.'[2]

Thus 'custom' or 'behaviour' was the original meaning of 'ethics', as well as that of 'morality'. But in the subsequent development of philosophy a distinction came to be made between 'ethics' and 'morality'. Morality, thus, generally refers to a set of beliefs about what one ought to do, how one should behave, whereas ethics or 'moral philosophy' to the rational or philosophical foundations of such principles. As William Frankena puts it, 'Ethics is a branch of philosophy; it is moral

[1] Paul Lehman, *Ethics in a Christian Context*, SCM Press, London, 1963, p. 23.
[2] Ibid., p. 24.

philosophy or philosophical thinking about morality, moral problems and moral judgements'.[1]

It is interesting to note, by way of anticipation, that *Dharma*, the comprehensive Hindu term for morality and ethics, as well as for much else, comes from the root *Dhṛ*, which means 'to hold together'. Thus the function of *Dharma* is to hold human society together, to give it stability, exactly what was conceived to be the function of 'ethics'. Right conduct then is essential if human society is to survive. Such conduct, however, may spring either from obedience to authority or convention or from reflection on the principles and truths underlying such convention; and *Dharma* comprises all these sources.

It may be useful to bear this not-too-sharp a distinction between 'morality' and 'ethics' in mind, for what we intend to do in the following pages is neither to prescribe a new set of moral principles nor, primarily, to criticize the moral beliefs and practices of either Christians or Hindus, but only to study the philosophical or theological foundations of their moral beliefs and practices. In other words, we shall be interested in comparing the 'philosophical thinking' of Christians and Hindus about morality, moral problems and the issues underlying moral judgements. By this we not only mean the specific views expressed by Hindus and Christians on such issues as were recognized to be ethical issues, but also those that logically follow from other kinds of opinions expressed by them which bear on ethical issues. This has to be so because many of the problems which we, modern students of ethics, regard as problems were not treated as such in traditional Hindu or Christian ethics.

It may now be desirable to consider in a few words the slight extension of scope that 'ethics' inevitably acquires in a theological or religious context. Professor Nowell-Smith rightly considers most of traditional ethics and almost all religious ethics as 'teleological'. He says:

'. . . The notion of doing one's duty for duty's sake hardly appears before Kant. Earlier philosophers thought it quite sensible to ask "Why should I do my duty?"; the obligation to do one's duty needs justifying and can only be justified by

[1] William K. Frankena, *Ethics*, Prentice Hall, Inc., New Jersey, 1963, p. 3.

showing that doing his duty is, in the short or long run, advantageous to the agent; indeed the classic treatises on the subject might be said to be mainly concerned with this justification.'[1]

On the whole, this point of view can hardly be challenged. Especially in the context of religious ethics, the teleological character of all ethical enquiry is very obvious. For example, the relevant question for Christian ethics, as given in the words of the Gospel is 'What shall I do to inherit eternal life?'[2] 'Eternal life', then, is the goal, and ethics or moral behaviour is only an aid or instrument for achieving this goal. Duty, thus, has always a supra-ethical reference which makes the former meaningful.

But it may not be out of place to state here that there is a sense in which much of Hindu ethics may be regarded as relatively 'deontological' rather than teleological. Of the four desirable ends—*Artha* (wealth), *Kāma* (pleasure), *Dharma* (righteousness or holiness) and *Mokṣa* (liberation)—the ultimately or really desirable are considered to be the last two—*Dharma* and *Mokṣa*. But it is realized that *Mokṣa*, the highest ideal, may not necessarily be everyone's ideal. Indeed it is thought that most people will not have reached the stage of evolution or spiritual enlightenment when the earnest desire to be liberated becomes the abiding passion. But *Mokṣa* or no *Mokṣa*, *Dharma* has to be performed. No one has a real option in respect of the latter. Hence for many, *Dharma*, and all that it stands for, is its own justification, whereas for the few who seek liberation or *Mokṣa*, the former is a means to this higher goal. Therefore, in so far as *Dharma* (duty in the most comprehensive sense) can be an end in itself, the Hindu view of ethics may in a sense be regarded as deontological. But this, however, does not alter the main position that religious ethics is, on the whole, teleological. For even in the Hindu view, the fact remains that the ultimate ideal is *Mokṣa*. The recognition that as a matter of fact most people will not seek it does not change the position that ideally this is what everyone ought to seek. And if so, then *Dharma* itself must derive part of its content or at least orientation from this higher goal of *Mokṣa*.

[1] P. H. Nowell-Smith, *Ethics*, Basil Blackwell, Oxford, 1957, p. 13.
[2] Ibid., p. 13.

Now it is this reference to and presupposition of a higher religious goal which extends the scope of the term 'ethics' in the context of religion. If the Ultimate Good is a non-ethical or religious goal, then whatever promotes approximation to this goal may, in a sense, be regarded as falling within the sphere of the ethical. If the highest goal is *Mokṣa* or 'eternal life', then all activity that is recommended by competent authority as leading to this goal may form part of the ethical ideal of the seeker. Thus acts of worship and prayer, for example, may be discussed under 'ethics' in a religious context, but will not form part of 'philosophical' ethics. In this extended sense of the term, it would be seen, it may be difficult not to include under ethics, for example, the systematic exposition of the various exercises for self-control that the Yoga system recommends as leading to self-purification (*Citta-Śuddhi*) and thereby to *Mokṣa*. This example is merely to emphasize the slightly wider sense that 'ethics' may be given in the religious or theological context.

To make our point clearer, let us approach this issue from another angle. Though we have accepted Professor Nowell-Smith's main contention that 'doing one's duty for duty's sake' hardly appears before Kant, it is doubtful if he is entirely right in saying that 'the notion of duty does not play the central role in traditional that it plays in modern ethics'.[1] A more accurate statement would perhaps be that though duty does play the central role, it is not 'duty for duty's sake'. This is at least true of the major religions. The emphasis on duty in Hindu, Christian and Buddhist ethics is unmistakable, though it is justified, by and large, on the ground that it is God's (in the case of Buddhism, the Buddha's) command. What is in fact distinctive about the concept of duty in religious ethics as against that in philosophical ethics is the inevitable addition of a separate category of duty—duty to God (or whatever takes the place of God). Philosophical ethics recognizes duty under only two heads—duty to society and duty to oneself. But this is just not enough for a system of religious ethics. Duty to God in the form of prayer and worship is always either specifically mentioned or covertly implied. If God is the final point of reference, then not only should ethics include worship and prayer, but it should also take account of specific attitudes to

[1] P. H. Nowell-Smith, *Ethics*, Basil Blackwell, Oxford, 1957, p. 13.

and interpretations of Godhead in a way that is generally out of question in philosophical ethics. Similarly, if ethics, or moral behaviour is only a means to the attainment of a higher spiritual end, then one or the other view of this higher end is likely to make all the difference to the orientation of the ethics, even though the higher end itself may not be a strictly 'ethical' goal. These considerations make the use of 'ethics' in a wide sense in the religious context almost imperative, for the 'spiritual' overplus of meaning that ethical terms acquire in a religious context cannot be accounted for if we use 'ethics' in its more limited sense.

It was considered important to draw attention to this wide sense of 'ethics' because more often than not it would be found necessary to use this term in its wider connotation in the course of our discussion of Christian and Hindu ethics. The necessity for introducing this distinction will be gradually driven home as we proceed with our enquiry. But just to give an example here, when we speak later of, say, the *ethics* of Ramanuja or of Shamkara in connexion with our analysis of Hindu ethics, the use of the term can only be justified in this wider sense. This is so because in the Hindu tradition *Dharma* and its implications are generally accepted by all, whatever their metaphysical views may be. Thus traditional *Dharma*, or the principles underlying the morals of men, will remain the same whether he is a follower of the non-dualism (*Advaita*) of Shamkara or of the qualified non-dualism (*Viśiṣta Advaita*) of Ramanuja. But since the conceptions of the ultimate reality and of the final goal (*Mokṣa*) are very different in these two thinkers, the orientation and emphases of the ethical thinking or, to be more precise, of their metaphysical thinking bearing on ethics, are bound to be different. Thus in the narrow sense of 'ethics', there is no ethics to be found specifically in their systems apart from their acceptance of *Dharma* and its implications. But in the wider sense there certainly is, for their conceptions of Godhead and human destiny are so different.

With this explanation of the meaning and scope of ethics, we now pass on to the meanings of the terms 'Christian' and 'Hindu'. Defining Christian ethics, Paul Lehman says:

'Christian ethics, as a theological discipline, is the reflection upon the question, and its answer: What am I, as a believer in Jesus Christ and as a member of his church, to do?'[1]

It is obvious, then, that 'Christian' according to him means 'a believer in Jesus Christ and his church'. This is a definition which, for practical purposes, sums up the meaning of the term, though it may not be considered an entirely adequate definition. For believing in Jesus Christ in just any form will certainly not do. Islam believes that Jesus was a prophet of God, but not that he *was* God. Or, say, a Hindu may extend his conception of incarnation, and believe that Jesus Christ was one of the various incarnations of God. But neither the Muslim nor the Hindu who believes as stated will qualify for being a Christian. It is important to believe not only that Christ was God but also that he was the one and only incarnation of God and much else besides.

The Nicene Creed, which has been described by Dr J. N. D. Kelly as 'one of the few threads by which the tattered fragments of the divided robe of Christendom are held together',[2] lays down what is involved in being a Christian. Let us quote from the Creed to outline some of the main points in the definition of a Christian:

I believe in *one God* the Father Almighty, Maker of heaven and earth, And of all things visible and invisible:

And in *one Lord Jesus Christ, the only begotten son of God*. . . . Begotten, *not made, Being of one substance* with the Father . . . who for us men and *for our salvation* came down from heaven, And was incarnate by the Holy Ghost of the Virgin Mary, And *was made man*, And *was crucified*. . . . He *suffered* and was buried, And the third day He *rose* again . . . And *ascended* into heaven . . . And he shall *come again* with glory *to judge* both the quick and the dead: whose *Kingdom* shall have no end.

And I believe in the *Holy Ghost*. . . . Who proceedeth from the Father and the Son . . . And I believe *one Catholick and Apostolic* Church. I acknowledge *one Baptism* for the remission

[1] Lehman, *op. cit.*, p. 25.

[2] J. N. D. Kelly, *Early Christian Creeds*, quoted by John Burnaby in his preface to *The Belief of Christendom* (A Commentary on the Nicene Creed), National Society and S.P.C.K., London, 1960.

of sins. And I look for the *Resurrection of the dead*, And the *Life of the world to come. . . .*[1]

We have here a statement of some of the basic tenets of belief that one must share in order to be called a 'Christian'.

Much as we might like to do so, it is not possible to explain here in greater detail what we have outlined as the important elements of a Christian's belief. We may note in passing that the emphasis on *one* is unmistakable at this stage of the development of Christian thought. The differences of interpretation and emphasis that resulted from the Christians' attempts to analyse what believing in Christ and His church involves have gradually given rise to a variety of churches and a diversity of creeds. But, unfortunate as it may be, we shall find that on the whole we shall have to leave out the differences and concentrate on the common ground, except in our second chapter, where the specific aim is to throw the spotlight on the variety of emphases and interpretations in Christian as well as Hindu ethics.

When we come to analyse what 'Hindu' means, the realization is forced on us that we are dealing with a very complex and difficult problem. Hinduism covers such a wide ground and means so many different things to different men that it is extremely difficult to come forward with a short and precise definition of the term. Dr Radhakrishnan's remarks in the opening sentences of his *Hindu View of Life* are indicative of the kind of difficulty that one has to face in defining Hinduism. 'To many,' he says, 'it seems to be a name without any content. Is it a museum of beliefs, a medley of rites, or a mere map, a geographical expression?'[2] It is perhaps generally known by now that 'Hindu' originally meant a geographical area, that which lay around and was contiguous with the river Sindhu in the northwest of India. This in due course came to denote the whole of India. Therefore, the term 'Hindu' signified all the various beliefs and practices that prevailed in this vast and variegated stretch of land. No wonder the term signifies so many things.

[1] The Nicene Creed, reproduced by John Burnaby, *op. cit.*, under the heading 'The Nicene Creed'. (Emphases mine.)

[2] Dr S. Radhakrishnan, *The Hindu View of Life*, George Allen and Unwin, London, 1963, p. 1.

But let us not despair. This variety of beliefs and practices is not the whole truth about Hinduism. There is much unity underlying this diversity. There are some fundamental beliefs which must be accepted by every Hindu. It is true that beyond the acceptance of these fundamentals the Hindu is in all other respects free; but there can be no compromise regarding these fundamentals themselves. And, what is more important, a Hindu is a Hindu by virtue of his belief in these. Without more ado, therefore, it will be desirable to state some of these underlying beliefs with a view to fixing the connotation of the term 'Hindu'. These are:

(1) Belief in the authority of the Vedas and other sacred writings of the ancient sages;
(2) Belief in the immortality of the soul and in future life;
(3) Belief in the existence of a Supreme God;[1]
(4) Acceptance of the theory of *Karma* and rebirth;
(5) The worship of ancestors;
(6) Acceptance of the social organization represented by the four main castes;
(7) Acceptance of the theory of the four main stages of life; and
(8) Acceptance of the theory of the four *Puruṣārthas* or Ends.

It may be possible to add more to this list; but the beliefs mentioned here are generally regarded as the most fundamental. We are now, therefore, in a position to answer the question, 'Who is a Hindu?' A Hindu is anyone who, irrespective of anything else he believes, accepts the above tenets and acts in conformity with these.

With the definitions of 'ethics', 'Christian' and 'Hindu', it is not difficult now to find out what 'Hindu ethics' or 'Christian ethics' can mean. Hindu ethics is the system of philosophical thought on moral problems which guides the community of

[1] It is true that the Mīmāṃsā and Sāṃkhya systems do not believe in a God, but the former venerates the Vedas almost as divinity itself, and the atheism of the latter is countered by the theism of the allied Yoga system. Moreover, there is hardly any practising Hindu today who does not believe in God in some form. It is therefore appropriate to incorporate belief in one God as a tenet of Hinduism.

Hindus knit together by the fundamental beliefs underlined above. Similarly, Christian ethics is the record of the philosophical thinking of Christians on moral problems.

THE PLAN OF THE WORK

It may be helpful to say a few words here about the plan we intend to follow in the rest of the book. What we shall do is to select some fundamental questions that are generally discussed in philosophical ethics and then find out what answers to these can be given by Christianity and Hinduism, and finally to compare and contrast these answers. Everyone may not agree with our selection of the most fundamental problems but it can be hoped that the problems selected will at least be considered important.

We shall start with the 'Nature of Christian and Hindu Ethics' in order to show that neither of the two is a uniform or homogeneous system representing a single line of ethical thinking. In the next chapter we shall discuss 'The Nature and Destiny of Man'. What view a religious system of ethics takes of human destiny is, we have seen, extremely important, for it is this view that largely shapes its views on other issues. The remaining chapters in the main body will be familiar topics discussed in religious and philosophical ethics. 'The Moral Law, Its Authority and Sources' (Chapter IV), 'The Content of the Moral Law: Virtues and Duties' (Chapter V), 'Moral Effort and Human Freedom' (Chapter VI), and 'Moral Failure and Responsibility' (Chapter VII) follow in the order indicated. Of these various topics, only 'Virtues and Duties' would appear to be one which is seldom discussed in philosophical ethics; but it will be included in view of its importance in religious and theological discourses. Freedom and Responsibility are generally discussed together in treatises on ethics, but in view of the many serious problems involved, and also owing to the fact that responsibility presupposes much more besides freedom, it will be convenient to discuss these two issues and their implications separately. The last chapter, of course, will sum up our arguments in the previous chapters, besides throwing light on matters not specifically discussed earlier.

Sources

Since the primary purpose of this work is neither Biblical interpretation nor the interpretation of the Hindu scriptures, we shall generally leave the interpretation of the main scriptures to acknowledged authorities in the field, except in cases where the available interpretations appear to be insufficient or unsatisfactory. In other words, we shall be relying mainly on secondary sources, that is, on works by other scholars of Hindu and Christian thought which relate to the subjects under our examination. References, however, to the Vedas, the Upaniṣads, the Mahābhārata and the Gītā amongst Hindu scriptures and to the Bible and the Nicene Creed and commentaries on them, amongst Christian scriptures, will frequently be made. As will be realized gradually, wherever there are differences of opinion among Hindu thinkers and scriptures with regard to specific issues, the position outlined in the Gītā will be adopted in preference to any others, unless there is sufficient reason to treat some other source as more authoritative. This will appear to be in keeping with the unique and most influential position that the Gītā enjoys among Hindu scriptures. Similarly, on the Christian side, the direct and unambiguous implications of Biblical passages will in general be preferred to church opinion. Moreover, since this work is an essay in comparative philosophy rather than theology, wherever independent and authoritative philosophical opinion will be available either in Hindu or Christian ethics, it will generally be adopted in preference to traditional theological opinion.

A Presupposition

To avoid getting involved in the considerable task of explaining elementary terms in either Hindu or Christian ethics, which would only complicate and delay coming to grips with the main issues, a general familiarity with the basic Christian and Hindu world-views will be presupposed. The immensity of the scope of the subject leaves no option in this respect. The more important and complex terms and theories, however, will be briefly explained wherever necessary.

An Apology

Since the aim of the work is to treat Hindu as well as Christian ethics as unique systems rather than as mere collections of creeds, it will naturally not be possible to pay much attention to denominational differences on most issues. The claim implicit in this approach is that there is a body of belief and practice which can generally be identified as 'Christian' or 'Hindu', without necessarily referring to this or that 'brand' of Christianity or Hinduism.

CHAPTER II

NATURE OF CHRISTIAN AND HINDU ETHICS

As a necessary prelude to our comparative study of Christian and Hindu ethics, it will be worthwhile to stress one very significant fact—the catholicity and heterogeneity of these two systems of ethics. Of Hindu ethics this observation will perhaps be readily accepted even by orthodox Hindus. But when asserted of Christian ethics it may initially appear to be of questionable validity, for Christian ethics is commonly assumed to be a homogeneous system, often described simply as 'the ethic of love', for instance. Such simple descriptions of Hinduism or Hindu ethics are rare. J. N. Sarkar states that Hinduism is 'that all-embracing but undefinable system of toleration or synthesis which shelters within its capacious bosom every form of belief and practice that will agree with its few general conventions'.[1] With reference to Christianity, however, if we remember the emphasis on *one* in our extract from the Nicene Creed, it may appear that a system of ethics based on this unity of belief can never admit of any diversity. 'Every form of belief and practice' certainly cannot be predicated of Christianity.

But whatever the appearances, the truth is that Hindu ethics is not all chaos and Christian ethics not entirely a picture of simplicity. The various forms of belief and practice within Hinduism have much more in common than its 'few general conventions'; and 'church history is littered with various interpretations of that holiness' which emerges from the life and teaching of the 'One Lord Jesus Christ'.[2] Sir Charles Eliot appears to understand better the true spirit behind the outward

[1] J. N. Sarkar, *India through the Ages*, p. 17, quoted by Sir P. S. Sivaswamy Aiyer in *Evolution of Hindu Moral Ideals*, Calcutta University Press, 1935, p. 2.
[2] J. E. Fison, *The Faith of the Bible*, Pelican Books, London, 1957, pp. 115 *ff*.

diversity of Hindu faith and morals as well as the so-called unity claimed on behalf of Christianity. Speaking of the variety in the beliefs and practices of Hindus, he writes, '. . . nothing is more surprising than the variety of its phases except the underlying unity'.[1] He continues:

'This power of varying in sympathetic response to the needs of many minds and growing in harmony with the outlook of successive ages, is a contrast to the pretended *quod semper, quod ubique, quod ab omnibus* of the Western Churches, for in view of their differences and mutual hostility it can only be called a pretence.'[2]

This is not intended to be either a reflection on the differences within the Christian church or a denial of the unifying power of the person of Jesus Christ, but simply a vindication of the truth that, for very understandable reasons, Christian faith and morals, like their counterparts in Hinduism, display an amazing variety and 'catholic comprehensiveness'.[3] The true character of Christian ethics would perhaps be suggested better if we were to say of Christianity what St Paul said of himself, that it was 'made all things to all men, that [it] might by all means save some'.[4]

To substantiate what we have been arguing so far it will be necessary to trace the background, composition and development first of Christian and then of Hindu ethics. We shall analyse some of the various elements in and influences on the ethical thinking of Christians and Hindus through the ages with a view to finding out what resemblance (or otherwise) there is between the general characters of the two ethics. Because of limitations of space this analysis obviously cannot be exhaustive and we shall have to be content with stressing what we consider to be the most significant features.

[1] Sir Charles Eliot, *Hinduism and Buddhism*, Routledge and Kegan Paul, London, 1954, I, p. xcvii.

[2] Ibid., p. xcvii.

[3] Fison, *op. cit.*, p. 115.

[4] 1 Corinthians 9:22. *The Holy Bible*, Two-Version Edition, Oxford University Press, London and New York, 1899.

SOURCES AND DEVELOPMENT OF CHRISTIAN ETHICS

In the words of Bishop Henson,

'Christian morality as we know it today is the result of a long process of development, in the course of which many contributions of varying origin, potency and ethical quality have been assimilated.'[1]

This position is fundamentally sound; but it ought to be added that the 'assimilation' has in some cases been far from complete. It has to be remembered that even such potent and powerful forces as Christian or Hindu ethics cannot really assimilate everything. In response to the demands of changing times they have often had to make room for ideas and ideals which did not always agree with the basic postulates of the systems. And to allow some belief or practice to co-exist is hardly what is meant by 'assimilation'. But we shall have occasion to come to this point later. For the time being let us proceed with our analysis of the various factors in the development of Christian ethics.

To quote a passage from Henson again,

'The range and character of original Christian morality were mainly determined by three factors—the tradition of Judaism, the teaching of Jesus, and the influence of Graeco-Roman society. From the first, Christianity received the conception of a moral law expressing the will of a Righteous God, and, in its essential contents, declared in the Decalogue. From the second, Christianity derived freedom from national limitations, a new and larger understanding of moral obligation, and, above all, a supreme embodiment of personal morality in its Founder. From the third, Christianity, by an inevitable reaction from its social environment, learned to emphasize the necessity of ascetic discipline, to assert the final authority of the private conscience, and to magnify the function and claim of the Christian fellowship.'[2]

Quoting this rather long passage from Henson need not oblige

[1] H. H. Henson, *Christian Morality*, Gifford Lectures, 1935–6, Clarendon Press, Oxford, 1936, p. 65.

[2] *Ibid.*, p. 137.

us to follow all the details in his analysis nor to agree with everything he has to say. But it may be desirable to adopt in our own analysis the general pattern suggested by him.

(a) The Judaic inheritance

Of all the sources which have shaped the nature of Christian ethics, the profoundest and most important has come from the parent system of Judaism. Jesus, the founder of Christianity, was himself a Jew and strove all his life to practise essential Jewish morality at its best, albeit in the light of his own insight into the system. 'I am not come to destroy, but to fulfill'[1] is a clear statement of the indebtedness of Jesus to the Jewish faith and its morals. He regarded himself merely as a reformer and restorer of the true perspective. It is obvious, therefore, that original Christian ethics must above all be considered a continuation of the finer side of Jewish ethics, a superstructure raised on the foundation supplied by the latter. Now, of what exactly did this foundation consist?

In the very first place, it must be recorded that Judaism had already come to accept a monotheistic faith and unquestioning belief in one supreme God who was not only kind and merciful but also 'terrible'.

'For the Lord your God is God of gods and Lord of lords, a great God, a mighty, and a terrible, which regardeth not persons, nor taketh reward.'[2]

Such was the Jewish conception of God. And naturally it evoked and inspired an ethical attitude essentially oriented toward love of God—love in gratitude for all 'these great and terrible things'[3] that God had done for the people of Israel. For 'Only the Lord had a delight in thy fathers to love them, and he chose their seed after them, even you above all people, as it is this day'.[4] And if this great and terrible God had bestowed this distinction of choice on the people of Israel, how could they turn ungrateful and not do what God required of them? Hence the Old Testament is unequivocal in declaring what these people were to do:

[1] Matthew 5: 17.
[2] Deuteronomy 10: 17.
[3] Deuteronomy 10: 21.
[4] Deuteronomy 10: 15.

'And now, Israel, what doth the Lord thy God require of thee, but to fear the Lord thy God, to walk in all his ways, and to love him, and to serve the Lord thy God with all thy heart and with all thy soul,

To keep the commandments of the Lord, and his statutes, which I command thee this day for thy good?'[1]

From the foregoing account of the then Jewish morality it would appear that it was an essentially simple and unsophisticated system. There was a single all-powerful and mighty God who was benevolent but at the same time terrible. This God had somehow come to take a fancy to the people of Israel and had done tremendous things for their salvation. Nothing could be more natural than to expect the people of Israel to obey the laws and commandments of this God as revealed to them through their Scriptures. God had promised salvation for the Jews, and the least that the Jews could do for their God would be to be grateful to Him for all this. God had wrought miracles for these people and promised to do much more only if these people were to tread in God's ways, to obey his commandments and to respect his law. This was, therefore, essentially an *ethic of gratitude for deliverance*,[2] even though this was reinforced by an appeal to the terrible nature of God, who had to be feared as well.

We must not forget, however, that this was the post-exilic, Mosaic interpretation of Jewish morality and was different from the spirit of the elaborate sacrificial system with its centre at Jerusalem and its essence in ritualism. This new insistence on allegiance to Divine law rather than to the national monarch was inspiring indeed, but none the less it was a change in perspective which was liable to give rise to conflict as, perhaps, in time it did. There was, on the one hand, the clearest possible recognition that

'The Creator was also the Author of the Moral Law, and, so the prophets had taught, had His witness in the human conscience.

[1] Deuteronomy 10: 12, 13.

[2] I am indebted to Dr W. A. Whitehouse (formerly of Durham University, Theology Department) for kindly discussing this topic with me.

The true knowledge of God drew with it a right understanding of His Will, obedience to which was the essence of morality.'[1]

But on the other hand, this appeal to conscience created perplexities for the feeble-minded, as it always does for the vast majority of human beings. This abstract conception of a moral law expressing the will of a righteous God and inscribed in the consciences of men might have been all right for the sage; but the ordinary man wanted something more tangible and concrete as a guide to his morals. The answer to these people was that this Law, apart from being written in the consciences of men, had also 'in its essential contents been declared in the Decalogue'.[2] This opened the door to the authoritarianism and literalism in Jewish ethics. If Divine Law was laid down in the scriptures, then obviously someone who claimed to know this law through his study of the scriptures was going to become an indispensable element in the moral guidance and instruction of the Jewish people. In time, therefore,

'Effective guidance had passed from the central sacrificial system at Jerusalem to the recently established organization of the Scribes, that is, to those who were the students of the Law, and who expounded it in the synagogues every Sabbath.'[3]

This was both a step forward and a step back—forward because of its orientation towards the understanding of morality in place of mere rituals and sacrifice, and backward because of its having in the long run the same demoralizing, authoritarian and dogmatic implications for essential morality as the sacrificial system with its priests and high priests had had.

As a result of the inevitable conflict between the ancient canonical writings and the faith and sensibility of the comparatively modern Jew, there had evolved a casuistry which in a way sought to make a compromise between the two, and was naturally more elastic and practical; being largely unwritten, it was known as the 'Unwritten Torah'.[4] And this casuistry aspired to be a complete guide in practice, a kind of manual of behaviour. It must be added that this urge to provide a detailed

[1] Henson, *op. cit.*, p. 66.
[2] *Ibid.*, p. 137.
[3] *Ibid.*, p. 69.
[4] *Ibid.*, p. 70.

and voluminous casuistry might in part have come from the example of Moses himself. For Moses does not rest content with his general exposition of the ethic of obedience to God in gratitude for deliverance, but was said to elaborate in great detail what this ethic implies according to him. As a result, the book of Deuteronomy does not contain only passages like '. . . thou shalt love the Lord thy God with all thine heart, and with all thy soul, and with all thy might',[1] but also the ones that lay down what is to be eaten and what is not. 'Thou shalt not eat any abominable thing. These are the beasts which ye shall eat: the ox, the sheep, and the goat. . . .'[2] This is followed by a list of animals which may be eaten and explains why one rather than the other is to be considered edible. The people of Israel are 'an holy people unto the Lord',[3] and therefore must not eat anything that defiles and makes one unholy. It should be easy to realize that if holiness involves not only one's response to God but also one's choice of foods and the like, the door is being opened for the voice of conscience to be replaced by an appeal to authority. There must be someone to decide what is permitted and what is forbidden; hence the need for the casuistry and hence the indispensability of the Scribes.

Now whatever the causes of its growth and whatever its original purpose, this Rabbinical casuistry undoubtedly became, in the course of time, 'over subtle, voluminous, morally enfeebling'.[4] It concealed the essence of morality and thus contributed to the development of the attitude of self-righteousness in the Pharisees. This was natural enough; for if holiness consisted in doing what was prescribed for all moments of life, if it meant following the scriptures and the Scribes and performing the various rites enjoined for various occasions, then the Pharisee could justifiably boast of his performance. He knew what must be done—or so he thought—and strove every moment of his life to keep the letter, even if not the spirit, of the Law. He scrupulously obeyed all the injunctions himself and was naturally prone to censure anyone who seemed to violate these. The ethics of the Pharisee had shifted the emphasis from the spirit of the law to its letter.

Even this sketchy account of the Jewish scene leaves no

[1] Deuteronomy 6: 5.
[2] Deuteronomy 14: 3, 4.
[3] Deuteronomy 14: 2.
[4] Henson, *op. cit.*, p. 71.

doubt as to the nature of the Jewish ethic. There was undoubtedly a clear recognition that there was a Moral Law whose author was none other than God himself and that morality consisted in obeying this Law. But when it came to the question of what this Law implied and who was to judge the implications of the Law, there were two different answers to be found in the tradition of the Jews. On the one hand, there was the tradition of prophets like Amos and Isaiah for whom morality consisted in showing gratitude to God for deliverance, with its appeal to conscience and its emphasis on the right attitude rather than on the diligent and scrupulous performance of rites and ceremonies. This was perhaps the essence of Jewish morality. On the other hand, there was the appeal to authority and the emphasis on ritual and ceremonial duty leading to a concealment and distortion of essential morality. These, then, were the two distinct ways in which duty continued to be understood and interpreted in Jewish society; it either signified the attitude of love and gratitude, with only a nominal concern for ritual, or else it consisted almost entirely in ritual and routine performances as prescribed by the canonical writings. Though one of these conceptions of duty did sometimes succeed in pushing the other into oblivion or insignificance, it will be reasonable to think that neither of them ever completely disappeared. Jewish morality, therefore, may be regarded as a compound of both these elements, and, perhaps, much more. But that there was a Jewish morality in the proper sense of the term is proved beyond doubt. The belief in a Righteous God, the awareness of a Moral Law or moral order imposed by this God which had to be respected, and the conviction that there was a life of holiness which ought to be lived—these and other elements had given the Jewish faith a truly moral orientation. And it was against this background and into tnis society that Jesus was born.

(*b*) *The life and teaching of Jesus*

As we have seen, Jesus was a reformer and not a destroyer of Jewish morals and faith. But what was it that needed this reform? The answer is that at the time of Jesus' appearance, Jewish morality was perhaps not quite what he would have liked it to be. Morality had no more remained a matter of the spontaneous choice and application of one's conscience but had become a somewhat lifeless code of do's and don't's which covered practically all moments of an individual's life. The essential morality of love and gratitude for deliverance had suffered a set-back and the perspective had been distorted. It was Jesus' task to restore the perspective. Besides, Jewish morality suffered from its narrow nationalism and parochialism. Even the best of the Jewish prophets had not succeeded in freeing themselves from their preoccupation with Israel, and their concern for deliverance was confined in its appeal to the people of Israel. Jesus converted this faith into a universal religion in which there was to be no distinction between the Jews and the Gentiles. Dr Claude Montefiore, a Jewish scholar, sums up succinctly the difference in the attitudes of the then Jews and Jesus in the following words:

'I think Rabbinic teaching was defective about the love of the foreigner and the idolater, and that Jesus might very well have said, "you all consider your neighbour to be only your fellow-Jew, but I tell you that the neighbour whom you are to love includes all men, the Roman and the Greek and the Syrian no less than the Jew". That would by no means have been needless teaching. . . .'[1]

It would be obvious from this that the task of Jesus was primarily that of purging the Jewish faith of its unnecessary ritualism, literalism and nationalism. E. W. Hirst rightly remarks that the 'originality' of Christianity was not so much in its content as in its '*note of authority*, its *emphases*, and its *religious setting*'.[2] He is of the opinion that the content of the Christian ethic is 'far from being entirely original'.[3] The Christian ethic, according to him, had been anticipated in broad outlines by some of the older religions, the closest approximation having occurred in pre-Christian Jewish literature—particularly in The Testaments of the Twelve Patriarchs, 'a book written, presumably, in the last quarter of the second century B.C.'.[4] He goes on to quote several authorities who

[1] Quoted by Henson, *op. cit.*, p. 100.
[2] E. W. Hirst, *Jesus and the Moralists*, Epworth Press, London, 1935, p. 13.
[3] *Ibid.*, p. 11.
[4] *Ibid.*, p. 12.

have tried to relate the New Testament ethic to its roots in this particular book. It is stated, on the authority of H. Maldwyn Hughes, for example, that 'in this book . . . we find for the first time in literature the union of the two commands to love God and to love our neighbour'.[1] This only emphasizes our earlier observations that the ethic of Jesus is primarily based on that of Judaism, and that the Jewish ethic in its finer and more essential aspect had much to be proud of. But unfortunately, at the time of Jesus' ministry, this lofty ethic of Judaism had been somewhat obscured and was in need of someone who could restore this suppressed legacy back to its rightful place. Thus Jesus had on his hands more the problem of right application of precepts than of innovation. From the Jewish tradition he took the 'conception of the moral Law as expressing the will of a Righteous God' and also the ideals of love and holiness, which, though found in the scriptures, were rarely allowed to take their central places in the moral life of the Jews. Jesus himself provided the 'larger understanding of moral obligation', and, above all, a living example of the moral ideal.

Where precisely, then, did Jesus differ from the guardians of the contemporary Jewish faith and morals? We can answer this question very satisfactorily in the words of Henson:

'Jesus broke with Pharisaism on the cardinal point of its mechanical conception of duty. . . . With increased insistence and more august authority, He echoed the protests of Isaiah and Amos against an established religion which had parted company with fundamental morality, and, in its emphasis on ritual and ceremonial obligations, had destroyed the true perspective of human duty.'[2]

This 'protest of Isaiah and Amos', it may be stated, was essentially nothing else but an exhortation to go back to the essential spirit of the ethic of Moses, given later in Deuteronomy. Jewish morality during the time of Jesus had almost parted company with fundamental morality in the sense that it was gradually forgotten that this ethic was an *ethic of gratitude for deliverance* that entailed whole-hearted love and surrender to

[1] E. W. Hirst, *Jesus and the Moralists*, Epworth Press, London, 1935, p. 12.
[2] Henson, *op. cit.*, p. 102.

the will of God and not merely the performance of ritual and ceremonial duty. Complete obedience to the will of God, love for God and a genuine concern for discovering what God required of men, coupled with the fear of God's wrath—this was the essence of morality and the mark of holiness. And all this was to be there because the redemption of men lay not in performing sacrifices and worshipping at an appointed hour at the shrine, but in the mercy and discretion of a God who was to be pleased not by mere ritual but by the performance of good deeds. Isaiah's advice is absolutely plain:

'Bring no more vain oblations; incense is an abomination unto me. . . .

To what purpose is the multitude of your sacrifices unto me? saith the Lord: I am full of the burnt offerings of rams, and the fat of fed beasts; and I delight not in the blood of bullocks, or of lambs, or of he goats.'[1]

What the Lord expects, according to Isaiah, is this:

'Wash you, make you clean; put away the evil of your doings from before mine eyes; cease to do evil;

Learn to do well; seek judgement, relieve the oppressed, judge the fatherless, plead for the widow.'[2]

This is the essence of morality and this is what is to be done in gratitude for God's promise of deliverance. This was perhaps the true spirit of the ethic of Jesus. He did not lay down specific details of conduct for his followers. The essence of his ethic did not consist so much in the following of commandments as in the attitude of total surrender of one's will to that of God in love and humility. 'Not what I will, but what thou wilt'[3] sets the tone of man's relationship with God.

Like Isaiah, Jesus shifts the emphasis from rites to 'righteousness'.

'For I say unto you, That except your righteousness shall exceed the righteousness of the scribes and Pharisees, ye shall in no case enter into the kingdom of heaven.'[4]

[1] Isaiah 1: 13, 11.
[2] Isaiah 1: 16, 17.
[3] Mark 14: 36.
[4] Matthew 5: 20.

The kingdom of heaven is the objective and none but God can grant this. If one seeks redemption from his sins, let him be righteous, let him love God and his neighbour. Love God and love your neighbour—'on these two commandments hang all the law and the prophets'.[1] God loves men and is prepared to forgive their sins and save them only if men would set their hearts on God, pray to Him and be thankful to Him. This is the spirit of Jesus' ethic which transforms the concept of obligation. Duty does not consist in meekly following tradition, but in getting oneself into the right relationship with God. He mocks the Pharisees for their perverted sense of values: 'Howbeit in vain do they worship me, teaching for doctrine the commandments of men.'[2] Yes, the true doctrine does not consist in the commandments of men but in love and gratitude to God and in doing good to others. For if we do good to others, redemption will be our reward. The logic of this assurance is plain:

'If ye then, being evil, know how to give good gifts unto your children; how much more shall your heavenly Father give the Holy Spirit to them that ask Him?'[3]

To conclude, then, these are the main details in which Jesus transformed the Jewish ethic of the time: he changed it from a narrow national to a universal ethic of love and forgiveness; he restored the proper sense and perspective of obligation, and freed morality from mere authoritarianism and superficial conventionalism; he tried to restore the value of individual human conscience in matters of morals: for the ethic of love and gratitude that he was preaching had to be the response of the human heart, of the whole personality of man, and not merely one's reaction to conventional rules. This ethic of love and gratitude had a very far-reaching consequence in determining the character of the Christian ethic and in giving it the catholicity that we intend to investigate. Perhaps the other very important factor in this respect was the complexity of Jesus' own insight and the many strands of his teaching and practice. But we shall come to this later. Meanwhile, let us examine the

[1] Matthew 22: 40.
[2] Mark 7: 7.
[3] Luke 11: 13.

third factor in the development of Christian ethics, namely, the Greek and Roman influences.

(c) *The Greek and Roman influences*

Our accounts of the ethics of the Jews and of that preached by Jesus should have made it amply clear that despite the misplaced emphases and orientation of the former there is nothing in it which may be essentially opposed to the spirit of the latter. In fact, Jesus had built on Jewish foundations. But when we come to consider the Greek influence on original Christian morality, the picture changes almost entirely. It is no more merely a difference of emphasis; we now examine the impact of an ethic which is different in kind. Not only the goal of moral effort was differently conceived by the Greeks; even the definition of moral life was different, and so was the means of achieving a virtuous life. To start with, unlike Jewish and Christian ethics, Greek ethics was not primarily God-oriented nor did virtue connote a surrender to God's will. The moral law did not derive its authority from the will of God but from human reason. Christianity does not share the Greek belief in the infallibility and self-sufficiency of human reason; hence there cannot be an appeal to human reason, but only to the redeeming love of God. That is good for man which God commands. Thus the 'prophets and Jesus never appeal to human reason or to human conscience', but only to the 'will of the Father'.[1] This is not so in Greek ethics. Here, though man is regarded as a compound of reason and passion, the conviction is always there that the distinctive and specifically human faculty is reason. Hence virtue consists in relegating the passions and leading a life of reason proper. The source and final arbiter of the moral life, therefore, does not lie in anything external, but in the reason of man himself. A properly acquired knowledge of the workings of reason will automatically bring with it a knowledge of right and wrong, of virtue and vice, and if the lead of reason is to be followed, the end will be a virtuous and happy life. Thus the goal of a moral life is happiness, *eudaemonia*. The model of a happy life is to be found within the human reason itself, and the achievement of this perfect, happy or virtuous life lies within the powers of man himself, unaided by any supernatural

[1] W. J. Verdenius, 'Plato and Christianity', *Ratio*, June, 1963, p. 24.

agency. In other words, what an aspirant for the virtuous life had to do was to let his reason take command of his entire life, to let his true rational self establish its ascendancy over his passions.

It is clear, then, that according to the dominant line of Greek thinking, the ideal enjoined was to become master of one's self, to acquire proper self-hood with the aid of knowledge and personal diligence. It was an ethic of self-autonomy, intellectualistic in conception and wholly anthropocentric. Christian ethics, on the other hand, was theocentric in as much as it regarded the achievement of a virtuous life primarily as a gift of God, definitely beyond the powers of man without the grace of the Almighty. Man could strive, of course, but without the redeeming grace of God he could never reach the goal of holiness. It was no longer a question of mere self-discipline or of knowledge. The only means of realizing virtue or righteousness was a complete and loving submission to the will of God, whose mercy would lead a man to his goal.

Thus we find an inherent opposition between the Greek ethic of 'natural virtues' and the Christian ethic of 'faith'. One contradicts the other, and the two approaches to ethical life are surely conflicting. Yet the new ethic of faith could not simply brush aside the established ethic of natural virtues, which had a tremendous appeal to enlightened minds. The Greek masters, especially Plato and Aristotle, had started exerting such a compelling force on thinking minds of the day that it was impossible for Christian ethic to displace the ethic of self-achievement enunciated by the Greeks. From this there resulted within Christian history a continual effort to reconcile and synthesize the two approaches. In the words of Jacob Taubes,

'The subsequent history of Western moral experience and thought may be described in terms of the tension between the symbols of "natural" virtue and "supernatural" faith. It is the story of a continuous effort to synthesize these fundamentally contradictory standards by classifying the Greek philosophic canon of virtues as the "natural" norm for human behaviour, while taking the Christian standard of faith, hope and love as a guide for the "supernatural" order of man.'[1]

[1] Jacob Taubes, 'Virtue and Faith', *Philosophy East and West*, April–July 1957, p. 27.

The problem for Christianity since has been that it has been presented with two opposing methodologies, neither of which could be dispensed with. Hence the leading authorities on morals in the West have been at pains to devise a way in which the Greek ethic of self-achievement could, without inconsistency, be accommodated inside the Christian ethic of faith. The anxiety on the part of theologians and moralists to bring Christian ethics into a meaningful relationship with philosophical ethics is nothing but the outcome of this earlier search for a compromise between Christian and Greek ethics, for it is an undisputed fact that Western philosophical thinking—whether in ethics or in metaphysics—is nothing more than a continuation of the Greek tradition. We may say that it is this desire for synthesis that has resulted in what Paul Lehman calls 'the Thrust of Christian Ethics toward Philosophical Ethics', the 'most influential' of these thrusts being the 'Revisionist thrust of Augustine', 'the Synthetic thrust of Thomas Aquinas' and 'the Dia-parallel thrust of Schleiermacher'.[1] The crux of the problem has been the irreconcilability of self-achievement with the belief in the grace of God. Therefore, there have been attempts to interpret the concept of grace in such a way that grace could be regarded as only a supernatural variant on the self-achievement story. In this way it has been possible to treat grace as merely reinforcing man's own effort at achieving maturity or perfection. Thus natural virtues have been the norm of human behaviour, and faith, hope and love have been regarded as giving shape to the gratitude by which a man prepares himself to receive the reinforcing power of God's grace. This is then the story of the co-existence of the ethic of self-achievement and the ethic of self-surrender, the ethic of 'natural' virtues and the ethic of 'supernatural' faith. The exact nature of this co-existence is summed up in a passage in Jacob Taubes' article, referred to above:

'The emphasis on either of these elements has continued to shift from time to time. In the classic period of Christian moral philosophy in the Middle Ages the edges of both the canons were dulled; in the doctrines of Pelagius, Erasmus, Montaigne

[1] Paul Lehman, *Ethics in a Christian Context*, SCM Press, London, 1963, pp. 253 *ff*.

and Hegel the religious statement was flattened out and formulated in terms of a natural philosophic canon. But in the teachings of Augustine, Luther, Pascal, and Kierkegaard the consciousness of contradiction between the two realms flares up.'[1]

It would appear from this that it has, on the whole, been an uneasy truce between the two canons within the wider framework of European and Christian morals. And, it may be added, that it has been this 'tension between an ethics of virtues and a life of faith that is the very denial of an ethics of virtues' which has given 'rise to the peculiar dynamics which marks Western moral philosophy and moral theology throughout its history'.[2]

We now come to another important influence on early Christian morality which may be termed Graeco–Roman. This was the Stoic philosophy founded by Zeno and propagated by three famous men during the days of the Roman Empire—Seneca, the statesman, Epictetus, the slave and Marcus Aurelius, the Emperor. Though the Stoic School was founded by Zeno in Greece, 'it was, however, when Stoicism passed from Greece to Rome that it became specially interesting from the point of view of Christianity'.[3] That some of the early teachers of Christianity, notably the Apostle Paul, were in close contact with the then leading Stoics is a 'historically established fact'. It is possible that as a result of these contacts the Stoics also were influenced by Christian teaching, and that 'the influence was reciprocal',[4] but it cannot be denied on any count that early Christian morality came under Stoic influence in a significant way. The most important Stoic influences on Christian ethics, perhaps, were the ethic of ascetic self-denial and the excessive stress placed on the life of reason. The Stoic insistence on the life of reason as against that of passion was so pronounced that the Stoic 'tried to rid himself as far as possible of emotion, and to cultivate "apatheia" or apathy'.[5] This element of asceticism could without much difficulty penetrate into the structure of Christian ethics for the simple reason that there were strong undercurrents of asceticism in the teaching of Jesus himself. In the words of J. E. Fison,

[1] Taubes, *op. cit.*, p. 27.
[2] *Ibid.*, p. 32.
[3] Hirst, *op. cit.*, p. 70.
[4] *Ibid.*, p. 73.
[5] *Ibid.*, p. 73.

'The holiness of monasticism was profoundly ascetic, and though its monastic expression was late in developing in the Christian church, *its ascetic emphasis was true to an indisputable element in* the life and teaching of Jesus Christ. He [Jesus] was himself unmarried. . . . He made the strongest possible demands on his followers for poverty, chastity, and obedience. He said it was almost impossible for a rich man to enter the kingdom of heaven.'[1]

He even went so far as to demand the 'hatred of kith and kin as a condition of loyalty to God'.[2] This leaves no room for doubt about the presence of an element of asceticism in Jesus' life and teaching. What the Stoic influence did was merely to sharpen this element in the teachings of the early Christians. One example from St John will show how at a very early stage asceticism had entrenched itself in Christian morality. No one can fail to notice the ascetic note in these verses:

'Love not the world, neither the things that are in the world. If any man love the world, the love of the Father is not in him.
For all that is in the world, the lust of the flesh, and the lust of the eyes, and the pride of life, is not of the Father, but is of the world.
And the world passeth away, and the lust thereof: but he that doeth the will of God abideth for ever.'[3]

A careful perusal of the history of early Christian morality makes it difficult for one to agree with Henson's refutation of Dean Inge's remark that 'early Christian ethics . . . were mainly Stoical' and that 'the Stoical ethics were taken over by Christianity'.[4] This cleavage which the early Christian writers created between the world and the Church remained discernible in Christian morality for hundreds of years with all its world-denying implications, most conspicuously in the monastic discipline. Stoic asceticism on the whole, however, reflected itself in the sexual morality of the Christians more than in any other sphere. Perhaps it was under this ascetic influence that Christianity tended to regard 'virginity' as the 'specifically

[1] Fison, *op. cit.*, p. 118 (emphasis mine).
[2] *Ibid.*, p. 119.
[3] I John 2: 15–17.
[4] Henson, *op. cit.*, p. 139.

Christian virtue, and the essence of all virtues'.[1] But it would be a mistake to think that Christian morality was ascetic only in its treatment of sex. The general note of Christian morality itself remained rather ascetic right up to the Middle Ages, and even now, in spite of the encroachments of materialistic and hedonistic philosophies, an ascetic interpretation of Christian ethics would not necessarily be regarded as heretical or scandalous. Whether or not Henson is correct in saying that 'the French revolution was directed against the ascetic character of Christian morality as well as against the dogmatic demands of Christian faith',[2] he is certainly not far from the truth so far as the ascetic character of Christian morality is concerned.

We may conclude, then that whatever its degree, asceticism is not foreign to the spirit of Christian ethics, and that this has to some extent been due to the influence of the Graeco–Roman philosophy of Stoicism. With this we must close our analysis of the Graeco–Roman influence on Christian ethics, for though Greece and Rome might surely have contributed other elements as well, it would be reasonable to think that the most significant of these have been the ones we have already discussed. With the above account of the main streams that helped to give shape to Christian ethics in its formative years, we shall now briefly discuss some of the chief re-orientations of and emphases on the various elements of this ethics in some of the later thinkers and interpreters.

(*d*) *Some later accents in the history of Christian ethics*

Of all the reinterpretations and emphases put on one or the other aspect of Christian ethics in its later days, perhaps the most significant was the intellectualistic interpretation of St Thomas Aquinas. Aquinas, with his deep roots in Greek, especially Aristotelian, thought, regards *beatitude* as the highest end of life, and considers the nature of this beatitude as essentially speculative. 'The act constituting beatitude must therefore be of a speculative nature, and this amounts to saying that this act must consist in contemplation.'[3] The attainment of

[1] Harnack, *History of Dogma*, III, 128, quoted by Henson, *op. cit.*, p. 197.
[2] Henson, *op. cit.*, p. 198.
[3] Etienne Gilson, *The Philosophy of St Thomas Aquinas*, trans. Edward Bullough, W. Heffer and Sons Ltd., Cambridge, 1929, p. 341.

beatitude is necessarily an intellectual operation and is identical with what Lehman might call the 'ascetic or contemplative crown of the Christian life at the end'. In his words,

'The discussion of the theological virtues at the beginning of the *Secunda secundiae*, and of the ascetic or contemplative crown of the Christian life at the end, with the treatment of the cardinal virtues in between, provides substantial confirmation of the fact that both the spirit and the letter of Thomas' argument are marked by the ascetic and mystical approaches to the Christian life which dominated the Middle Ages.'[1]

It is needless to emphasize that this intellectualistic interpretation of Christian ethics by Aquinas has exercised a considerable influence, especially in Catholic moral theology, and has become the favourite of those who wish to adopt some form of strictly rationalistic ethic without having to discard their Christian faith. We may feel tempted to quote a sentence from Lehman about the quality and significance of Aquinas' achievement. He says:

'It was Aquinas who made room for *all* men within the household of faith. And he did it by an ingeniously contrived synthesis of reason and faith, nature and grace, Aristotle and the Bible, rational and theological virtue, moral philosophy and Christian ethics.'[2]

Perhaps not as abiding or as important an influence as that of Aquinas, but nonetheless a very significant one has been that exerted by the work of St Thomas à Kempis of the late Middle Ages. In his celebrated work, *Imitation of Christ*, the emphasis shifts to an altogether new element: 'the central place in Christian piety and behaviour is occupied by the Passion of Christ'.[3] This 'Passion Mysticism'[4] may not have been a completely new element within Christian ethics but the emphasis was certainly new, and might possibly have given rise to tendencies within Christian ethics which quite often led to

[1] Lehman, *op. cit.*, pp. 39 *f.*
[2] *Ibid.*, p. 257.
[3] *Ibid.*, p. 39.
[4] *Ibid.*, p. 39.

what William James calls the 'theopathic condition'[1] of the mind. Lehman's analysis of the source as well as the consequence of this new emphasis seems to be a very fair statement of the position. 'It must be admitted,' he says,

'that this concentration upon the Passion of Christ contributed to the understanding of the sacrificial character of the love of God. But it must also be noted that this "Passion Mysticism" was nourished by the Bride figure of the Song of Songs as well as by the Crucifixion. The effect of this was to sensualize and even to sentimentalize the love for Christ, a consequence confirmed not only by medieval mysticism but by evangelical hymnody, particularly the Passion hymns.'[2]

This underlines a fact seldom realized, namely, that sensualism or sentimentalism in the love of God is not, or at least has not been, quite alien to the spirit of Christian piety and behaviour.

A mention of Kant in course of this enumeration of the sources of Christian ethics may surprise some, but it is generally admitted these days that though the critical philosophy of Kant was founded ostensibly on independent sources, his deep roots in Christian thought were a formidable influence in shaping his thought. On the other hand, he has himself influenced considerably Christian ethical thinking since his day. This is brought out clearly in the following passage from Lehman:

'The Aristotelian search for the Good has chiefly influenced Christian thinking about ethics through the formative mind of Thomas Aquinas. But if classical eudaemonism may be said to be nearer to the ethical thought of Roman Catholicism, a parallel claim may be made as regards the critical philosophy and the ethical thought of the Reformation.'[3]

The deontological ethics of Kant might have had their roots in the Christian call to do the Will of God, and the Categorical Imperative might have been the rationalistic counterpart of the Christian Divine Imperative, but it cannot be denied that

[1] William James, *Varieties of Religious Experience*, Longmans Green, 1929, p. 343.

[2] Lehman, *op. cit.*, p. 39.

[3] *Ibid.*, p. 172.

the renewed stress by Kant on absolute obedience to the Imperative has added a new relevance to the arguments of the theologians and Christian moralists regarding absolute submission to the Will of God—the Divine Imperative.

The temptation to extend this analysis to modern exponents of Christian ethics, like Emil Brunner, Reinhold Niebuhr, Karl Barth and Dietrich Bonhöffer, may be great, especially in view of the fact that the subtleties of their arguments and the variety of interpretations may lend further support to our thesis that Christian ethics is comprehensive and elastic. But it seems quite reasonable to believe that all these thinkers—though differing in matters of detail—have generally adopted one or the other of the various positions we have already discussed. Moreover, it seems reasonable to suppose that the case for the elasticity of Christian ethics has been adequately expounded in the foregoing. Then again, consideration of the claims and counter-claims as to whether modern science has influenced modern Christian ethics or the latter made the former possible adds increased complexity to a problem that is already amply complex. Both kinds of claims are made, and the controversy is not, and perhaps cannot be, settled as to whether scientific advances transformed the Christian outlook or the Christian tradition helped the growth of science. But it may perhaps be desirable to remember the note sounded in this 'biting epigram' of T. H. Huxley:

'When there is a new thing in science, they first say "It's impossible!" Then they say, "It's against the Bible." Then they say, "We knew it all the time."'[1]

Though our analysis is by no means exhaustive, it is hoped that it may still demonstrate one thing: any oversimplification of the content of Christian morality betrays an ignorance of the diverse factors that constitute it. The fact is that whatever its original creed—and even that was not simple—Christian ethics today is a highly complex phenomenon which contains diverse elements and is subject to various interpretations, capable of catering to the tastes of various individuals and groups within a highly extensive and comprehensive framework. With this account of

[1] Quoted by S. C. Carpenter in *Christianity*, Penguin Books, London, 1953, p. 134.

the constituents of Christian ethics, we must now turn to Hindu ethics and examine what the picture is like there.

SOURCES AND DEVELOPMENT OF HINDU ETHICS

Hindu ethics displays a much greater variety and is constituted of many more elements than we have been able to trace in Christian ethics. This is quite understandable, for Hinduism has always accepted, almost as a part of its creed, that human beings are differently constituted and that among them there are innumerable differences of temperament, training and level of aspiration. This being so, the ethical goal will obviously be approached in various ways, and the ethical ideal will always be subject to various interpretations. It is this recognition of differences in temperament and training that has been responsible for the growth of some of the well-known Hindu social institutions such as the *Varṇa-Āśram Dharma*, or the institution of class and stages in life. But apart from this, an equally, if not more, important factor in shaping Hindu ethics into its highly complex and comprehensive character has been the extreme, sometimes even unquestioning, reverence of the Hindus for the Vedic and Upaniṣadic literature. The vast range of this literature contains various strands of thought, some of which may be considered inconsistent with others. But in his extreme regard for authority, the Hindu has tended to regard every idea muted in this literature as equally sacred and, therefore, equally worthy of allegiance and attention. When some of these ideas and ideals have been found to be mutually conflicting, the natural reaction of the Hindu moralists and men of learning has been to regard each of them as alternatives rather than to discard any of them in favour of the other. Synthesis and compromise rather than criticism and elimination have been the guiding principles of Hindu teachers and commentators. Compromise has quite often been possible only at the cost of consistency, and the net result for the character of Hindu ethics has been elasticity rather than exclusiveness, and infinite complexity rather than well-defined simplicity. Almost every form of belief and practice within Hinduism can be traced to ideas and concepts either implicitly or explicitly laid down within this immense literature, so that Hindu ethics, unlike Christian ethics, has received little by way of foreign influence. Hindu ethics is almost entirely an indigenous growth. Our analysis of the constituent elements of Hindu ethics, therefore, will have to follow a slightly different pattern from that of our analysis of Christian ethics. We shall not enumerate the various influences from different sources but rather take account of the significant ethical concepts found in each of the important groups of Hindu literature.

The main groups of religious literature in the Hindu tradition are (*a*) the Vedas and the Brāhmaṇas, (*b*) the Upaniṣads and (*c*) the Epics and Purāṇas. Our account of the ethical concepts will, accordingly, have these three main heads. But the Bhagavadgītā, though only a part of the third group, occupies in Hindu literature a singularly important place and has exercised a considerable constructive influence on the Hindu mind. It would be proper, therefore, to discuss the ethical ideas of the Gītā under a separate head. This will complete our account of early Hindu ethics. To this will be added a section dealing with the main emphases in the later development of the ethical thinking of the Hindus in which we will comment on the thought of such thinkers as Shamkara and Ramanuja.

(*a*) *The ethical concepts in the Vedas*

Like so much else in the intellectual and religious heritage of the Hindus, their thinking about ethics must be traced back to its beginnings in the Vedas, particularly the Ṛg Veda. Of the four Vedas, the two more deserving of attention for our purposes are, of course, the Ṛg and the Atharva, but in view of the fact that the latter mostly presupposes and enlarges on the former, our account will by and large concern itself with the ethical ideas of the former. It should be remembered that the earliest of the Vedas were probably composed nearly three thousand years ago, or even earlier, and so it would be absurd to regard them as treatises on ethics. It is not at all surprising, therefore, that 'any system of ethics that might be discovered in the Ṛg Veda is of a very rudimentary sort'.[1] What is actually remarkable is the presence in the Vedas of some concepts which suggest an extremely well-developed moral consciousness. Commenting on the conception of *Ṛta* in the Ṛg Veda, John Mackenzie observes,

[1] John Mackenzie, *Hindu Ethics*, Oxford University Press, 1922, p. 7.

'Yet it is very significant that at this early stage we should find such a unifying conception as that of Law or Order, pervading all things, expressing itself in the order of nature and in the manifestations of man's religious life, and tending to be associated with one Supreme God.'[1]

E. W. Hopkins, concluding his investigation of 'The Vedic Idea of Sin and Law', has this to say about the ethical content of the Ṛg Veda:

'Morality is an expression of divine law; sin is opposition to that law. The sinner is one who is out of harmony with the higher spiritual environment which encompasses and controls the world.'[2]

It should be clear from the above remarks that though the Vedas contain on the whole quite a number of accounts of what appears to us to be obscure and occult ritual and sacrifice, there is undoubtedly an ethical orientation of religious thought and practice.

This recognition of a moral element, though implied in even the very concept of bright, beneficent gods, '*Devas*—shining, fair as opposed to *Rākṣas*, meaning injurers who go about by night'[3], is noticeable above all in the conception of *Ṛta*, the Moral Law or Order, pervading the entire universe. *Ṛta* means fit or orderly as the English word 'good' originally meant or as the German '*guoti*' means. *Anṛta*, its opposite, means falsehood or bad. *Ṛta*, therefore, stands for harmony or a moral order in the world.[4] It is true that *Ṛta* is used in a very comprehensive sense; it represents not only the moral order but also the natural order as well as the 'ordered course of the sacrifice'. But it must be made clear that, though manifested in these various orders, *Ṛta* is a unity. The moral implication and orientation of the concept of *Ṛta* becomes clearer when we take note of one particular observation made by Henry Lefever. He is of the opinion that *Ṛta*, though objective, is still ideal in a sense. While making this point he says:

[1] John Mackenzie, *Hindu Ethics*, Oxford University Press, 1922, p. 7.
[2] E. W. Hopkins, *Ethics in India*, Yale University Press, 1924, p. 44.
[3] *Ibid.*, p. 2. [4] *Ibid.*, p. 2.

'It is in the sphere of human conduct, however, that the difference between ideal and actuality is most strongly marked. However regular the operation of *ṛta* in the natural world may be, it is expressly stated in IX, 73, 6 (R.V.) that the wicked "travel not the pathway of *ṛta*". Man, as Betty Heimann remarks, is distinguished from nature in that he is placed before the alternatives, to act in accordance with *ṛta* or not.'[1]

Now the moral significance of *Ṛta* is important because this is the concept which has given rise to two other Hindu concepts which have a primarily ethical bearing. These are the concept of *Dharma* and the Law of *Karma*.

It is universally recognized these days that *Dharma* is a very complex concept and is, therefore, variously translated and interpreted. But this should not lead us into believing that it is vague or ill-defined. As G. H. Mees suggests, *Dharma*, like many of the conceptions of ancient cultures (India, Greece, Rome, etc.) and like the modern word 'law', is indeterminate rather than vague. And his reason for stressing this distinction is that in his opinion 'indeterminateness does not preclude inner clarity, whereas vagueness is the opposite of clarity'.[2] Thus the ancient Hindus allowed *Dharma* to stand for various things not because of their failure to define it but because of their effort to name that all-embracing principle which would cover all aspects of a man's life; therefore, it quite naturally took different meanings in different contexts. Though it would be possible to distinguish between these various aspects of *Dharma*, let us not lose sight of the fact that in the ultimate analysis there could be only one *Dharma*—the fundamental Law or Order, varying in manifestation and application but one in essence. Dr Bhagvan Das' definition of *Dharma*, quoted and highly commended by G. H. Mees, may convey the full extent of the elasticity in the meaning of the term. According to him, *Dharma* is

'. . . that which holds a thing together, makes it what it is, prevents it from breaking up and changing it into something else; its characteristic function, its peculiar property, its funda-

[1] Henry Lefever, *The Vedic Idea of Sin*, London Mission Press, Travancore, India, 1935, p. 7.

[2] G. H. Mees, *Dharma and Society*, Luzac and Co., London, 1935, p. 3.

mental attribute, its essential nature, is its *dharma*, the law of its being. . . . Briefly, *dharma* is characteristic property, scientifically; duty, morally and legally; religion with all its proper implications, psycho-physically and spiritually; and righteousness and law generally, but duty above all.'[1]

Since there will be several occasions for more detailed examinations of this concept, we shall close this discussion of it for the time being with the observation that *Dharma* primarily signified the Moral Law, and is essentially the same as the Jewish 'Torah'.

The other concept with an eminently ethical significance which, along with *Dharma*, was derived from the Ṛg Vedic *Ṛta* was the Law of *Karma*. We may say that the Law of *Karma* signifies that there is a uniform moral law governing the actions of men and the rewards and punishments appropriate to such actions. In very simple terms, this law is an explicit credal recognition of the truth implied in the commonly known proverb, 'As you sow, so you reap'. It would perhaps not be misleading to suggest that this law might be described as the counterpart in the moral field of the Law of Conservation of Energy, for it implies that every action—good or bad—that we perform inevitably generates certain subtle potencies which determine our character and circumstances in our future lives. In other words, it is impossible for us to escape the consequences of our actions. The germs of this principle are already noticeable in the Ṛg Veda and the Atharva Veda wherein it is recognized that the 'sin cannot be escaped.'[2] This law provides a clear incentive to righteous conduct, for if it is impossible to escape the consequences of actions and if only right conduct can lead to beneficial results, there would naturally be an urge to do what is considered good.

It should be remarked that the Law of *Karma* is only a special manifestation of the eternal moral order, *Dharma*, and that the two concepts are allied and complementary. In the words of Mees,

'Dharma is Karman, but much more than that, for it is not only

[1] Dr Bhagvan Das, *The Science of Social Organisation*, as quoted by Mees, *op. cit.*, p. 11.

[2] Hopkins, *op. cit.*, pp. 48 *f.*

the tendency due to past and present work, but also the divine tendency hidden in the inmost being of man, to unfold in the future. Dharma is the law of his unfoldment, the divine inner potentiality. If Karman implies law and bondage, Dharma holds the element of Divine Grace and the principle of freedom. Karman is a law of cause and effect, Dharma is largely ethical and religious.'[1]

This mutual interrelatedness of *Dharma* and *Karma* is often lost to view even by able commentators, thus leading to unsatisfactory understanding of both these concepts. But we need not dwell on this point now.

What is worth special notice at this stage is that both these concepts, but primarily *Dharma,* have reference to a divine agency. This divine power whose laws *Dharma* and *Karma* represent is often extolled in the Vedic hymns as the highest and the first among gods. Though each one of the various gods, being part of the divine organization of things, is more or less responsible for the maintenance of *Ṛta,* it is above all Varuṇa who is more often than any other god associated with *Ṛta* as its guardian. The henotheism of the Vedas becomes especially manifest in the context of *Ṛta.* Though many gods are mentioned and invoked, there seems at the same time to be clear recognition of the ultimate overlordship of one over the rest. Though Indra is often declared in the Ṛg Veda to be the chief God, Varuṇa is the deity especially related with prayers for moral guidance. Varuṇa is even referred to in the characteristic Christian way as Holy Father (*Pitā Yajatras*).[2] Thus we notice not only that the ethics of the Vedas is God-oriented, but also that there is a clear movement toward monism, which finally establishes itself in the philosophy of the Upaniṣads.[3] In the words of Hopkins,

'. . . the bright gods, like the parts of a kaleidoscope, rearranged themselves and became united into one whole. At the very end of the Ṛg Veda the personification of Right Order as a divine personal power, preceded by such parallel statements as that

[1] Mees, *op. cit.,* p. 20. [2] Hopkins, *op. cit.,* p. 42.

[3] On the strength of several statements in the Ṛg Veda it is possible to argue that Vedic thought was monistic from the start; but this makes no difference to the essential ethical implications.

the regular succession of days is in accordance with the statutes "of Varuṇa" and "of Ṛta" (Order), leads to Great Order being invoked as a God along with other deities.'[1]

According to this passage, *Ṛta*—the foundation of *Dharma* and *Karma*—is not only being referred to the highest of the Gods, but is being itself transformed into the highest Divinity. This should leave no room for doubt as to the ethical character of the Vedic faith.

We must confess, however, that owing to the development of certain 'magical' and occult practices in the later Vedas, some writers on Hinduism have come to believe that the essentially ethical character of the Ṛg-Vedic faith is not only impaired but lost completely in later Vedic thought. To give only one example of such thinking, let us examine Mackenzie's opinion. Soon after expressing his admiration for the concept of *Ṛta* and its ethical significance in a passage quoted earlier, he relapses into a mood of lamentation:

'But unfortunately, long before the Vedic period ended other conceptions had arisen and displaced it, and in the history of Indian ethical thought it has not been upon the idea of an over-ruling God, righteous in Himself, seeking righteousness of His people, and helping them in the attainment of it, that the moral life has been grounded.'[2]

That Mackenzie's dismay is unwarranted will perhaps be clearer as we proceed with our analysis. For the present we shall content ourselves with the observation that *Dharma* has always been the basis of moral life in Hinduism, in spite of all appearances to the contrary. Mees, for example, is of the opinion that 'in the different periods of Indian history Dharma, and not Moksha, came on the whole foremost as ideal and was considered as supreme'.[3] No student of Indian religious thought can deny that in India there have been other conceptions of deity than the one of which Mackenzie speaks, but it will at the same time be impossible for anyone to forget the tremendous role of *Dharma* in the life of the Hindu. And if we remember

[1] Hopkins, *op. cit.*, pp. 40 *f.*

[2] Mackenzie, *op. cit.*, p. 7.

[3] Mees, *op. cit.*, p. 26.

the connection of *Dharma* with *Ṛta*, it will be seen that there is no cause for Mackenzie's lamentation. Hopkins may be nearer the truth when he says,

'. . . A lower order of magic submerged the loftier thought of the Ṛg Veda (in the post-Ṛg-Vedic period), yet it could not do away with the ethical consciousness already awakened, nor did it entirely suppress the idea that morality was an expression of spiritual worth divinely implanted in man.'[1]

It will not be unreasonable to conclude from all this that the ethics of the Vedas was on the whole not very unlike the ethics of the Jews before the advent of Jesus. Like that of the Jews, the ethics of the Vedic Hindus was primarily God-oriented, and there was a distinct recognition of a divine Moral Order or a Moral Law, conformity with which was the essence of moral life. But when it came to the interpretation of the Law in the context of actual practice, two different emphases attracted people's attention. There were those who thought that morality consisted of discharging one's duties—ceremonial, ritual, and sacrificial—to the gods and the 'fathers'. The emphasis here on ceremonies and sacrifice resulted from the tendency to interpret the scriptures literally. But it has to be confessed that this literalism, with its stress on occultism and sacrifice, is by no means the only approach to the ethico-religious goal. Perhaps the more important and essential element in the Vedic ethic is that of love and worship offered to the gods in complete submission. For the recognition is there that the gods are loving and benevolent and guard those who worship and love them. The statement that 'the Gods further him that loves them and like suitors rejoice in him who loves the Brahma',[2] sets the tone of the personal relationship that the Vedic Hindu desires to have with his gods. In fact, the ethic of love and obedience that was later adopted by the theistic schools has its roots in the Ṛg Veda itself. As Hopkins says, 'The *Bhakti* or loving devotion, which some scholars imagine to be only a late development of Hindu religion, is already evident in the Ṛg Veda, even in its dangerous trend toward eroticism . . .'.[3]

[1] Hopkins, *op. cit.*, p. 62.
[2] Ṛg Veda, I, 83, 2.
[3] Hopkins, *op. cit.*, p. 8.

To summarize then, the Vedic Hindus had a clear recognition of a Moral Order or Moral Law. This Law was considered to have been laid down by God, that One Existent, That Truth which, in its wider connotation, had been breathed into the very constitution of the universe. Men were regarded as being under obligation to obey this law. This was to be done in one of two ways. Since this Order was reflected even in the right performance of sacrifices, one who performed these sacrifices and the ceremonial duties laid down in the scriptures would achieve his goal of eternal happiness in heaven. The other way of attaining this goal was to love and worship the gods—to please the gods: for they were the guardians of the Law. Magic and sacrifice, according to this view, were merely 'the means employed to express the worshipper's submission and faith'.[1]

'With obeisance, sacrifice and oblation, O Varuṇa, we deprecate thy wrath. . . . Loose from us the sins we have committed (remove thy fetters) and (by abiding) *in thy law* may we be sinless before Aditi.'[2]

Freedom from sins, thus, is the goal; the two ways in which this can be achieved are by compelling the gods through magic and sacrifice or by pleasing and winning the favour of the gods, the keepers of the Law, through love and devotion.

Before closing our account of the ethics of the Vedas, we ought to take note of one other Vedic concept which perhaps introduced into later Hindu ethics an altogether new and significant element. This is the concept of *Tapas* which occurs in the Ṛg Veda itself. It is said, for example, that 'it was through *Tapas* that the Primal Being began to create'.[3] *Tapas* means 'heat' and, as Mackenzie suggests, later 'came to be applied specially to the heat or fervour of devotion'.[4] Mackenzie also notes, however, that in at least one of the *Sūktas* in the tenth book (of the Ṛg Veda) one begins to notice association of this word with the familiar ascetic austerity. In the Atharva Veda and the Brāhmaṇas it is the latter association of *Tapas*, that is, ascetic austerity or self-mortification, which is more often in evidence. A belief was generated that by austerity and

[1] Hopkins, *op. cit.*, p. 34.
[2] Ṛg Veda, I, 24, 14–15.
[3] *Ibid.*, X, 129.
[4] Mackenzie, *op. cit.*, p. 14.

penance one could compel the gods, nay, even become a god. The significance of this concept lies in the fact that it formed the basis for the ascetic strain in Hindu ethics, and perhaps formed the core of *Haṭha Yoga*, the path of ascetic austerity for the attainment of *Mokṣa*.

(*b*) *The ethics of the Upaniṣads*

The above account of the ethical concepts in the Vedas is far from exhaustive. What we have done is to have taken note of some of the more significant concepts, but the significant ones are surely not the only ones. As a matter of fact, almost all the later movements and tendencies in Hindu religion and ethics are believed to have been contained, either implicitly or explicitly, in the Vedas. It is important to remember this, for later Hindu ethics—whether it be that of the Upaniṣads or of the Gītā or of any other source—presupposes the Vedas and is built on Vedic foundations. No section of orthodox Hindu religious and ethical literature has ever consciously or deliberately tried to depart from or contradict the Vedas. This does not mean that Hinduism has had no new ideas since the Vedas. It only means that whatever new ideas have been there have been shown, with varying degrees of consistency, to be in conformity with Vedic teaching.

It is against this background that we shall discuss the ethical ideas in the Upaniṣads. The highest goal is no longer eternal happiness in heaven, as it had been for the common man in the Vedic times, but liberation from the trammels of transitory existence and re-attainment of the inner essence of the soul. Rituals are no longer considered sufficient for the attainment of the goal. Their place is taken by mystic contemplation coupled with right conduct. But in spite of all this change in perspective and the consequent change of emphases in matters of morals, it would still be wrong to suppose that the Upaniṣads are primarily concerned with ethics. As Hopkins says,

'. . . in this philosophy (the relation of human soul to All-soul) ethics is taken for granted; the real questions are concerning metaphysics, so that we may be thankful for such hints as are given in regard to the sages' opinions on morality.'[1]

[1] Hopkins, *op. cit.*, p. 64.

But we must be careful not to fall prey to the misconception that the sages of the Upaniṣads did not recognize the importance of morality. In fact, while it is true that the Upaniṣads regard *Mokṣa*, or liberation, as the highest goal, they insist that this cannot be achieved without leading a virtuous life. It is categorically asserted that 'He who has not ceased from immoral conduct can not obtain God through the intelligence'.[1] Innumerable other passages can be quoted to show that the philosophy of the Upaniṣads, though primarily concerned with metaphysical questions, is essentially highly ethical in character.

It is in the Upaniṣads, in fact, that the transition from *Ṛta* to *Dharma* becomes complete, and it is here again that the mutual interrelatedness of the various concepts with ethical import, like those of *Dharma* and *Adharma*, *Karma*, *Saṃsāra* and *Mokṣa*, begins to be noticeable. All these concepts now begin to fall into a coherent pattern and impart significance to one another. A passage from J. A. B. Van Buitenen very clearly brings out this interconnection among these concepts:

'. . . Dharma is all that activity that a man, if he is to live fittingly, is required to contribute to the fixed order of things, to the norm of the universe which is good and should not be altered. Adharma is the exact opposite: acts contrary to the established order in the widest sense of the word. The acts performed by man exist, once performed, forever, carrying their latent potential (Karma) to a new scene where they will materialize in new circumstances for man to live in (Saṃsāra).'[2]

In other words, *Saṃsāra* means an endless cycle of births and deaths for man in accordance with the Law of *Karma* which is unsparing in its application, until, by a supreme moral and spiritual effort, he rises above the Law and attains liberation. It is not difficult to see that all these other concepts—*Mokṣa, Saṃsāra, Karma*—are related to *Dharma*. *Dharma*, being the norm and the established order of things, the violation of its spirit, i.e., *Adharma*, naturally and inevitably binds man to *Saṃsāra* through the instrumentality of the Law of *Karma*, and

[1] Kaṭha Upaniṣad, I, 2, 24.

[2] J. A. B. Van Buitenen, 'Dharma and Mokṣa', *Philosophy East and West*, April–July 1957, p. 36.

it is from *Saṃsāra* that liberation is sought. It is important to remember that if it is the lack of *Dharma* which causes continued bondage, then release or *Mokṣa* can only be attained through the performance of *Dharma*.

At this stage, perhaps, it will be desirable to analyse the meaning of *Mokṣa* and its implications, for in the Upaniṣads *Mokṣa* becomes the supreme ethico-religious goal. This should be obvious from the above discussion of the interconnection of all the ethico-religious concepts in the Upaniṣads. *Mokṣa,* we may say, has two aspects. Negatively, it means release from the cycle of births and deaths (*Saṃsāra*). On its positive side, however, it implies the recovery of the true nature of the soul, the knowledge of which is obscured by *Māyā,* or Cosmic Ignorance. The Soul, being spirit by definition, attains liberation by realizing that it is different from body, life, and mind, all of which are non-spiritual. The material body that every soul assumes must be treated as an accretion, and the essence of the human soul must be supposed to lie much deeper than we normally imagine. As long as the realization of this essence through a supreme moral effort and genuine transcendental wisdom does not take place, we shall go on identifying ourselves with our bodies, and will remain subject to the dictates of the bodily passions and desires, as though *these* were the real constituents of our true self. This, it may be incidentally remarked, is reminiscent of the sharp division between reason and passions occurring generally in the whole of ancient Greek philosophy but especially in the philosophy of the Stoics.

To continue our account of *Mokṣa,* however, this loss of perspective regarding the true nature of the human soul leads to a perversion of insight and ideals. Once we have identified ourselves with our bodies, we naturally look at things from a narrow angle and tend to act in selfish and indulgent ways, with undue attachment to things transitory and perhaps, in the last analysis, unreal. This attachment and craving in turn makes us subject to the Law of *Karma* and binds us to the chains of *Saṃsāra.* Our release, then, lies in a fresh realization of the essential character of the soul. Once we succeed in doing this, we cease to be slaves to our bodies and their passions, and consequently we cut the very roots of *Karma* and *Saṃsāra.* We become one with our essence again; we regain the lost glory of the self. And this is a goal which can be realized primarily by the acquirement of transcendental knowledge (*Viveka Jñāna*), discriminating between the spiritual and the non-spiritual, and a gradual withdrawal from the snares of the body and the senses, though, as we saw earlier, this must necessarily involve following the path of *Dharma*. In this acquirement of *Mokṣa*, which is sometimes interpreted as 'obtaining God',[1] the mercy or grace of God is occasionally invoked. For example, we are told:

'He is not to be obtained by instruction, nor by intelligence, nor by much learning. He is to be obtained only by the one whom He chooses; to such a one He reveals His own person.'[2]

After the realization of the goal, i.e. *Mokṣa*, action does not cease altogether; it only ceases to have potency to bind the soul again, for the liberated one does not act from hankering. It is needless to emphasize that the liberated man who has realized the inner essence of things is hardly likely to act in an immoral or anti-social way. 'The man who has wisdom,' says the Mahābhārata, 'does not sin; he ceases to do evil and through his wisdom annuls the evil of his former life.'[3] Thus *Mokṣa* does not mean inactivity or immorality; it is the culmination of a continuous moral effort through a series of lives and deaths.

It is interesting to note that some writers have seen a kind of opposition between *Dharma* and *Mokṣa*. If *Dharma* means the order of the universe, the power that sustains the world, and if *Mokṣa* means release from the world altogether, then clearly the latter is a negation of everything that is governed by *Dharma*. As Van Buitenen says,

'*Mokṣa*, "release", is release from the entire realm which is governed by *Dharma*, that is, in the picturesque phrase, the Egg of Brahmā (*Brahmānda*). It stands, therefore, in opposition to *Dharma*, but the opposition is of another kind than that of *Adharma* to *Dharma*. . . . *Adharma* is sheer lawlessness. . . .'[4]

[1] Kaṭha Upaniṣad, I, 2, 23.
[2] Muṇḍaka Upaniṣad, III, 2, 3.
[3] Mahābhārata, XII, 270, 20.
[4] J. B. Van Buitenen, *op. cit.*, p. 36.

Mokṣa, therefore, does not contradict *Dharma*; it only transcends the latter's realm. It is, in short, a higher spiritual ideal conceived to comprehend and yet to go beyond *Dharma*. The relationship between *Mokṣa* and *Dharma* can perhaps be better expressed in this way:

'Saying it in Christian terms, we might perhaps call Mokṣa the Kingdom of Heaven, and Dharma, in its highest aspect naturally (ruling Artha and Kāma), the Kingdom of Heaven on earth, for which few are chosen, since most see Dharma only in its lower aspects.'[1]

This description by Mees could not be excelled.

To summarize, it is not difficult to see that the contribution of the Upaniṣads to the ethics of the Hindus is on the whole similar to the Greek contribution to Christian ethics. Like its counterpart, it is primarily anthropocentric and intellectualistic. It does sometimes talk of grace but generally tells of self-achievement, and the emphasis on knowledge is unmistakable. Though the Hindu understanding of the knowledge that leads to liberation may tend more toward the intuitive than the intellectual, it is knowledge or wisdom that is emphasized. With this observation, however, we must pass on to the content of the next important group of writings, the Epics and the Purāṇas.

(c) *The ethics of the Epics and Purāṇas*

In the course of our discussion of the ethical concepts in the Vedas we observed that *Bhakti* or devotion to the deity, even in its erotic blend, is already to be found in the Ṛg Veda itself. In the Epic period, *Bhakti* becomes a distinct and powerful cult. In a way, therefore, the ethic of the epics presents nothing new, but the emphasis is again new and has far-reaching consequences. This emphasis is a natural and logical development in so far as it promised to provide an alternative to the highly philosophical and abstract monism of the Upaniṣads. The strict monism and impersonalism of the Upaniṣads could hardly be expected to satisfy the religious aspirations of the common man, however appealing it might be to the philo-

[1] Mees, *op. cit.*, p. 26.

sopher. Hence there must have been the need for an ethic of faith and love centred round the personality of a supreme and benevolent God with whom the devotee could come into a personal relationship. The seeds of this ethic, as we have seen, are contained in the Vedas, a fact that enables us to understand that this development was neither abrupt nor discontinuous with the past. The emergence of this ethic in an organized form was perhaps aided by the success of Buddhism, as some people have suggested. In the words of Hopkins, once again, ' "The god who had been a man" was of all others best fitted to enter the lists in a struggle for supremacy with the idealized Buddha, now worshipped over all India as a divine being'.[1]

Thus arose the devotional cults based on the belief in incarnation. Popular heroes like Rama and Krishna were regarded as the incarnations of God, who was believed to have taken human forms in order to rid the universe of its *Adharma*, or unrighteous element. The theological presuppositions of this cult, with some notable differences, strongly resemble those of Christianity. There is the same stress on complete loving submission to the will of a God whose mercy is the only means to deliverance. 'Come to me as your refuge; I will release you from all sins,'[2] declares Śrī Krishna. This seems to strike the same note as the Pauline 'justification by faith'. This is, in other words, an ethic of faith, hope and love. In keeping with the spirit of this ethic, the Upaniṣadic meaning of *Mokṣa* undergoes a change. *Mokṣa* in the *Bhakti* schools no longer means a merger of the individual soul with the Ultimate Absolute, *Brahma*; it now means life everlasting in communion with God. The close similarity between the theological tenets of this cult and those of Christianity will be made even clearer if we consider one passage from Rudolf Otto in which he states the similarity of views between Christianity and some forms of *Bhakti*-religion:

'What is the good conferred in salvation by Christianity? Communion with the living personal God. What is the means of salvation? Grace, *gratia* and *gratia sola*, which lays hold of the lost, rescuing and redeeming him. Now these are the very

[1] Hopkins, *op. cit.*, pp. 171 *f.*
[2] Gītā, 18, 66.

slogans and distinctive terms of those forms of Bhakti-religion of which we are to speak.'[1]

This ethic of self-surrender, it should be noted, is in conflict with the Upaniṣadic ethic of self-achievement. But, as we saw earlier, some Upaniṣads do speak of grace and thereby provide additional support for the theocentric ethic of the *Bhakti* schools. The compromise effected was to leave the ethic of self-achievement for the few enlightened philosophers, and to make the ethic of faith and self-surrender the guide for the common man. Whatever the conflicts between the approaches of the *Bhakti* schools and the Upaniṣadic seers in this respect, we must not lose sight of the fact that *Dharma*, or the moral Law, is placed in the very centre of things, for Śrī Krishna says, 'Know that Dharma is my beloved first-born mental son, whose nature is to have compassion on all creatures. . . .'[2] This leaves no room for antinomian interpretations of the ethic of faith.

(d) The ethics of the Bhagavadgītā

Our survey under this head is a continuation of our analysis of the ethics of the Epics and Purāṇas, for as we stated earlier, the Gītā is part of the Mahābhārata, one of the two great epics of ancient India. But in view of the extraordinary impact of the Gītā on the minds of the Hindus, we have decided to mention briefly the outstanding features of its ethics. As is well known, the Vedic and Upaniṣadic groups of literature had, by the time the Gītā was written, become immensely vast, and contained a host of ethical concepts and religious creeds which were not always mutually compatible and, thereby, could have become sources of perplexity to the practising Hindu. To give just one example, there was considerable wrangling as to whether knowledge or devotion or sacrifice was the means to deliverance, whether ascetic renunciation (*Nivṛtti*) or the discharge of one's moral and social duties (*Pravṛtti*) was the better approach to the goal. The most outstanding contribution of the Gītā is its work of synthesis of all these concepts and creeds, which has since become the model for every religious thinker or leader in

[1] Rudolf Otto, *India's Religion of Grace*, quoted by John Mackenzie in *Two Religions*, Lutterworth Press, London, 1950, p. 106.
[2] Mahābhārata, Asva. Parv, 54: 11–17.

India. The Gītā is an ingenious effort to bring the best of all these creeds together, and is perhaps largely responsible for the catholicity of the Hindu's faith and morals. In the words of Dr Radhakrishnan,

'The Gītā takes up the various creeds and codes that were already competing with each other and transforms them into aspects of a more inward religion, free, subtle, and profound. If popular deities are worshipped, it must be understood that they are only varied manifestations of the One Supreme. If sacrifices are to be offered, they must be of the spirit and not of material objects. A life of self-control or disinterested action is a sacrifice. . . . The Gītā teaches the doctrine of the *Brahman-Ātman* which the followers of the Upaniṣads seek and proclaim. The Yoga of concentration is useful but the Supreme is the Lord of Yoga. The dualism of the Sāṃkhya is taken over into non-dualism, for *puruṣa* and *prakṛti* are the two natures of the Supreme Lord, Puruṣottama. He alone dispenses grace. He is the true object of devotion. For Him must all work be done. Saving wisdom is of Him. The traditional rules of Dharma are to be followed because He established them and He upholds the moral order. The rules are not ends in themselves, for union with the Supreme is the final goal. The teacher of the Gītā reconciles the different systems in vogue and gives us a comprehensive eirenicon which is not local and temporary but is for all time and all men.'[1]

We should be excused for this lengthy quotation, for, as we believe, it would help to bring out clearly the various elements in the synthesis of the Gītā.

The other distinctive feature of the Gītā is its emphasis on what may be called a Kantian ethic in a religious setting. This new ethic might have helped to turn the tide against asceticism and renunciation (*Nivṛtti Mārga*) by its authoritative and forceful exposition of the view that *Mokṣa* could be attained by discharging one's duties in life, and need not necessarily entail ascetic self-denial. Since the moral law or *Dharma* was established by the Lord, man has an obligation to do what is enjoined

[1] Dr S. Radhakrishnan, in his introduction to the translation of the Gītā, George Allen and Unwin, London, 1960, pp. 74 *f.*

by this law. But he must act from the sole consideration that this is his duty, not from the motive of reward. There is in fact a renunciation involved here too, but this is the renunciation of the fruits of man's actions and not of actions as such. This ethic of 'Duty for Duty's sake' is an important element in Hindu thought and has provided the rationale for the endeavour toward *Mokṣa* along with an active life in the world.

In view of the fact that all later Hindu thought in ethics and religion has based itself on one or the other of the various elements found in the literature discussed above, our analysis of the constituents of Hindu ethics could, with sufficient reason, end here. But considering the profound influence of Shamkara and Ramanuja on later Hindu thought and practice, it appears that any account of Hindu ethics which does not include these two illustrious figures is bound to be incomplete. Hence we shall consider briefly the emphases and orientations given to Hindu thought by these two.

(*e*) *Landmarks in the development of later Hindu ethics: Shamkara and Ramanuja*

The importance of Shamkara in Hindu thought can easily be appreciated if we realize that quite often Hinduism itself is identified with the non-dualism (*Advaita*) of Shamkara. In fact, it would not be wrong to think that the frequent characterization of Hindu ethics as such as 'world-and-life denying'[1] is largely due to this identification. His description of the world as illusion (*Māyā*) and his forceful exposition of the view that the ultimate destiny of the individual soul is the merger into the All-soul (*Brahma*) has had such tremendous impact that at times people have been misled into thinking that there is nothing more in Hinduism. Shamkara, the St Thomas Aquinas of India, advocates an intellectualistic and contemplative ethic which culminates in the mystical merger of the individual soul in the All-soul, *Brahma*. Though he does not deny the existence of the world nor of the personal God on the practical plane, (*Vyāvahārika Sattā*), he does tend to reject these on the ultimate plane, (*Pāramārthika Sattā*). For the final realization of the

[1] This phrase is used by Albert Schweitzer to contrast, for instance, the 'world-and-life-affirming' optimism of Western thought with the 'world-and-life-denying' pessimism of Indian thought in his books *Indian Thought and its Development* and *Civilisation and Ethics*.

identity or non-difference of the individual soul with the Absolute, which is what *Mokṣa* means to Shamkara, knowledge or wisdom is the ultimate means. But he does not deny the initial value of either action or devotion. For him '*karma*' (action or duty) and '*bhakti*' (devotion) 'are means to spiritual freedom',[1] stepping-stones, as it were, to the attainment of saving knowledge. This emphasis on knowledge as the means of liberation and the interpretation of liberation or *Mokṣa* itself as the final realization by the individual soul that 'I am Brahma (*Ahaṃ Brahma-asmi*)' is only a more eloquent and uncompromising version of the Upaniṣadic ethic.

Ramanuja, on the other hand, interprets the 'three great sources (*Prasthānatrayī*)' as implying an ethic of love and submission to a personal God. He regards God as full of auspicious (*Śubha*) qualities of all sorts, especially mercy or kindness. Man's liberation, according to him, consists in an eternal life in communion with God which can be attained primarily by the grace of God that dawns as a consequence of man's unquestioning faith and genuine devotion to God. This ethic of love and gratitude, it must be said, has had a much wider appeal in India than the non-dualism of Shamkara which has been confined to the coterie of philosophers. The ethic of love and submission, through a host of poet saints like Vallabha, Chaitanya, Nanak, Kabir and Dadu, has permeated the whole fabric of life in India, and has established itself as the ethic of the masses. And the credit for this must go as much to Ramanuja as to any other source.

Much as we might like to include in our analysis the re-interpretations of Hindu ethics by modern thinkers like Tagore, Vivekananda, Aurobindo, Gandhi and Radhakrishnan, we are obliged, for two reasons, to suppress this temptation and close the account here. Firstly, the space at our disposal does not seem to allow any further extension of this analysis. Moreover, all these thinkers have generally adopted one or the other of the main lines of ethical thinking already discussed, with suitable modifications in the light of modern circumstances and knowledge. As a result, though the emphases have changed, ancient and medieval lines of ethical thinking have generally been the guidelines of modern thinking in Hindu ethics.

[1] Radhakrishnan, Translation of the Gītā, *op. cit.*, p. 73.

CONCLUSION

It seems to be time to summarize what we have been discussing so far in order to bring into sharper focus the main theme of our argument. Our account of the constituents of Hindu and Christian ethics has not been quite exhaustive, but it may be hoped that it has not been too sketchy either. Our whole effort would be justified only if it were reasonably obvious by now that our hypothesis about the nature of Christian and Hindu ethics is borne out by evidence, i.e. that both Christian and Hindu ethics are catholic, comprehensive and elastic. Huston Smith, writing on Islam, says that 'the creed of Islam wastes no words'.[1] We maintain that it will be extremely difficult, if not impossible, to say the same either of Christianity or of Hinduism. The latter are not well-defined systems of ethics, but contain systems within systems, a variety of ethical concepts and creeds, not necessarily mutually compatible. They are great reservoirs of ethical ideas from which their adherents can draw for consumption what they find suited to their tastes. In other words, by calling someone a Christian or a Hindu, though we undoubtedly derive some general information about his beliefs, we cannot with any certainty predict his principles and practice in the field of morals. As we have seen, there is such a wide range of ethical concepts and practices within either Hinduism or Christianity that the sheer fact of being an adherent of one of these faiths does not necessarily commit anyone to any specific kind of ethical thinking. A Christian is free to build his moral values around the nucleus of either mysticism or monasticism, eudaemonism, formalism, utilitarianism or even sacramentalism and ritualism so long as he places the ethic of love in the centre and accepts some basic dogmas of the Christian faith. And let us remember that a Christian, in giving his ethical thinking an ascetic or intellectualistic or any other orientation, need not be guilty of scandalous originality, for he can, in most cases, quote quite respectable authority for his own interpretation.

This applies even more aptly to Hinduism. A Hindu can make his choice of moral values from a vast range of these which he may find in his scriptures and tradition. In fact, it must be

[1] Huston Smith, *The Religions of Man*, Harper, New York, 1964, p. 210.

admitted that Hinduism goes to much greater, almost absurd, lengths in emphasizing its non-doctrinaire approach to moral practices and beliefs. For example, Dr Radhakrishnan claims that 'the theist and the atheist, the sceptic and the agnostic may all be Hindus if they accept the Hindu system of culture and life'. This amount of latitude would clearly not be allowed to a Christian, for whom a set of dogmas demands unconditional acceptance. It seems, therefore, that there may be a difference of degree between the two, but both Christianity and Hinduism are by and large catholic and comprehensive in their ethical thinking.

This diversity and elasticity of Christian and Hindu ethics needs explanation, the former perhaps more than the latter. For as we have stated earlier, recognition of the diversity in tastes and temperaments of people is almost a credal belief in Hinduism. Christianity, on the other hand, is supposed to have started as a simple faith, with the emphasis on unity rather than diversity. Yet the astounding thing is that this initially simple faith has had to make room for a variety of ethical concepts and practices in course of its two thousand years of existence and expansion. In our opinion three factors may be regarded as chiefly responsible for the present diversity of Christian and Hindu ethics.

(*a*) *The diversity of sources*

As our analysis should have shown, the sources of both Christian and Hindu ethics are too many, resulting in an inevitable diversity of interpretation and emphasis. But it may be held that since Christianity is rooted in its founder, Jesus Christ, he is the ultimate source, and his teaching the final arbiter in all matters of Christian faith and morals. This however, does not seem to help as much as it promises to, for it side-tracks the main problem. The main problem for Christian scholars and theologians through the ages has been that of determining what exactly Christ's teachings were and what they meant. And the diversity of interpretations and emphases is largely due to the fact that it has been very difficult to do this. Christ's ministry was brief; his utterances were cryptic and by no means mutually consistent. J. E. Fison, in his brilliant analysis of 'the catholicity of Jesus Christ', lists the various elements in the 'holiness of Jesus', which includes the esoteric, prophetic, ascetic, natural, supernatural, sacramental, mystical and many others.[1] In view of this, it is not at all surprising that Christian ethics should contain a diversity of elements. The truth is that this many-sided holiness of Jesus has been subject to various emphases and interpretations at the hands of later scholars and commentators who have stressed one of these elements at the cost of the other with the result that each of these has an equal claim to be regarded as genuinely Christian.

(*b*) *The diversity of the human material*

It is a well-known fact that India has assimilated, in course of its long history, people of practically every race, colour and culture. This process of assimilation has inevitably led to a tolerance of the customs and beliefs of aliens by recognizing these as somehow forming part of Hinduism. It is perhaps this factor which eventually led to the Hindu's emphasis on diversity as a fact of life. Christianity, similarly, has been forced to give way to all kinds of customs and beliefs in the course of its expansion through various continents. To quote only one example of this compromise, it is well known that the caste system of India has not left unvarnished the Christian community in India. Until recently there were separate churches for the converts coming from the class of 'untouchables'. Moreover, what Hinduism has overtly recognized as a creed has been covertly in operation within Christianity, namely, the diversity in the tastes and temperaments of people. This, to an extent, accounts for the infiltration of alien concepts and practices.

(*c*) *Love and gratitude capable of various interpretations*

Almost the whole of Christianity and the main stream of Hinduism can be described as the religion of love and gratitude. And it is a notorious fact that love and gratitude can be expressed in more than one way. It can be the relationship of love between father and son, or between friends, or between lover and beloved. The first of these, which characterizes the whole of Christianity and some sects of Vaisnavism, is perhaps the purest and loftiest expression of the love of the Almighty, but

[1] Fison, *op. cit.*, Chapter III, pp. 115–28.

the last one of these can, and has led to erotic expressions, sometimes resulting in absurd aberrations. Eroticism, though more common in Hinduism, is, however, not confined to it alone. Marguerite Marie Alacoque, St Gertrude and St Theresa are illustrations of the erotic blend of love within Christian history. William James quotes the following passage as an illustration of what he calls the theopathic condition of the mind. This passage describes the transports of Margaret, a Catholic nun:

'. . . But to be loved by God! and loved by him to distraction (*aimé jusqu'à la folie*)! Margaret melted away at the thought of such a thing. . . . She said to God, "Hold back, O my God, these torrents which overwhelm me, or else enlarge my capacity for their reception".'[1]

It would be seen then that the description of Christian ethics as the ethic of love has only the deceptive appearance of simplicity. In reality, however, the ethic of love lends itself to various shades of meaning and thus becomes a source of diversity and elasticity within a certain faith. This is as true of Hinduism as of Christianity.

[1] William James, *op. cit.*, p. 343.

CHAPTER III

THE NATURE AND DESTINY OF MAN

Reinhold Niebuhr, in *An Interpretation of Christian Ethics*, says,

'The distinctive contribution of religion to morality lies in its comprehension of the dimension of depth in life. . . . A religious morality is constrained by its sense of a dimension of depth to trace every force with which it deals to some ultimate origin and to relate every purpose to some ultimate end.'[1]

In other words, the ethical activity that the adherent of a religion undertakes has validity or value only in so far as it promotes the ultimate end as conceived by the religion in question. This ultimate end or final destiny is what imparts meaning and significance to the ethical endeavour of man. It follows, then, that the religion which fails to establish a meaningful relationship between the ethical ideal it preaches and the ultimate end it prescribes fails not only as a satisfying religion but also as a system of ethics. It is important, therefore, that we consider the Christian and Hindu views of the ultimate end or final destiny of man in order that we may estimate their value as systems of religious morality. It needs no arguing, however, that the destiny of man depends on his essential nature and capacities.

We shall, therefore, open our discussion in this chapter with the consideration of the Christian and Hindu views of the nature and status of man. This, however, entails a consideration of the how and why of creation itself, for man only occupies a place in the created universe, and his nature and capacities can be explained only in the context of creation.

[1] Reinhold Niebuhr, *An Interpretation of Christian Ethics*, SCM Press, London, 1936, pp. 15*f*.

THE CREATION MYTHS

In every religious tradition we find stories about how and why the world came into existence. To some adherents of any of these religions these stories may appear to be literal accounts of the act of creation, but to some others they seem to be only symbolic or metaphorical representations of the basic facts about creation. In view of this, it would be more appropriate to call these stories 'myths', for myths are 'tales which are not literally true'.[1] Now any discussion of these creation myths inevitably raises many knotty problems. The answers to some of these problems or detailed discussion of any of their aspects is clearly beyond the scope of this essay. We intend to touch on only those aspects of this issue which, in our opinion, have some significant bearing on the main theme of our present enquiry, that is, the nature and destiny of man. Let us start with the traditional Christian story.

(*a*) *The creation myth in the Christian tradition*

The Genesis narrative opens with the words,

> 'In the beginning God created the heaven and the earth.
>
> And the earth was without form, and void; and darkness was upon the face of the deep. And the Spirit of God moved upon the face of the waters.
>
> And God said, Let there be light: and there was light.'[2]

We do not have to go into further details of this narrative to realize that before this act of creation there was nothing else apart from God. What is asserted unequivocally in this account, then, is that God created out of nothing. In other words, God did not just shape a pre-existing matter, as Plato, for example, believed; He produced the world out of sheer nothingness, as it were. He is the sole and sufficient cause of the world. This raises the issue of whether the world can be said to have a beginning or to be eternal. Now it must be said that creation *ex nihilo* implies not only 'the popular idea of creation (involving on the one hand a beginning of the world)', but also 'the creation

[1] A. Flew and D. Mackinnon, *New Essays in Philosophical Theology*, SCM Press, London, 1963, p. 171.

[2] Genesis 1: 1–3.

of the theologians on the other (a recognition of man's absolute dependence on God)'.[1] Before deciding which of these implications is relevant for our purposes, it would perhaps be desirable to mention St Thomas' views as to whether the world had a beginning. In the words of Etienne Gilson,

St Thomas maintains (therefore) the possibility of proving the creation *ex nihilo* of the universe, wherein he is . . . resolutely opposed to Averroës and his followers; but, in conceding, like Maimonides, the logical possibility of a universe created from all eternity, he refuses to confuse the truths of faith with those which can be the objects of proof. In this way he achieves in his teaching the harmony which he sets out to establish between the authentic doctrine of Christianity and whatever undoubted truth is contained in the philosophy of Aristotle.[2]

Thus it would seem that the 'authentic doctrine of Christianity' asserts the beginning of the world in time. This question of the beginning of the world in time, however, may be of significance to the students of the history of science or of metaphysics. For our purposes, the more significant aspect of the doctrine of creation *ex nihilo* lies in its 'insistence on absolute dependence (on God) and this rejection of any sort of dualistic account of the universe'.[3] This is what we called the theologians' idea of creation. The significance of this idea lies in the moral suggestions and overtones it has. As evidence of the moral suggestions entailed by this idea, Anthony Flew quotes Emil Brunner's statement that in recognizing God as 'MY creator and the creator of all things I become aware that I am . . . his servant, his property, because all that I am and have I have from him, because not only I but all that is has been created by him'.[4] In the words of J. S. Whale,

'The Christian doctrine of creation is a symbolic assertion, not that the world was made by the Great Artificer as a carpenter makes a box, but that man in all his felt finitude comes from God and goes to God; he is not surrounded by a sheer abyss of nothingness. God, the God and Father of our Lord Jesus

[1] Flew and Mackinnon, *op. cit.*, p. 185.
[2] Gilson, *op. cit.*, p. 151.
[3] Flew and Mackinnen, *op. cit.*, p. 173.
[4] *Ibid.*, p. 173.

Christ, is the ground and goal of all that is. All is of God—our creation, preservation and all the blessings of this life; the redemption of the world, the means of grace and the hope of glory. He is the first and the last and the living One.'[1]

It should be obvious that such a view of creation will inevitably imply certain moral attitudes—attitudes such as, in the words of Flew again, 'This is God's world . . . [and] we should behave, as it were, as guests and borrowers: not as owners who have a right to do what they like with their own'.[2] It follows from the above discussion that there are three points of cardinal importance in the traditional Christian account of creation which may deserve special notice by students of Christian ethics. These are (1) the insistence on absolute dependence, (2) the rejection of any real fundamental dualism, and (3) the suggestion of certain conduct and attitudes as appropriate.

Though once again this is a metaphysical problem which does not primarily concern us, we shall still make a passing reference to the question of why, after all, God created the universe. This is important because the purpose that God had in creating the world is bound to have a bearing on the destiny and the ethical ideal of man. St Thomas' answer to this question, in the words of Etienne Gilson, is

'that good tends naturally to diffuse itself beyond itself; its characteristic feature is to seek to communicate itself to other beings to the extent to which they are capable of receiving it. What is true of every good being in proportion as it is good, is eminently true of the Supreme Good which we call God.'[3]

Thus the reason for creation is the superabundance of goodness in God 'whose perfection overflows and spreads over a hierarchy of participating beings'.[4] If we substitute love for goodness, we may rephrase this explanation, but the essential argument will be hardly changed. God is love and love, like good, or perhaps even moreso, seeks to communicate itself to other beings *to the*

[1] J. S. Whale, *Christian Doctrine*, 5th impression, Fontana Books, London, 1963, pp. 13*f.*

[2] Flew and Mackinnon, *op. cit.*, p. 173.

[3] Gilson, *op. cit.*, p. 141.

[4] *Ibid.*, p. 141.

extent to which they are capable of receiving it. Thus love and goodness form the very fabric of the world, and so must determine the ethical ideal and final destiny of man.

(b) Creation myths in the Hindu tradition

The use of the plural, myths, is deliberate here, for in the Hindu tradition there is more than one myth regarding the act of creation, though quite a few of these myths differ from each other in only minor details and not on the main theme or its essential implications. In the words of Sir Charles Eliot,

'Hindu cosmogonies are various and discordant in details, but usually start with the evolution or emanation of living beings from the Divinity and often a reproductive act forms part of the process, such as the hatching of an egg or the division of a Divinity into male and female halves. In many accounts the Deity brings into being personages who continue the work of world-making and such entities as mind, time and desire are produced before the material world. But everything in these creation stories is figurative.'[1]

It may be desirable to mention briefly in this context what is perhaps the oldest and the most celebrated one of these 'stories'. This is contained in the famous *Puruṣa Sūkta* of the Ṛg Veda (X, 129). According to this account, the world and all that is in it has emanated from the One Primeval Man (*Puruṣa*). This *Puruṣa* is both immanent and transcendent, for 'the finite world only accounts for one-quarter of his being, the remaining three-quarters constitute immortality . . .'.[2] The act of creation was started by *Puruṣa* being offered as an oblation at the great primeval Sacrifice, and thus the world may be said to be a result of this act of self-immolation by *Puruṣa*. The whole universe then is only a part of God, and, naturally, cannot exist independently of God.

Fascinating as they might be, it will be neither possible nor profitable for us to dwell at length on these 'various and discordant' details of the creation stories. It is possible, however, to make some observations which may be generally acceptable to all or most schools of Hindu thought. It must be said first

[1] Sir Charles Eliot, *Hinduism and Buddhism*, I, Book II, p. 43.
[2] Professor R. C. Zaehner, *Hinduism*, Oxford University Press, 1962, p. 57

of all that the idea of creation *ex nihilo* is more the exception than the rule with Hinduism. The more common concept seems to be that God creates in the sense of arranging, ordering or manipulating elements that are themselves eternal. The Nyāya-Vaiśeṣika theory of creation, for example, holds that there are eternal constituents of the universe—the four kinds of atoms (of earth, air, fire and water) and the five substances (*Ākāśa*, space, time, mind and soul)—which can neither be created nor destroyed. God only arranges these various eternal constituents into composite substances in accordance with the requirements of *Karma*. The Mīmāṃsā, which does not believe in a God, holds that this arrangement of atoms can be brought about by the Law of *Karma* itself. The Sāṃkhya, which again is atheistic, believes in the evolution of everything but souls from the unconscious primordial stuff, called *Prakṛti*. It is important to note, however, that in the allied system of Yoga, God or *Īśvara*, is brought in to co-ordinate and give direction to the process of evolution. In the Gītā, on the other hand, the dualism of the type advocated by Sāṃkhya is transformed into a monism, and the two ultimate entities—*Puruṣa* and *Prakṛti*—are conceived as being only different aspects of the Supreme Person, *Puruṣottama*. Thus matter, though distinct from spirit, is co-eval with it as part of the Supreme. This is the explanation adopted by Ramanuja also, the most influential of the Hindu theists. *Cit* (spirit) and *acit* (matter) are both constituents of the Lord, *Īśvara* or *Brahma*. It would thus be clear that according to most influential schools of Hinduism, matter and spirit are both equally primordial and hence the question of creation *out of nothing* does not arise.

The second point on which there is complete unanimity among all schools of Hinduism is that there can be no question of the world having a beginning in time. With its belief in cyclic creation it tends to subscribe to what for St Thomas was a mere logical possibility, that is, that the universe is created from all eternity (*Anādi*).

We are, however, still to emphasize what for our purposes is the most important implication of the Hindu cosmology. This is that despite the differences in other details, every school of Hinduism (except of course the atheistic Sāṃkhya and Mīmāṃsā) unhesitatingly declares the utter dependence of the world and especially man on God. Even those systems which advocate some kind of pluralism on the ultimate plane (Madhva and Nyāya, for example), insist that *Paramātman*, or the Supreme Self, is the sovereign, and therefore everything is ultimately dependent on Him. All these systems conceive the human soul to be separate from but dependent on God. Only Shamkara believes in the ultimate identity of the *Ātman* with *Brahma*; but even he has to concede that the *Atman*, being merely a part of *Brahma*, cannot be independent of the latter. Thus even though God creates with pre-existing material, and though the souls are eternal and unborn, nothing can conceivably exist independent of God. This fact of dependence on God is brought out even more forcefully by the popular Hindu belief that the trinity of Brahmā, Viṣṇu and Maheśa, as different aspects of the same Supreme Lord, is responsible for not only the creation but also the preservation and destruction of the universe.

Regarding this absolute dependence, which the Christian doctrine of creation is interpreted to imply, the utterances of the Gītā leave us in no doubt whatsoever that it is the same in Hinduism. Śrī Krishna declares,

'(I am) the goal, the upholder, the lord, the witness, the abode, the refuge and the friend. (I am) the origin and the dissolution, the ground, the resting place and the imperishable seed.'[1]

If God is the ground of everything that is and happens, then utter and absolute dependence could be the only response to Him. This is brought out also by the sentiments expressed by the many poet-saints of India who have played an instrumental part in giving direction to religious piety amongst the multitudes in India. The moral overtones of this sense of absolute dependence, once again, are the same in Hinduism as they were found to be in the case of Christianity, that is, that since this is God's world, we ought to behave as guests, borrowers, or even servants, rather than as owners who have a right to do what they like with their own. The very opening verse of the Īśa Upaniṣad strikes this note when it says,

[1] Gītā, IX, 18.

'(Know that) all this, whatever moves in this moving world, is enveloped by God. Therefore, find your enjoyment in renunciations; do not covet what belongs to others.'[1]

The same attitude characterizes the ethic of the Gītā which declares,

'Whatever thou doest, whatever thou eatest, whatever though offerest, whatever thou givest away, whatever austerities thou dost practise, do that (O Son of Kuntī-Arjuna), as an offering to Me.'[2]

Thus the attitude of absolute dependence and the suggestion of certain conduct and attitudes as appropriate are common to both Hinduism and Christianity, as following from their doctrines of creation.

About the why of creation, once again many answers are offered. Two terms are most frequently mentioned in connexion with this explanation of the ultimate mystery. These are *Māyā* and *Līlā*. *Māyā* is generally understood to mean the 'power which enables Him to produce mutable nature'.[3] Though there may be differences of opinion about this meaning, it may reasonably be held to be the view of most of the theistic schools and certainly of the Gītā. In the Purāṇic literature, however, and in much of the *Bhakti* sects there is an equally frequent mention of the second of these terms, that is, *Līlā*. *Līlā* means sport, and thus creation is attributed to Divine sport. This may seem to be a very un-Christian way of speaking about the creative act of God, if it is supposed to mean a callous, purposeless and indifferent act on the part of God. But this is definitely not the real meaning of the term. Sport, in the context of creation, only signifies a certain exuberance which overflows into an act of creation. And this is because God is supposed to be loving, and so the exuberance is the exuberance of love and affection. In the words of Dr Radhakrishnan,

'The one Godhead . . . is also the Supreme Living God, loving the world and redeeming it by His grace. Why is the world

[1] Īśa Upaniṣad, 1.
[2] Gītā, IX, 27.
[3] Radhakrishnan, Introduction to the Gītā, p. 42.

what it is with its graduated hierarchy? We can only say, it is the nature of the Supreme to express itself in this way.'[1]

The Nyāya-Vaiśeṣika explanation of creation, however, attributes creation to the desire (*Icchā*) of *Īśvara* or God, under certain accessory conditions (*Sahakārī*). But God is not supposed to have created the world for any selfish purpose, 'but for the good of all beings'.[2] That the *Līlā* of God is no mere whim would be realized if we remember the Nyāya-Vaiśeṣika belief, shared by most Hindus, that God creates in accordance with the requirements of the Law of *Karma* in order that the souls might have the chance to enjoy or suffer the consequences of their actions. The world thus becomes a moral stage on which nothing happens by sheer chance.

It seems then that whether in Hinduism or in Christianity, the explanation of the why of creation is either in terms of good or of love, though it is often confessed that these are mere humble efforts to understand or pierce the divine mystery. This tendency to regard the how and why of creation as an ultimate mystery, though more common in Hinduism, is not, however, absent from Christianity. Bernard Iddings Bell's remarks on Christianity are worth quoting in this connexion. He says, 'Almost the first thing to be noted about Christianity is that it is a religion based on agnosticism. . . . It makes no attempt to explain the unexplainable or, as the negro pastor said, "to unscrew the inscrutable".'[3] This remark on Christianity, it may be confidently said, applies equally well to Hinduism.

MAN—HIS NATURE AND STATUS

The above accounts of creation provide the background in which we now must consider in some detail the nature and status of man. This would involve the investigation of such questions as: what is the constitution and the essential nature of man? what is he capable of? and what is his status in the hierarchy of beings in this created universe?

[1] Radhakrishnan, Introduction to the Gītā, pp. 39 *f.*

[2] S. N. Das Gupta, *A History of Indian Philosophy*, Cambridge University Press, 1922, I, 324.

[3] Bernard Iddings Bell, *Religion for Living*, John Gifford, London, 1939, p. 40.

(*a*) *The Christian view*

In the words of A. C. Bouquet,

'Christians are committed officially to a very high belief in the potential greatness of man. He is a little lower than God (Ps. viii). He is made in the image of God (Gen. i). The spirit of man is the candle of the Lord (Prov. 27). Yet Christians are equally committed to the belief in man's utter need of God. Man needs God. Man cannot be all that he ought to be, or fulfil his grand possibilities, if he tries, as he so often does, to be the artist of his own social and individual life—"on his own", so to speak—apart from the life of God.'[1]

This passage practically sums up the main points in the Christian doctrine of man. But let us examine in greater detail some of the key phrases used and their implications. To start with, what is the exact significance of the phrase 'in the image of God'? Linguistically, perhaps, it can only mean that man bears a certain amount of resemblance or likeness to God. This may mean that man, though not quite God, does, to some extent, possess the attributes and powers that are supposed to belong to God. Presumably, it is only a figurative way of speaking about what Bouquet calls the 'potential greatness of man'. Among other things, this potential greatness implies that just as God rules or has dominion over all His creatures, so man was made to have '. . . dominion over the fish of the sea, and over the fowl of the air, and over the cattle, and over all the earth, and over every creeping thing that creepeth upon the earth'.[2] The difference between man and God, however, must not be lost sight of. God's dominion over the universe is final and absolute, that is, He exercises this in His own right as the creator of the universe, whereas in the case of man, this privilege or power is there simply because it has been delegated to him by God. It follows, then, that man can enjoy his powers only so long as he enjoys the confidence and love of God, something like the situation of the ambassador of a country, who can represent the interests of his country only so long as he enjoys the confidence

[1] A. C. Bouquet, *Comparative Religion*, Sixth edition, Pelican Books, 1962. p. 257.

[2] Genesis 1: 26.

of his country's government. This, as we shall see later, has important ethical implications.

Meanwhile, let us ask what else is entailed by man's being created in the image of God. Since God is a creator, man's likeness to God may also imply the power of creativity on a limited scale. But, perhaps, the most significant implication of the phrase 'in the image of God', at least ethically, is man's awareness of it. As J. S. Whale puts it,

'He is lifted above all earthly creatures in being made in the image of God, and in being aware of the fact. He is aware that the Creator is the Eternal Love who calls men into existence that their willing response to his love may fulfil his creative purpose. This responsible awareness which God created in man (*Ansprechbarkeit*, addressability, or answerability, as Brunner has called it) is man's greatness and his fatal temptation. As Brunner observes, this responsibility or addressability was not a task, but a gift; not law, but grace.'[1]

To summarize, then, the Christian view is that man is God's creature, but a privileged one in so far as he has been created in the likeness of God. This means that he has been endowed with intelligence, with the power of creativity on a limited scale, and with the power to reciprocate God's love, but above all, with a sense of responsibility, an awareness that all his powers and privileges are gifts of God rather than his absolute rights. In status, therefore, he seems to occupy an intermediate position—definitely above the other creatures of the earth but below that of the celestial creatures, like the angels, for example. The fact is that man can achieve almost anything and is potentially capable of everything, provided he does not forget that he is, after all, only a creature and is embodied like the rest.

This question of man's being embodied and merely a creature raises the question of immortality, and, perhaps, of pre-existence. If man is only a creature and is embodied like the rest of the creatures, as surely he is, and if he is also immortal, as Christian theology insists, then it follows that immortality can belong only to his soul, for it surely cannot be his body's. The

[1] Whale, *op. cit.*, pp. 41 *f.*

popular notion is that in physical death only the body dies, and the soul survives in some form, for after the Day of Judgement it is the soul which either reaps the reward of eternal communion with God or suffers eternal damnation in hell. Now, what exactly is meant by 'soul', and in what sense is it immortal?

Once again, we seem to be faced with a very difficult metaphysical problem whose solution is beyond the scope of our enquiry. Leaving aside all metaphysical subtlety, however, it can be safely asserted that the belief in a soul is a concrete representation of man's conviction, or, we might say, fond wish, that there is more in the constitution of man than meets the eye. That one part of man, his body, is perishable cannot possibly be questioned, for after all, this part of man is only made of 'dust'. '. . . For dust thou art, and unto dust shalt thou return'[1] is the verdict of God. But whatever this phrase might have meant in early Judaism, later Judaism and Christianity regarded this as referring merely to the 'body' of man. Yes, the body of man is made of dust and so it must return to dust. But what about the Spirit or Soul—the Divine in man? This surely survives physical death, or, in other words, is immortal. How and when the concept of immortality entered into Christianity is extremely difficult to find out, nor is it our task, but it is certainly true that in St Paul's interpretation of Resurrection there is clear evidence of belief in immortality of the soul. We are not suggesting that St Paul was the first in the Christian tradition to have talked of soul and the immortality of the soul, but, in the words of S. D. F. Salmond, 'It is in Paul's Epistles above all others that it is set forth as the specifically Christian doctrine'.[2] Without going into further detail, we may conclude, then, that St Paul's doctrine of Resurrection, and all later Christian theology, implies that man is an 'embodied soul' and that though the body is perishable, the soul is immortal. This immortal soul can obviously not be identical with the mind, as we understand the latter today, though there are many instances in the history of Western philosophy and theology where no real distinction has been

[1] Genesis 3: 19.

[2] S. D. F. Salmond, *The Christian Doctrine of Immortality*, T. and T. Clark, Edinburgh, 1913, p. 437.

maintained between the mind and the soul. But this statement, perhaps, is not quite relevant here. What is relevant is that the authentic Christian doctrine on this issue happens to be that the soul, though created, is immortal at the same time. We shall have occasion to refer to the difficulties in the belief in *created but immortal souls*. For the time being, let us pass on to another allied problem.

We have seen that the Christian doctrine of Resurrection implies a theory of immortality. Does it also imply a theory of pre-existence? Almost all Christians today will certainly exclaim a vigorous 'no' in answer to this question. But let us remember that belief in pre-existence is not quite as foreign to Christian thinking as is generally imagined. Origen, for example, one of 'the leaders of early Christian thought' '. . . took the idea of *pre-existence* definitely and seriously' and believed that 'every individual is born with an inherited burden of failures and sins, not inherited from Adam but from his own previous life'.[1] It is true that Origen's teaching on this point has been gradually and definitely lost on the Christian world, and it cannot, therefore, be accepted as genuine Christian belief. But it may be urged that his explanation in terms of pre-existence and after-life may appear to many a better explanation of the continuity of the soul's existence after bodily death than the belief that the bodies of the dead are literally to be 'raised' before the final Judgement. Origen, understandably, 'repudiates with indignation the notion that the *bodies of the dead* are to be "raised" and to exist for ever'.[2] Resurrection of the dead does not seem to explain what happens to the immortal soul after the death of the body. In what form is the soul preserved, as it must be, till the Day of Judgement? If it is assumed that it takes another, perhaps subtle form, then rebirth in some form is clearly implied. And this seems to be an unavoidable alternative if the 'raising of the dead' is not to mean a fresh creation by God.

To sum up, then, Christianity believes that man is potentially great. He is a complex of body and spirit, of which the former is perishable but the latter immortal. Thus it believes that the soul can be created, yet immortal. Its concept of the immortality

[1] S. H. Mellone, *Leaders of Early Christian Thought*, The Lindsey Press, London, 1954, p. 97.
[2] *Ibid.*, p. 95.

of the soul and its belief in the resurrection of the dead contain implicitly the idea of pre-existence and rebirth, as it was worked out by Origen, but official Christianity somehow shies away from this belief.

(*b*) *The Hindu view*

Let us state at the outset that the Hindu view about the nature, composition and status of man is strikingly different from that of Christianity in many details; but this is not to say that the Hindu view of man's status or his capacities is contrary to, or even essentially different from, the Christian. The fact is that the metaphysical and ontological constituents of the story are different, but, as we shall see later, the ethical substance is by and large the same.

Hindu metaphysics has worked out in much more elaborate detail the nature and composition of man than perhaps Christian theology has. According to most authoritative Hindu accounts, man is a compound of (1) a human form or body (*Deha* or *Śarīra*) which includes the ten external organs (*Bāhyakaraṇas*)—five sensory and five motor; (2) life (*Prāṇa*); (3) mind (*Manas*), which is a kind of co-ordinator between knowledge and action; (4) intellect (*Buddhi*), which is the organ of ascertainment and decision; (5) ego (*Ahaṃkāra*), which is responsible for the feeling of 'I and mine' (*Abhimāna*); and, of course, (6) a soul (*Ātman*). It should be clear from this enumeration that in the Hindu tradition the mind, the intellect and the ego are definitely recognized to be different from the soul or self and hence there can never be any question of confusing the soul or *Ātman* with the mind at all. It would follow, then, that with the decomposition of the body only the adjuncts of the body can die; it does not affect the soul in any way.

What, then, is the nature of the soul or *Ātman*? The Gītā returns an unequivocal answer to this:

'He (the true self or Ātman) is never born, nor does he die at any time, nor having (once) come to be will he again cease to be. He is unborn, eternal, permanent and primeval. He is not slain when the body is slain.'[1]

[1] Gītā, II, 20.

That this soul or self is immortal is obvious from the above passage, and does not therefore have to be established. But there is another phrase in this passage which ought to be taken careful note of. It says that 'He (Ātman) is never born' either. This undoubtedly implies that there can be no question of the *Ātman* having been created at all. It is an eternal entity and has co-existed along with God from eternity. But this does not mean that it is an independent entity. In the words of Dr Radhakrishnan, 'It is *everlasting as a Divine form* and derives its existence from God'.[1] It is no doubt separate from God, but from only part of God. Thus the *Ātman* in man is literally and really the Divine spark in man, what St Paul perhaps means by the Christ that 'liveth in me'.[2]

It will be seen that whatever the other advantages or disadvantages of this theory, it certainly avoids the inconsistency of created but immortal souls. But in keeping with our intention to avoid controversies of a metaphysical nature, we shall not discuss in detail the difficulties of the doctrine of created but immortal souls. We shall simply point out that to quite a few great minds, including that of Bradley, this doctrine seems to involve a plain contradiction.[3]

What is relevant for our purposes here is the fact that Hinduism believes in eternal and immortal souls. Those eternal souls, once they have entered *Saṃsāra*, or the world-process, assume various bodies, including those of animals and plants. It is clear that Hinduism regards animals as well as plants as being possessed of souls. This, once again, is in sharp contrast to the traditional Christian belief wherein only human beings are supposed to have souls. This belief, incidentally, though helpful in boosting the status of man, has obvious limitations. For instance, 'it seems to be assumed that such a complex mind as a dog's can be explained as a function of matter, whereas there is something in a child which cannot be so explained'.[4] It will be seen that, howsoever flattering this belief might be to man's ego, it does not seem to fall in line with modern scientific and evolutionary ideas. Hinduism, on the other hand, treats the

[1] Radhakrishnan, INTRODUCTION TO THE GĪTĀ, p. 107 (emphasis mine).
[2] Galatians 2: 20.
[3] For a detailed analysis, see Eliot, *op. cit.*, pp. liii to lvi.
[4] Eliot, *op. cit.*, p. liii.

souls of all living-beings as potentially equal, though it asserts that all the souls are not equally evolved and capable of promoting the soul's ultimate good. In fact, only the human soul is capable of liberation (*Mokṣa*).

Anyway, to proceed with our main story, each individual soul, once it has entered *Saṃsāra,* passes through a series of progressively more complex bodies until it reaches the human level on its evolutionary march. Until the human stage has been reached, the soul's passage from one body to another is determined by some kind of automatically operating natural law. But since the soul has taken a human form, it comes under the jurisdiction of a moral law—the Law of *Karma*. Henceforward it is man's own actions that govern the course of his existence and status in a future life. Our actions in this life generate certain potencies which, for better or for worse, determine what kind of existence our souls will have after the decomposition of the present body. If we have led a good life and have attained moral worth, we shall most certainly be born in circumstances more congenial to the attainment of spiritual freedom, and we shall be a step nearer our ultimate goal. And if we continue to live morally, the day would inevitably come when we should have realized our divine worth, and thus be liberated from the flux of life, called *Saṃsāra*.

To summarize, then, Hinduism teaches that the soul is eternal and immortal. Once involved in the world-process, a body of some sort becomes a necessary adjunct for the soul, but the same body is neither necessary nor convenient for an indefinite period of time. Accordingly, when one body becomes old, or when the spiritual and moral progress of the soul necessitates a more complex body, the soul passes into a new body after discarding the old one.

'Just as a person casts off worn-out garments and puts on others that are new, even so does the embodied soul cast off worn-out bodies and take on others that are new.'[1]

Pre-existence and transmigration are, therefore, necessary postulates of the Hindu view of life. What is, thus, an exceptional point of view in Christianity is the general rule in Hindu thought.

[1] Gītā, II, 22.

It is remarkable, however, that these rather important differences on the metaphysical and ontological plane do not lead to as much difference in the moral implications of these doctrines as one would imagine. In other words, the Hindu doctrine about the nature, status and capacities of man is not, as some might expect, fundamentally different from the Christian. To start with, like the Christian, the Hindu view accepts man's complete dependence on God, even though it does not regard the soul as a creature. The consensus in the Hindu tradition is for treating the soul as a separate, eternal but dependent entity. To repeat the words of Dr Radhakrishnan, the soul is '*everlasting as Divine form and derives its existence from God*'. It is obvious, then, that the uncreated existence of the soul does not absolve it of its responsibility or accountability to God. The soul is a part of God, as it were, and, like any other part, can have no reality in isolation from the whole, that is, God.

Coming once again to the status of man, we find the Hindu view much the same as the Christian. Though the souls of all creatures are alike in the sense that they are all eternal and primordial, this does not mean that a man is the same as a monkey or a moth. We have already seen that the embodied soul reaches the human stage at the very highest phase in its evolutionary course. Assumption of a human body, therefore, is the crown of achievement for the soul so long as it is embodied and unliberated. But undoubtedly there are gods and goddesses and angels who are in a way higher up than men in the hierarchy of beings, though it is remarkable that even gods have to be reborn as men if they desire liberation, 'for it is only through a human incarnation that *Mokṣa* or final liberation can be achieved'.[1] In this respect, then, men are more privileged than even the gods. But on the whole man's status in Hinduism, as in Christianity, is intermediate, i.e. above all other beings of the earth but below that of the gods and angels.

Man's potential greatness, similarly, is undisputed. By virtue of his possession of a divine soul, man becomes divine. But it may be objected that this is true of every other being, and, therefore does not impart any uniqueness to human existence. This is true to an extent, and morally significant, because this implies that every living being should be treated with sympathy

[1] Zaehner, *op. cit.*, p. 82.

and respect. But if we remember that in the scale of evolution the human stage is the last and the highest, we will see that man, rather than any beast, is more likely to regain his lost divinity. The liberation of a beast, though possible, is a miracle, whereas that of a human being is just what it ought to be. This is why we hear so many of the poet-saints of India singing of the utter futility and wretchedness of their lives, because they are tortured by the awareness that they have failed to make the best of the gift of a human existence (*Mānava Janma*).

But the greatness of man is not unqualified. This very greatness constitutes a potential threat or temptation. In the Christian tradition man's temptation lies in his forgetting the fact of creaturehood and his tendency to place himself in the position of God. In the Hindu tradition the same story is told in different words. Among all the beings man is the only one who has intelligence and ego (*Buddhi* and *Ahaṃkāra*). If the ego, this faculty which creates the awareness of 'I and mine' (*Abhimāna* or pride), is suppressed, or, even better, given up, spiritual freedom is the reward, but if the ego is let loose, it can create desires and hankerings in man which will bind him more and more firmly to *Saṃsāra*. In other words, both Hindu and Christian traditions emphasize the responsibility of men, as moral creatures, to strive to avoid falling prey to the temptations of false pride and to work for their salvation in fear and trembling.

MAN—HIS FINAL DESTINY: REDEMPTION OR LIBERATION

We have seen that both Christianity and Hinduism speak of salvation as the ultimate destiny of man, and, to that extent, can be described as religions of redemption. But what exactly does this concept of redemption mean? What is redemption sought from, and why? These are the questions that will engage our attention in the next few pages. A tentative answer to the question 'why redemption?' seems to be suggested by our analysis of the nature and status of man in the previous section. We have seen that both Christianity and Hinduism emphasize the *potential* greatness of man. And the very emphasis on the use of the term 'potential' seems to imply that in actuality man has, for one reason or the other, lost some of his greatness, at least temporarily. How this happened and what can be done to recover what has been lost are some of the most fundamental issues that Christianity and Hinduism have had to wrestle with. We shall now be reviewing, briefly, the common ground of Christian and Hindu thinking on these issues.

(*a*) *The Christian view*

We have mentioned earlier that Christians are committed 'officially to a very high belief in the potential greatness of man', but we noted at the same time that they are equally 'committed to the belief in man's utter need of God'. We also mentioned that, in fact, man's potential greatness, his having been created in the image of God, is also 'his fatal temptation'. It is a temptation because man might overrate his greatness and thereby forget the fact of his 'utter need of God'. His potential greatness might tempt him to do away with God, or, in other words, he might try to become God Himself. In his self-pride he might lead a life of defiance and rebellion against the Creator. And this is precisely what has happened, according to the Biblical narrative. Adam ate of the forbidden tree, the tree of the knowledge of good and evil, in defiance of the explicit command of God. By so doing, he tried to become God. In the words of Genesis 3: 23,

'And the Lord said, Behold, the man is become as one of us, to know good and evil: and now, lest he put forth his hand, and take also of the tree of life, and eat, and live for ever: therefore the Lord God sent him forth from the garden of Eden, to till the ground from whence he was taken.'

This has been traditionally called the story of the Fall. About the exact consequences of the Fall there are differences of opinion among theologians. But this much is agreed—that man's Fall, symbolized by this act of defiance, was a great spiritual catastrophe which erected a barrier between God and man and which has ever since stood in the way of man's communion with God. 'Therefore the Lord God sent him forth from the garden of Eden' leaves no doubt about the displeasure of God and the consequent act of punishment. This act of defiance is man's greatest sin, and it is as a result of this sin that he is being forced to live in isolation from God.

Thus the root of the trouble lies in the will of man, who, not being content with his finiteness, misuses his freedom and tries to take the place of God and thereby falls a prey to temptation and sin. As Reinhold Niebuhr puts its,

'. . . The basic source of temptation . . . resides in the inclination of man either to deny the contingent character of his existence (in pride and self-love) or to escape from his freedom (in sensuality). Sensuality represents an effort to escape from the freedom and the infinite possibilities of spirit . . . an effort which results inevitably in unlimited devotion to limited values.'[1]

But whatever the source of sin, a sinful state of existence is far from desirable. We shall have further occasions to work out in detail the connotation and implications of sin. For the time being, we shall be content to state that the story of the Fall, and the consequent sin has been interpreted generally in one of two ways. To some it has meant a literal account of the Fall of Adam, the first ancestor of man, from his state of original perfection, and has generally signified a burden of inherited guilt and sin which every man has inevitably to carry in so far as he is a descendant of the First man. But there are others, especially among modern interpreters of Christianity, to whom the Fall of Adam merely symbolizes the character of man's will and his proneness to defy God, the assertion of his self-will. In the words of J. S. Whale, for example,

'The idea of a Fall from an original state of perfection is really a limiting conception, a theological *Grenzbegriff*. It is not a scientific statement about the dawn of history. The Fall is symbolism, necessary to the intellect, but inconceivable by the imagination . . . it describes the quality rather than the history of "man's first disobedience".'[2]

It would seem, then, that sin really consists in man's placing his own will in opposition to God's will. It is this tendency in man

[1] Reinhold Niebuhr, *The Nature and Destiny of Man*, Nisbet, London, 1941, I, 197.

[2] Whale, *op. cit.*, p. 49.

which is generally referred to as man's depravity or sin. But, as Bouquet says,

'This will in itself is no more evil than the "cool self-love" of which Bishop Butler speaks in one of his sermons. But its over-emphasis leads to a nearer and narrower good being preferred to a higher, remoter and more ultimate good, and this exaggerated self-love is what is called carnal freedom or more shortly "sin" (German, "*Sünde*"), i.e. that which sunders or separates from fellowship with God.'[1]

It should be obvious by now that the tragic consequence of sin consists mainly in its sundering or separating man from the fellowship with God. And the agent of this tragedy is the exaggerated self-love or ego of man, the exaggerated feeling of 'I and mine', what the Hindu calls *Ahaṃkāra* or *Ahaṃ*. In other words, man's bondage lies in his ego, which prevents him from visualizing the higher goal of communion or fellowship with God by narrowing his perspective. If this is so, it follows that his deliverance consists in re-establishing communion with God by shunning this life of sin and by making God's will supreme.

The foregoing discussion has attempted to answer one of the questions that we undertook to investigate—the Christian conception of the why of redemption; in other words, why man is in need of redemption at all. Man was created in the image of God, 'recreated in the image of the Son', and was meant to live in communion with God. As a result of his sin, this communion was made ineffective; and so the need for redeeming man from sin so that he could live in fellowship with God. It is clear that redemption, then, primarily means redemption from sin. Man must repent for his sin, submit his own will to the will of God, live a life of righteousness and love so that the merciful God could, once again, accept the lost sheep back into his fold. 'What is aimed at,' then, 'is freedom from sin, and the acquisition of holiness.'[2]

Thus the unequivocal answer that a Christian would return to the question 'What is redemption sought from?' would be

[1] Bouquet, *op. cit.*, p. 257.
[2] Donald Mackenzie, *Encyclopaedia of Religion and Ethics*, edited by James Hastings, T. and T. Clark, Edinburgh, 1912, V, 472.

that it is 'from sin?' Redemption from sin, because 'the world of sin . . . is alienation from the life of God through wicked works, the consequent darkening of the conscience and understanding. . . .'[1] Once redeemed from sin, the way would be open for a life in communion with God; organically viewed, the Kingdom of God. It may, however, be doubted whether redemption from sin is the entire connotation of the Christian doctrine of redemption. We shall, therefore, try to examine below whether there is anything more implied by this doctrine. In other words, we shall see whether the Christian doctrine of redemption also entails redemption from this world.

It is a well-known fact that the early Christian faith was largely apocalyptic. There was definite anticipation on the part of Jesus himself and some of his followers that the end of the present world was near, and that this would be followed by the Kingdom of God.

'And the stars of heaven shall fall, and the powers that are in heaven shall be shaken.

And then shall they see the Son of man coming in the clouds with great power and glory.'[2]

Appeals to people to be righteous were made in this context, for it was presumed that the end might come any time, and that, therefore, those who wanted eternal happiness were expected to keep themselves in readiness. After Jesus' crucifixion, some of his disciples were genuinely disillusioned that the prophecy had not come true. This is what the Kingdom of God meant to the contemporaries of Christ. It would be reasonable to conclude then that Christianity, at least in its beginnings, preached not only redemption from sin but also redemption from this world itself. It is true that 'this primary meaning of redemption has come to be missed in Protestant doctrinal construction',[3] but there are many modern scholars who regard this to be genuine New Testament teaching. In the words of A. G. Hogg,

[1] Donald Mackenzie, *Encyclopaedia of Religion and Ethics*, edited by James Hastings, T. and T. Clark, Edinburgh, 1912, V, 471.

[2] Mark 13: 25, 26.

[3] A. G. Hogg, *Redemption from this World*, Cunningham Lectures, T. and T. Clark, Edinburgh, 1922, p. 13.

'Too commonly redemption means for us only redemption from sin, or even only redemption from punishment, whereas by those who first experienced redemption through Christ it was conceived of as redemption from the many-sided tyranny of an evil world-order, of which guilt and moral impotence were only factors, although doubtless the most outstanding and momentous factors.'[1]

Or as Sydney Cave puts it,

'The consummation of the Kingdom would not come by the gradual education of the race, nor even by the progressive influence of the Church. It would come by the power of God. *The Kingdom was the heavenly realm* in which men might share already the life which is eternal and triumphant. *To be a member of the Kingdom is thus already to be redeemed from the world.*'[2]

Whatever, therefore, the Protestant and post-modernist interpretations of redemption, it is not altogether fanciful to suggest that the Christian conception of redemption also entails redemption from the world. In fact, this presumption will help to explain better the other-worldliness and the derogatory references to the world that are to be found in many of the leaders of early Christian thought.

(b) The Hindu view

We start our analysis of the Hindu view of man's destiny with the examination of a passage in the Gītā. It says,

'A fragment (or fraction) of My own self, having become a living soul, eternal, in the world of life, draws to itself the senses of which the mind is the sixth, that rest in nature.'[3]

In this passage, 'a fragment of My own self' refers to the individual soul, the *Ātman*, which, as we mentioned earlier, is divine. The next phrase, however, 'having become a living soul,

[1] A. G. Hogg, *Redemption from this Word*, Cunningham Lectures, T. and T. Clark, Edinburgh, 1922, p 13.

[2] Sydney Cave, *Redemption Hindu and Christian*, Oxford University Press, 1919, p. 231 (emphases mine).

[3] Gītā, XV, 7.

eternal, in the world of life', seems to demand some explanation. The problem is that if the *Ātman* is divine, how does it come to be involved 'in the world of life', the world of becoming (*Saṃsāra*)?

This problem has been one of the most vexing to religious thinkers and philosophers in India, and consequently there are many answers given to this problem. Leaving aside the views of the philosophical schools for the time being, we shall try to concentrate on the common elements in the explanations given by the main religious schools. The commonest tendency among these schools, of course, is to treat this as part of the divine mystery which is beyond man's comprehension. But if something must be said in explanation of this phenomenon, all the schools, including the orthodox systems of philosophy, seem to agree on one thing—that the embodiment of the soul and its consequent involvement in *Saṃsāra* is due to ignorance, or *Avidyā*. *Avidyā* is a cosmic principle, as much a part of the constitution of the universe as anything else. When the soul is affected by *Avidyā*, it forgets its real divine essence and descends, as it were, into the fray of *Saṃsāra*, the world of life and becoming.

It is interesting to note here that there seems to be an obvious contrast between Christianity and Hinduism in this respect. We have noted that Adam's Fall lies in his eating of 'the tree of the *knowledge* of good and evil', whereas in Hinduism the soul's bondage comes about by its association with the principle of *ignorance*. Whereas Christianity considers man's attempt to be God as the main cause of his fall, in Hinduism it is man's forgetfulness of his divinity that is regarded as his bondage. But let us not be misled by these apparent differences of the two explanations, for the result in each case is the same. The Fall makes man subject to bodily death, decay and disease; so does bondage, brought about by ignorance. The Fall creates a chasm between man and God, and bondage makes man oblivious to his divine essence through a false identification with his bodily adjunct, or, in other words, it makes him forget his real nature. Nor is it much use asking why there is ignorance, for it would be like asking why God planted the tree of knowledge in the garden of Eden. God, being the omnipotent creator of the universe, could have refrained from creating a situation in which man could disobey Him, as much as He could have created a universe without the cosmic principle of ignorance. Why He chose to do otherwise, only He knows. The usual Christian answer that God deliberately allowed the possibility of disobedience on the part of man because He wanted man to surrender to His will, of his own free choice, smacks of a naïveté, for it pretends to know everything, including the mind of God. In fact, this pretence may be said to spring from the same pride and conceit of man which Christianity regards as the cause of the Fall. Hinduism is generally content with ascribing at least some part of the work of God to the sphere of mystery.

Excusing ourselves from this digression, however, we must return to the point which is relevant for us. And this is that the bondage of the soul is due to ignorance. We have noticed that despite the technically different explanations given of the Christian doctrine of the Fall and the Hindu doctrine of bondage, the consequences of the two are more or less the same. This becomes more obvious when we work out the moral implications of the Fall on the one hand and of bondage on the other. According to the Hindu belief, once the delusion of the *Ātman* has started, it must undergo the whole cycle of births and deaths until it reaches the human level, where, as we said earlier, it becomes distinctly possible for man to rise above the domain of *Karma* by a supreme moral and spiritual effort. But not every man succeeds in so doing. What stands in his way, then? Nothing but his exaggerated 'I and mine' consciousness, his ego (*Ahaṃkāra*) that refuses to face the fact that he is only a 'fragment' of God and that wrongly 'looks upon himself as the sole agent'.[1] 'Such a perverse mind,' (*Durmati*), lives in a world of make-believe, and by its limited vision and selfish hankerings falls a prey to desires which prove its undoing through the instrumentality of the unsparing *Law of Karma*. At the human level, therefore, the Christian and Hindu stories about the failing of man are the same. Both the systems declare that man's enemy is his false pride, his ego (*Abhimāna*), what we, in the phrase of Niebuhr, called 'unlimited devotion to limited values'.

It goes without saying, then, that if man's bondage is due to his falsely regarding himself as the sole agent of all his activity

[1] Gītā, XVIII, 16.

and all his achievements, his redemption will lie in the widening of his perspective. He must come to realize that it is not he but the Almighty, the Supreme Person (*Puruṣottama*), who is the doer, the agent of everything that happens, albeit only in His lower aspect as *Prakṛti* or nature. Whosoever realizes that the Supreme is 'the taste in the waters', 'the light in the moon and the sun' and 'the sound in ether and the manhood in men',[1] ceases to be selfish, a slave to desires. All his work, all his devotion and all his attention are then directed to the Supreme which paves the way to his rediscovery of the lost glory of the *Ātman*.

'He who does work for Me, he who looks upon Me as his goal, he who worships Me, free from attachment, he who is free from enmity to all creatures, he goes to Me. . . .'[2]

This is Lord Krishna's advice to Arjuna.

We ought to take careful note of the phrase 'he goes to Me' in the passage quoted above. This emphasizes the fact that on its positive side *Mokṣa* or liberation means, according to most theistic schools, the *Ātman*'s going to God, living in eternal communion with God. It is true that Shamkara interprets *Mokṣa* as merger with *Brahma*, but, as we noted earlier, though Shamkara's interpretation is very vigorous and commands the attention of most thoughtful Hindus, he cannot be regarded as the representative of the large majority of Hindus on this issue. This privilege must indeed belong to Ramanuja. According to Ramanuja, *Brahma* is not a qualityless Absolute, but the personal Lord possessed of all auspicious qualities. And *Mokṣa* is not identity with this Absolute but eternal bliss in communion with Him. *Mokṣa* is attained by submission or by a kind of gradual self-surrender to the loving Lord. In fact, according to Ramanuja the attitude of love to God is fundamental to the very being of the *Ātman*.

But it cannot be denied that the negative side of *Mokṣa* means release or redemption from the world, *Saṃsāra*. This world, with all its evils and suffering, is not the ideal abode for the eternal soul. Hence bliss cannot be obtained except by transcending the world. This attitude, however, as we have seen,

[1] Gītā, VII, 8.

[2] Gītā, XI, 55.

is not an exclusively Hindu attitude. If the ultimate end is communion with God, or a Kingdom of God in Heaven, then attachment to this world is a sheer perversion. And this is as much true of Hinduism as of Christianity. It is well known that Christianity, both early and medieval, has treated this world as an inferior sphere of existence which must be transcended. Liberal Christianity, of course, will protest against this interpretation of Christianity, but we do not have sufficient ground to treat Liberal Christianity as the most representative form of Christianity. Niebuhr is perhaps right in saying that Liberal Christianity invests 'the relative moral standards of a commercial age with ultimate sanctity by falsely casting the aura of the absolute and transcendent ethic of Jesus upon them'. Yes, it is true that redemption from the world is not in tune with the aspirations of a commercial age, but that is no reason why the evidence of the scriptures and of tradition should be disregarded.

The evidence of history supports the view that redemption in Christianity can legitimately be taken to imply redemption from the world. Commenting on the pessimistic character of Hinduism and Buddhism, Sir Charles Eliot says,

'It is generally assumed that these (pessimism etc.) are bad epithets, but are they not applicable to Christian teaching? Modern and medieval Christianity—as witness many popular hymns—regards this world as vain and transitory, a vale of tears and tribulations, a troubled sea through whose waves we must pass before we reach our rest. And choirs sing, though without much conviction, that it is weary waiting here. This language seems justified by the Gospels and Epistles.'[1]

If the world is vain and transitory, there naturally would, and should, be a desire for redemption from the world.

If we were now to summarize briefly our discussion so far, these essential facts would seem to emerge. First, though creation is ultimately a mystery, both Hinduism and Christianity tend to attribute it to the nature of God, either as loving or as good or both. Man is above all other creatures, and is really divine, but yet dependent on God. When, in excess of self-

[1] Eliot, *op. cit.*, p. lix.

pride, man forgets this fact of dependence, he becomes subject to suffering and evil. This can be stopped by a fresh realization of the fact of man's dependent status. This realization itself is a slow and difficult process, involving not only the right kind of knowledge but also an attitude of complete, willing submission of one's own will to that of God. This attitude of submission itself entails the highest possible regard for the will of God, as understood by man through his own intelligence and through revelation. And if man thus keeps on doing the will of God, and ceases to be a slave to selfishness and false pride, he ultimately regains his lost greatness and attains eternal communion with God. He is redeemed. It seems to us that the above summary of man's nature, status and final destiny represents the essence of Christian as well as Hindu views on this subject. Differences of terminology and narrative details between the Christian and Hindu stories are many, but it is fair to conclude that once we have crossed the barrier of terminological and technical details, the essential core of Christian and Hindu thinking does not appear to be so very different.

THE RELEVANCE OF MORAL EFFORT TO THE RELIGIOUS END

After examining the Christian and Hindu views on the nature and destiny of man, it would perhaps be desirable to conclude this chapter with a brief examination of how, if at all, these two religions make room for ethical endeavour in the context of the transcendent religious ends they prescribe. For as Niebuhr rightly points out, 'the ethical fruitfulness of a religion is determined by the quality of tension between the historical and the transcendent'. He suggests two considerations in judging this 'ethical fruitfulness' of a religion: (1) first, whether it is 'truly transcendent' and (2) second, whether it can impart significance to the historical.[1] If for 'historical' in the second criterion we substitute 'ethical', we then have the following two questions: (1) Are the religious ends prescribed by Christianity and Hinduism 'truly transcendent'? and (2) Can these religious ends impart significance to the 'ethical'?

It does not need much arguing to prove that both Christianity

[1] Niebuhr, *An Interpretation of Christian Ethics*, p. 15.

and Hinduism prescribe religious ends which are truly transcendent. We have seen that both these religions are religions of redemption, and, as we argued earlier, redemption does ultimately imply redemption from the world. Moreover, the positive content of redemption is conceived as communion with God. Christianity speaks of a Kingdom of God in Heaven, and Hinduism, though generally speaking of *Mokṣa*, does occasionally speak of eternal bliss in heaven, *Svarga* or *Vaikuṇṭha*. Though there may be numerous people who would like to argue with Tolstoy, for example, that the Kingdom of God is within every man's own soul, and that, therefore, this term does not have any other-worldly reference, it is unquestionably true that Christian tradition has by and large regarded the Kingdom of God as a realm transcending this world. Even the Kingdom of God *on Earth* refers to an ideal, a future possibility which is certainly not to be found in the world as it is, with all its sin and suffering, and is to that extent transcendent. Similarly, though there are schools of thought in India which advocate the possibility of *Jīvanmukti*, or liberation here on this earth, there can be no doubt that *Mokṣa* has in general been conceived to be a state which certainly is not of this world, and is, therefore, a transcendent goal. Thus it is possible for us to answer the first question in the affirmative, that is to say, that the final destiny of man as conceived by Christianity and Hinduism is truly transcendent.

Now, precisely because we have answered the first question in the affirmative, the second question becomes extremely important. The ethical ideal advocated by Christianity is righteousness or holiness, and Hinduism appeals to its adherents to be virtuous or righteous, *Dharmātmā*. Now the question is that if the ultimate end of man is something that involves transcending the world, or is other-worldly, as is the case with both Christianity and Hinduism, why should there be a demand for any kind of ethical endeavour, which is necessarily confined to this world? This simply amounts to asking: What is the relevance of moral effort in this world to the transcendent and other-worldly religious end?

It is difficult to see how else any transcendent religious goal can be related to an ethical life in this world except by treating the latter as a necessary preparation or stepping-stone to the former. And this is exactly what is done by both Christianity and Hinduism. Holiness or righteousness, necessarily involving good conduct and the pursuit of certain values, is regarded by Christianity as the precondition of fellowship with God. In Luther, perhaps, the emphasis on holiness is not so pronounced as in Catholicism, for Bishop Nygren states this difference: '. . . in Catholicism, fellowship with God on God's own level, on the basis of holiness; in Luther, fellowship with God on our level, on the basis of sin'.[1] But despite this change of emphasis, it cannot be denied that Luther demands holiness or righteousness, as involving good conduct. Similarly, Hinduism regards the performance of *Dharma* as a necessary condition to the attainment of *Mokṣa*. And in this respect even Shamkara, who denies the ontological reality of the world, would have nothing different to say. Antinomianism apart, there seems to be no doubt that both Christianity and Hinduism regard a moral life as an absolute pre-condition of eternal happiness in the world hereafter.

[1] Quoted by Lehman, *op. cit.*, p. 40.

CHAPTER IV

THE MORAL LAW, ITS AUTHORITY AND SOURCES

Toward the end of the last chapter we tried to answer the question of how Christianity and Hinduism, with their conceptions of the transcendent and other-worldly human destiny, can still insist on the necessity of leading a moral life in this world. And our answer to this question was that both these systems made room for ethics by stipulating that an ethical life was a pre-condition or an essential preparation for the attainment of the highest spiritual end, i.e. redemption or *Mokṣa*. This was, however, only part of the answer. This question will be more adequately answered in the course of this chapter. To anticipate, we will see that not only is leading a moral life important but that in fact we do not really have an option once we adopt either the Christian or the Hindu view of the nature of the creative act and of man's place in the created world. We have seen that the acceptance of the view that this is God's world leads to the acceptance of the implication that in matters of conduct in this world it is God's will, and not ours, which must be regarded as the final word. And morality, they would argue, is nothing but doing what God expects us to do. We have, therefore, an absolute obligation to do what God commands, and we can flout these only at our own risk.

In other words, if the creatorship of God is conceded, it would follow that the world cannot be viewed as a mere fortuitous combination of elements; it must indeed be regarded as a kingdom of ends. And we, as 'guests and borrowers' in God's world and as beings who cannot live independently of God, have a duty to do only what promotes these ends in so far as we know what they are.

It would seem to follow, then, that Christians as well as Hindus would generally consider the very nature of the relationship between man and God as one which makes demands on man in the form of a consciousness of duty. This would be vindicated as we proceed further with our enquiry. Meanwhile, we shall presuppose that it is the concept of Duty which perhaps forms the nucleus of Christian and Hindu ethics, and accordingly we shall start our discussion with an analysis of the concept of duty. Now, the word 'duty' may be used in one of two senses: (*a*) a subjective sense and (*b*) an objective one.

(*a*) In the words of H. D. Lewis, 'The subjective duty is that duty that appears so to some particular person, and a man can be said to have done his duty in the sense that really matters so far as his moral worth is concerned if he is loyal to his own moral end or ideal'.[1] This sense of duty seems to presuppose a well-formulated end or ideal on the part of the individual which may or may not be shared by others. Loyalty to this ideal is the individual's duty, and the only significant problem it presents is that of interpretation in particular circumstances.

(*b*) The other sense of duty, however, implies duties of a kind that would be considered as duty by anyone, irrespective of his private ideals, if only the individual understood or were made to understand the broad connotation of duty. To quote Lewis again, 'The objective duty is the course of action which he would consider his duty if he understood aright, the duty that we have in mind when we say that some honest or well-meaning person has done what is wrong'.[2]

Duty in this objective sense presupposes a certain objective 'realm' or 'order of values' which is regarded as making demands on us. The unique feature of this demand is that the awareness of this demand is, in the words of Professor Maclagan, 'not simply a consciousness of being "under obligation" in a quite general and empty way',[3] but one that is always specific and commands our absolute allegiance. The moral demand or duty has an authoritativeness that makes it an imperative. The moral law is, in the inimitable phrase of Kant, a Categorical Imperative. Consideration of duty in this sense, therefore, involves a discussion of this Imperative or the Moral Law and its impli-

[1] H. D. Lewis, *Morals and the New Theology*, Victor Gollancz, London, 1947, p. 36.

[2] *Ibid.*, p. 36.

[3] W. G. Maclagan, *The Theological Frontier of Ethics*, George Allen and Unwin, London, 1961, p. 54.

cations. In the pages to follow we shall, accordingly, devote our attention to such questions as arise in connexion with the Moral Law.

There are three main questions that deserve consideration in this context: (1) What is the nature and source of this Moral Law in Christianity and in Hinduism? (2) From what does this Law derive its authority? In other words, what makes this Law obligatory or binding on us? It will be seen that this question entails the discussion of the theory or theories of obligation either specifically formulated or implied in the ethical thinking of Christians and Hindus. (3) What are the sources of the knowledge of this Law? In other words, how does an individual come to know the contents and implications of this Law? Let us now proceed to the consideration of the first of these.

THE NATURE AND SOURCE OF THE MORAL LAW

(*a*) *Christianity*

We have seen in a previous chapter that Christianity inherited from Judaism the concept of a Moral Law which expresses the will of a Righteous God and which has been laid down in the Decalogue for the guidance of all men. This belief was later reinforced by the Stoic concept of a World-Reason or *logos* which governs and determines the working of all natural phenomena. In fact the Stoics, in their emphasis on this World-Reason, were merely giving a more systematic expression to a general belief, prevalent in all previous Greek thought, in the conception of an eternal law of which the moral law was later regarded as only an aspect. This conception of 'a fundamental law, a divine common *logos*, a universal reason' that 'holds sway' can be traced back in Greek thought to Heraclitus, the 'Obscure Philosopher' (536–470 B.C.).[1] Thus starting from Heraclitus, this idea of an eternal or fundamental law was adopted in one form or another, and with various degrees of emphasis, by almost all the leading ancient Greek thinkers until it finally crystallized in the philosophy of the Stoics, through whom it eventually gave rise to the Christian concept of Natural and Moral Law.

[1] H. A. Rommen, *The Natural Law*, Thomas R. Hanley, trans., B. Herder Book Co., St Louis and London, 1949, pp. 5 *f*.

One passage in Rommen's book *The Natural Law* more or less sums up the development of the Christian Natural Law from its general Greek and, particularly Stoic, origins:

'The metaphysical natural law of Plato as well as the more realistic one of Aristotle formed the high-water mark of moral and natural-law philosophy in Greek civilization. Stoicism, on the other hand, in a remarkable eclectic synthesis of single principles drawn from many philosophers, furnished in its system of natural law the terminology or word vessels into which the Church Fathers were able to pour the first conceptions of the Christian natural law and to impart them to the world of their time.'[1]

The Stoics, particularly Cicero, had already popularized the idea of the *lex nata* or the law within us, so that the natural-law philosophy of the Early Fathers had no difficulty in blending this *lex nata* with the Jewish Torah, and then making this an important element of their teaching. This is the background in which we must understand the words of St Paul wherein he declares that the natural law is inscribed in the hearts of men:

'For when the Gentiles, which have not the law (of Sinai), do by nature the things contained in the law, these, having not the law, are a law unto themselves:
Which shew the work of the law written in their hearts. . . .'[2]

This conception of the natural and moral law has been an important element in Christian thinking ever since the days of St Paul and the Fathers of the Early Church. In the words of Rommen,

'The Fathers of the Early Church made use of the Stoic natural law, finding in its principles "seeds of the Word", to proclaim the Christian doctrine of the personal Creator-God as the Author of the eternal law as well as of the natural moral law which is promulgated in the voice of conscience and in reason.'[3]

[1] Rommen, *op. cit.*, pp. 11 *f.*
[2] Romans 2: 14, 15.
[3] Rommen, *op. cit.*, p. 35.

St Augustine replaced the eternal, impersonal world-reason of the Stoics by the personal all-wise and all-powerful God, and declared that eternal law had its source in the will of God. Natural moral law, according to St Augustine, is precisely this divine law with reference to man, so far as the latter participates in the divine law. He was of the opinion that

'The eternal law dwells as blind necessity in irrational nature. As oughtness, as norm of free moral activity, it is inscribed in the heart of man, a rational and free being. It appears in the moral, rational nature of man; it is written into the rational soul.'[1]

In St Augustine, then, there is an effort to base the natural moral law in the natural reason of man, so that the intrinsic immorality of determinate actions consists not so much in the violation of the law as in the variance with natural reason. St Thomas tries to continue the basic approach of Augustine in this respect, but he also relates the eternal law to the wisdom of God. In so doing, he succeeds in showing that the eternal law or the natural moral law is not merely the pure will of God, but only a consequence following from the nature of God, and, therefore, amenable to the nature of man in so far as man is a rational being, made in the image of God. St Thomas' concern is to base morality on something internal or intrinsic to man rather than on the command of an external authority; and he does so by bringing in rationality as the common ground between the natures of the law-giver, God, and man for whom the law is intended. He, in fact, takes recourse to his theory of the ultimate identity of being, good and truth. Being, truth and goodness, according to him, are convertible, so that 'Good is to be done' means the same thing as 'Realize your essential nature'. It is clear that the eternal law, on the whole, and the natural moral law, as a special application of the former, has its source, according to St Thomas, in the will of God. But since there is no opposition between the will and intelligence of God, the Perfect Being, the law may as well be said to have its source in the intelligence or wisdom of God. 'The eternal law, then, is the governance of the world through God's will in accordance with

[1] Rommen, *op. cit.*, p. 38.

His wisdom.'[1] St Thomas, however, it should be remarked, does not rest content with laying down the general rule for moral actions. With his characteristic spirit of synthesis, he also goes on to demonstrate that the derivatives or particular norms of morality, deducible from the natural moral law, are identical with the Decalogue or Ten Commandments. The details of this demonstration, however, may be left out at the moment. What is worth noting is that Aquinas believes that there is an eternal divine law which, in the domain of free, rational beings, becomes the natural moral law. This law is derived from the wisdom or reason of God, and, since men are rational, corresponds to the nature of man.

But this effort of Aquinas to emphasize the primacy of intellect and to base morality on something intrinsic to the nature of man, i.e. his reason, though perhaps the most influential line of thinking in Christian ethics, is by no means the only one. With Duns Scotus, for example, the principle of the primacy of the intellect gives way to that of the will, and thereby starts a new train of thinking in Christian moral philosophy. For Scotus morality depends on the will of God. A thing is good not because it corresponds to the nature of God, or, analogically, to the nature of man, but because God so wills. This trend of thought leads almost to a kind of positivism in William of Occam, for whom 'law is will, pure will without any foundation in reality, without foundation in the essential nature of things'.[2]

Without going into further details—which the considerations of space do not permit—we may conclude that all later Christian ethics accepts natural moral law as an aspect of the divine eternal law which has, obviously, its source in God. This eternal law is implanted in the very constitution of things and represents their law of being. The natural moral law is the same law as applied to the conduct of human beings. There is no difference of opinion whatsoever as to the source of this law. It is God; but, as we have seen, there are differences as to whether the source lies in the pure will of God or in His nature as the All-wise being. This difference, however, is relevant not here but further on in our analysis when we shall be considering the theories of obligation. So leaving it aside for the

[1] Rommen, *op. cit.*, p. 45.
[2] *Ibid.*, p. 59.

time being, we shall now pass on to the consideration of the Hindu concept of the Moral Law and its source.

(b) *Hinduism*

The concept corresponding to the eternal law as well as the natural moral law in Hinduism is that of *Dharma*. While discussing the nature of Christian and Hindu ethics in an earlier chapter, we noted that *Dharma* was an all-embracing, universal principle which manifests itself in various forms in various spheres. We have also seen that *Dharma*, with its wide variety of meanings, is to be regarded as 'inderterminate' rather than vague, and we argued that this indeterminateness might possibly have been purposely allowed to enter into the connotation of *Dharma* by the ancient Hindus, for *Dharma* is regarded as the very foundation of the universe. The universe, with its many spheres and aspects, naturally requires its foundation to manifest itself in various forms. The Mahānārāyaṇa Upaniṣad states that 'it is by Dharma that the whole world is held together (parigṛhīta)'[1] and again that *Dharma* 'is the world's foundation'.[2] Thus there is no doubt that *Dharma* is nothing but the eternal law which governs the whole world and holds it together.

Dharma, then, is that all-inclusive eternal principle which in its broadest sense constitutes the very fibre of the world and is reflected as the moral law in the field of human conduct. It is written in the minds of men and is revealed through the scriptures. Max Müller's description of *Ṛta*, from which, we know, the concept of *Dharma* has been derived, refers to both aspects of *Ṛta*—*Ṛta* as eternal law and *Ṛta* as the moral law. He describes *Ṛta* as the

'. . . straight line which, in spite of many momentary deviations, was discovered to run through the whole realm of nature. We call that *Ṛta*, that straight, direct or right line, when we apply it in a more general sense, the Law of Nature; and when we apply it to the moral world, we try to express the same idea again by speaking of the Moral Law, the law on which our life is founded,

[1] Mahānārāyaṇa Upaniṣad, 78, 6.
[2] *Ibid.*, 79, 7.

the eternal Law of Right and Reason, or, it may be, "that which makes for righteousness" both within us and without.'[1]

If this is true of *Ṛta*, it needs no arguing that the same must be true of *Dharma*.

G. H. Mees lists at least sixteen different ways in which the term *Dharma* has been used in the scriptures, but it should be remembered that all these meanings are allied and interrelated. Some of these meanings are: *Dharma* as impersonal principle or order or law; *Dharma* as the moral and social duty of man; *Dharma* as merit; *Dharma* as Divine justice; as common law; as convention, etc.[2] The fact is not that there are so many separate meanings of *Dharma* but that there are various applications of the same principle. It should, however, be noted that all of these meanings of *Dharma* have a moral overtone, for *Dharma*, above all, is the Moral Law.

Innumerable passages can be quoted from the scriptures to show that *Dharma* has been universally regarded as the cosmic principle which holds the equilibrium of the universe, and which, therefore, must not be disturbed. The underlying belief is that moral conduct on the part of man, or righteousness, strengthens *Dharma*, the foundation of the world, whereas immorality undermines it and gradually leads to the destruction of not only the sinner but also the world, if sin and unrighteousness begin to prevail. For instance, Manu says, 'Dharma being violated, destroys; Dharma being preserved, preserves: therefore, Dharma must not be violated, lest violated Dharma destroys us'.[3] In the famous passages of the Gītā which explain the why of Incarnation there is left no doubt that divine Incarnation takes place primarily to restore the balance of *Dharma* over *Adharma*.

'Whenever there is decline of righteousness and rise of unrighteousness, O Bharata (Arjuna), then I send forth (create, incarnate) Myself.

For the protection of the good, for the destruction of the wicked and for the *establishment of righteousness* (*Dharma saṃsthāpanārthāya*), I come into being from age to age.'[4]

[1] Max Müller, quoted by Mees, *op. cit.*, p. 9.
[2] See Mees, *op. cit.*, pp. 4 *ff*.
[3] Manu, VIII, 15.
[4] Gītā, IV, 7, 8 (emphasis mine).

Quite often, however, scholars are misled into identifying *Dharma* with the several duties of the classes and stages of man (*Varṇa-Āśrama*). That *Varṇa-Āśrama Dharma* is a part, perhaps even the most important part, of *Dharma* cannot be denied. But we ought not to forget that *Dharma* is primarily eternal and moral law, and to identify it with any one aspect of *Dharma, Varṇa-Āśrama Dharma* for example, is like identifying the whole with one of its parts. *Varṇa-Āśrama Dharma,* like *Yuga Dharma* (the *Dharma* of a certain age) and *Āpad Dharma* (the *Dharma* of unusual or critical circumstances), is only one part of *Sanātana Dharma* (Eternal Law).

The conclusion, then, is that *Dharma* is both eternal law and natural moral law which manifests itself in various forms in various contexts, and appears different from different angles of vision. G. H. Mees' summing up of this all-inclusive principle is so illuminating that it may be worthwhile quoting a rather long passage from his book:

'Dharma is seen by men according to the different stages of their development, or to the colour of their character, which is related to the special field they are working in, and the special psychological angle from which they are wont to look at it. The religious man will see Dharma as the divine law of God, the ethical person will see it as the inner principle that affords standards of good and evil, the lawyer will see it as law, as a plan of protection of right and security, the psychologist will stress tradition, common law and the social mind, the philosopher will see in it the consciousness of kind or the consciousness of unity, by its nature impelling man in the long run to manifest "kindness" or unity, the idealist will see it as the ideal, the realist as the law behind the existent show of life, the practical mystic will see in it the force impelling to brotherhood, building the community and bringing about harmony in unity.

But in truth it is the principle at the bottom of and contained in all these manifestations, and underlying all these conceptions.'[1]

As to the source of this eternal law, *Dharma*, the consensus of opinion in Hindu thought is (with the exception of the atheistic

[1] Mees, *op. cit.*, p. 22.

schools such as Sāṃkhya and Mīmāṃsā) that this law is God-given, and that *Dharma* is nothing but, to use a phrase we employed earlier, 'God's governance of the world through God's will in accordance with His wisdom'. But as against those who conceive a personal source of the law, called the *Pauruṣeya-vādins*, the Mīmāṃsā school regards it as Impersonal Law without any personal source. The followers of this school, therefore, are called *Apauruṣeyavādins*. This school refuses to be dragged beyond the Scriptural Imperative for a more ultimate ground. They accept *Dharma* as revealed in the scriptures as the final word and leave it there. But, as we have maintained elsewhere, the dominant note in Hinduism is one of belief in a Personal God who is the creator and Lord of the universe; it would be reasonable to believe that most Hindus would consider *Dharma* to be God's law for the governance of the world.

THE AUTHORITY OF THE MORAL LAW

We have so far been examining the Christian and Hindu concepts of the Moral Law. After having discussed, however, that both Christianity and Hinduism believe in a Moral Law and that both, with certain exceptions on the Hindu side, regard the Moral Law to be God-given, it is now important to find out why, in the opinions of Christians and Hindus, it is necessary to respect this Law. In other words, what justification do Christians and Hindus give in support of a moral life? As we said earlier, this is the same as asking what theories of obligation are put forward by the two religions.

(*a*) *Christianity*

While discussing the Christian conception of natural moral law, we had occasion to point to a difference in the approaches of Aquinas and Duns Scotus as to whether a thing was good because it corresponded to the nature of God or simply because it was God's will. This controversy itself throws a hint toward the answer to the question: What is the real seat of authority of the Moral Law? Is it the pure will of God or the will of God as informed and determined by His rational nature? Here we already have the seeds of two of the most important theories of obligation formulated by Christian theologians. In fact, we shall see later that these may not be two theories so much as two different emphases on the same theory. For both these theories base the Moral Law ultimately on the will of God. And this is perfectly understandable. For in the Christian tradition the highest good is the godhead. In the words of Rommen, 'The highest good is the Godhead, purest Being. God's honour and glory, to which the whole of creation bears witness, are also its highest end.'[1] If Godhead is the highest end, it naturally follows that God's will should be the final word and its own justification. There is no doubt that in the Christian tradition duty or moral obligation is explained primarily and ultimately by an appeal to God's will or command for us. And we shall be examining the implications of this theory.

But though this is the main theory, attempts are sometimes made to provide 'extraneous support' for the moral demand from 'contextual considerations'.[2] For example, it may be argued or implied that though the authority of the moral demand follows from the very fact of its being God's command, this authority may be further reinforced by observing that there is something in the nature of the world itself which makes morality meaningful and worthwhile. The argument, in other words, is 'that the universe must be friendly to the doing of our duty if there is to be any sense in doing it'.[3] Theories which try to explain the moral demand on this or other similar postulates may be called 'contextual', in the phrase of Professor Maclagan. It would be interesting to examine one or two specimens of such contextual theories.

Professor Maclagan, in his admirable analysis, remarks that the basic postulate of contextual explanations—namely, that the universe must be friendly to our sense of duty—may be presented in either a crude or a refined form. He takes up first 'its very familiar crude form' which amounts to saying that the universe is so constituted that 'the good man will be rewarded and the evil punished'.[4] It is clear that support for the moral demand is here derived from the conviction or hope that it ultimately pays to be moral because 'the universe' 'looks after the interests of the dutiful'.[5] Professor Maclagan rightly dismisses this as too crude a theory. This theory is extremely

[1] Rommen, *op. cit.*, p. 202. [2] Maclagan, *op. cit.*, p. 64.
[3] *Ibid.*, p. 57. [4] *Ibid.*, p. 57 [5] *Ibid.*, p. 57

prudential and is aptly derided as 'training ourselves in commerce and not in godliness'.[1]

It must, however, be added, in all fairness to Christian ethical thinking that no Christian thinker today would seriously consider explaining duty on these lines. It is true that most Christian theologians do make some reference to rewards. In fact Jesus himself promised all kinds of rewards for the virtuous. But the rewards are promised, if one may say so, as something that will follow automatically our doing the will of God. The primary appeal is the latter, not the former. God's will is to be done not because of considerations of personal advantage but because it is God's will.

The 'refined' version of the contextual explanation implies that we cannot really claim purely moral motives for doing our duty if we act from considerations of reward and punishment. But as a matter of fact, some kind of belief in the friendliness of the universe is essential, at least as an incentive towards the realization of our moral ideals. Maclagan concedes that this is more refined but adds pungently that therefore it is 'only a more refined error'.[2] He counts in this very category 'the closely related suggestion that we can even *define* morality in terms of what the universe is friendly towards'.[3] The example he gives of such thinking is a passage from Stephen Neil's *Christian Faith To-day* (Penguin Books, London, 1955, p. 42), in which the latter says:

'Some attitudes and actions run along the grain of the universe, and others run contrary to it; this is really what is *meant* by describing some attitudes and actions as moral and others as immoral.'[4]

It is not difficult to see that the above passage defines as 'moral' those actions which 'run along the grain of the universe'. This is certainly not a good definition, for into the already considerably difficult problem of what is moral and why we should be moral it introduces another very difficult element—that of discovering what runs along the grain of the universe. But even leaving aside the quality of this definition as a definition, one would feel constrained to agree with Professor Maclagan that

[1] Maclagan, *op. cit.*, p. 58.
[2] *Ibid.*, p. 60.
[3] *Ibid.*, p. 60.
[4] *Ibid.*, footnote, p. 60.

these contextual theories, however refined, tend to be prudential. He himself does not seem to be a champion of Kantian rigorism. For he concedes that 'moral devotion . . . requires belief in a universe friendly to the extent that in *some* measure our ideals can be realized in it.'[1] But he feels that 'what is intended by those who look for friendliness in the universe as a condition of the reasonableness of the moral demand is clearly more than this'.[2]

Thus since all contextual considerations seem to impart to morality a prudential tinge, it is clear that they do not succeed in providing the extraneous support they intend to provide to the claims of duty. Moreover, even if such extraneous support could be had in a legitimate sense, it would still be of a secondary order. An appeal primarily to the will of God would for a Christian be the only legitimate explanation of duty. Hence, let us now turn to this main theory.

This main theory of the moral law and its obligatoriness is the one that insists that the law is authoritative simply because it is God's will. Most Christians will be quite content with giving the explanation that the moral law is God's command for us which, as His creatures, it is our duty to follow. Clearly, then, our primary and, perhaps, only duty is to obey God's command. This theory may safely be regarded as the most representative of Christian theories of obligation. As Cardinal Mercier says,

'In the opinion of most Christian moralists since the time of Kant, moral duty admits of only one possible explanation, namely the authority of God, the supreme Legislator of the moral order as He is of the physical. If there is a difference of opinion it is only on the question whether it is His essence, His intellect, His will, or His intellect and will combined, which gives the obligatory character to the moral law.'[3]

We must not forget, however, that the shades of difference referred to in the last sentence do not relate to the essential

[1] Maclagan, *op. cit.*, p. 60. [2] *Ibid.*, p. 60.

[3] Cardinal Mercier (*et al.*), *A Manual of Modern Scholastic Philosophy*, authorized translation by T. L. Parker and S. A. Parker, Third English edition, Fifth impression, Routledge and Kegan Paul, London, 1950, Vol. II, p. 238.

position that it is God's will or command to which we owe our obligation. The moral law is God's will without doubt; the differences of opinion occur as to whether it is God's will, pure and simple, or God's will as determined by His essence, intelligence, etc.

It must be said in defence of this theory that it is free from the confusion of values from which some of the previously considered ones suffer, for it restricts itself to God's will as the source of obligation. But, nevertheless, it raises important questions. In what sense is our duty commanded by God? Is it in an 'objective' sense or in a 'subjective' sense, or both? What might sometimes happen, and in fact does happen frequently, is that a misguided conscience may think of something as duty which might actually be different from, if not also positively contrary to, the objective sense of duty. And in such circumstances, it will be difficult to decide whether man with his conscience has or has not disobeyed God and thereby incurred sin. This is the serious problem posed by this theory. If our obligation to moral effort follows from the mere fact that it is God's will, then it makes 'the obligation to obey God', the 'one solitary underived moral obligation'.[1] And it is always possible to misread God's will. We have seen how Duns Scotus' emphasis on the pure will of God leads to a kind of moral positivism or even nihilism. For the implication of the basic view of William of Occam, which we quoted earlier, seems to be that sin does not contain 'any intrinsic element of immorality or what is unjust, any inner element of injustice; it is an external offence against the will of God'.[2]

It is here that the superiority of St Thomas' explanation begins to show itself. By basing the moral law in the very essence of God, he succeeds in guarding against these positivistic misinterpretations of the moral law. He does not deny that it is God's command that matters, but he insists that God's command itself must have a rational basis, for He is an all-intelligent being whose commands cannot but be rationally comprehensible. This reference to divine intelligence or essence, apart from ensuring the intrinsic morality of God's command, also makes morality subject to rational criticism and evaluation.

[1] Maclagan, *op. cit.*, p. 67.

[2] Rommen, *op. cit.*, p. 59.

The justification sometimes put forward for the Christian ethics of love, or Agapism, is that we are made in the image of God, and since God is the *loving and merciful* Father, it follows that we ought to be loving as well. This simple philosophy of imitating our Creator in matters of conduct is, in spite of its indefiniteness, all right so far as it goes. But when people begin to argue, and some do, that we ought to love because in loving we are 'so living as to be well-pleasing to God',[1] then the justification for a moral life is no more the imitation of God but the anxiety to please God. The implication of this theory is that we ought to love because this would be pleasing to God. Now, quite clearly this theory makes 'god's pleasure, considering simply as His pleasure, the overriding consideration',[2] and thereby with a single stroke robs morality of its rational element which St Thomas tries so hard to preserve.

Another theory often presented seems to be based on what may be called an imperfect understanding of the spirit of Kant's philosophy. The Kantian prescription of 'reverence for the moral law' is accepted by some people as a premise. But they go on to add that the feeling of reverence or respect, in the proper sense of the term, can only be aroused by a *personal* reality. As Professor Maclagan states the argument of the supporters of this theory:

'Our experience when we are conscious of "the moral law" is, at least implicitly, the experience of confrontation by a *personal* Holiness; that is to say, by God. The sanctity of "the moral law" is its "irradiation" by the sanctity of a God who is its Author.'[3]

The essence of this argument is that love and reverence for God, who is the author of 'the moral law', not only involves but is the necessary condition of respect for the moral law. But the exponents of this argument, though quoting a Kantian phrase, ignore something much more fundamental which unfortunately takes the life out of their argument. Kant himself insists that the reverence must be for the law itself. It is true that if we believe in a *personal* reality as the law-giver, we would normally have a reverence for this person, but as Professor Maclagan

[1] See Maclagan, *op. cit.*, p. 78. [2] *Ibid.*, p. 76 [3] *Ibid.*, p. 79.

says, 'there is a distinctive reverence for the moral law that is not reducible to reverence for a person'.[1] The moral life, we may conclude, gains nothing from relating the moral law to a personal God who is its author, except perhaps imparting a feeling tone to morality which is so sadly lacking in Kant. Our objection to the above argument still remains that it is a Kantian argument on an un-Kantian foundation.

With this summary of Christian theories of obligation, we now return to Hindu theories of the justification of moral life.

(*b*) *Hinduism*

Examining Hindu theories of moral obligation, we come across the same, or nearly the same, kinds of arguments as we encountered while taking account of Christian theories. We have for example, one particular theory of obligation given by the Naiyāyikas which can possibly be described as prudential. For the Naiyāyika *Vidhi* or Scriptural Imperative 'derives its force from a sanction, viz, *iṣtasādhanatva* or conduciveness to good. The obligatoriness of the Imperative is . . . thus the moral worth or excellence of its end appealing to the consciousness of the agent.'[2] In a complicated explanation, distinguishing between the obligatoriness and the objective authority of the Imperative, the Naiyāyikas make the point that 'The objective authority arises from the intrinsic worth or value of the end or good, while obligatoriness is due to this objective value being subjectively appropriated through a particular *Kāmanā* or desire'.[3] But it is not difficult to see that whatever the value of desire or *Kāmanā* as a psychological factor in leading to action of some sort, making the Moral Imperative itself subject to a desire or ulterior end makes no contribution to the purity and autonomy of the moral law itself. It is difficult to help the feeling that according to this theory the Imperative can be obligatory only when it is considered as leading to the end that the agent has in mind. This theory thus brings in the consideration of the agent's desire. For example, it is suggested that some of the Vedic injunctions about the performance of certain sacrifices can be binding on those who desire happiness

[1] Maclagan, *op. cit.*, p. 80.

[2] S. K. Maitra, *The Ethics of the Hindus*, Calcutta University Press, 1925, p. 130.

[3] *Ibid.*, p. 131.

in heaven. It is clear, therefore, that this theory tends to make the moral law, as laid down in the scriptures, a means to an end which itself may vary, and is to that extent prudential rather than properly moral.

It is because of this that the Mīmāṃsā school is very critical of this Nyāya theory. Kumarila, for example, is of the opinion that 'the end, consequence or *phala*, determines only the motive and choice, but not the obligatoriness of the Imperative'.[1] He feels that the end, at least in some cases, comes into operation only after the choice and hence cannot be the cause of the obligatoriness of the Imperative. But it is to be remembered, however, that Kumarila himself does concede that the end is to be reckoned as an essential part of the whole process that leads to volition. According to him, whatever the class of actions, whether they are *Kāmya* (optional) or *Nitya-Naimittika* (compulsory daily and occasional), the end is surely involved. For example, the end involved in the *Nitya-Naimittika* actions would be the avoidance of the sin (*Pratyavāya*) that would follow on non-performance. 'But,' he insists, 'it is not because of the *phala* or consequence, but because he is *Niyuktapuruṣa* or morally appointed by the Imperative that the latter binds him.'[2] In other words, the agent must perform these compulsory duties simply because they are his *duties*, though undoubtedly the performance of these will also bring certain consequences which may, in the first place, determine our volition. In this theory, then, we find the seeds of a gradual transition from the prudential to the purely moral theory of obligation.

The tendency to develop a purely moral theory that we noticed in Kumarila seems to be more or less crystallized in another thinker of the Mīmāṃsā school, Prabhakara, who, incidentally, is regarded as the exponent of a separate school within the Mīmāṃsā system. The Prabhakara school of Mīmāṃsā is of the view that *Niyoga* or Scriptural Imperative must be its own end. The moral Imperative as laid down in the scriptures itself 'constitutes the sanction, the motive as well as the moral authority of the *Vidhi*'.[3] There is nothing external to which an appeal need be made or from which the Imperative can derive its authority. On the contrary, they say, where the

[1] Maitra, *op. cit.*, p. 132. [2] *Ibid.*, p. 133. [3] *Ibid.*, p. 134.

agent is impelled by desire for the consequence, as in optional duties, the Imperative becomes *Udāsīna*, i.e. morally neutral. According to them, in the case of those unconditional duties which may properly be regarded as *duty* the Imperative is self-authoritative or self-realizing, while in the case of the *Kāmya*, or optional actions, it is without any imperative character, 'its function being merely to establish a relation of means and end between the act and the consequence to be attained thereby'.[1]

It cannot be denied that this is a great improvement on the theories of obligation put forward by the Naiyāyikas as well as by Kumarila. But we must confess that even Prabhakara's theory suffers from a certain prudential tinge. And there are two reasons for this. Firstly, because, in spite of his uncompromising attitude on the definition of duty, Prabhakara is still limited by the general Mīmāṃsā conception of *Dharma*. *Dharma* is regarded by this school as *Alaukika Śreya Sādhana*, or the means to the attainment of a certain supernatural essence, *Apūrva*. It follows then that if *Dharma* is a means to some supersensuous end, it cannot any more enjoy the full autonomy that characterizes or should characterize the moral law. Moreover, Prabhakara introduces into his theory one other element which seems to give it a slightly prudential bearing. He says that not every scriptural injunction constitutes *Dharma*. Only those of them which lead to *Artha* (and not to *Anartha*) can result in *Dharma* through their supersensuous effects or *Apūrva*. The Prābhākaras define *Artha* as that which does not produce pain in excess of pleasure. *Dharma*, according to them, is only a specific form of this generic good, namely, that which does not produce an excess of pain over pleasure. It will be easily seen that this introduction of the consideration of pleasure and pain in the determination of *Dharma* imparts to the Prābhākara theory of obligation a definitely utilitarian character.

One interesting theory of obligation seems to be implied in Ramanuja's attempt to deduce the moral virtues from the supposed character of God, since God is here regarded as the moral ideal.[2] In other words, Ramanuja advocates the view that in any circumstance we ought to behave as we expect God to behave in a similar situation. For example, we ought to be kind to the distressed, forgiving to the offender, of help to the

[1] Maitra, *op. cit.*, p. 137.

[2] *Ibid.*, p. 22.

weak and so on because in similar circumstances God would be doing the same. This is reminiscent of the Christian theory of *imitatio Christi*, considered earlier, that we ought to love because we are creatures of the loving Father. And therefore, we may only repeat the comment we made on that occasion. Surely we ought to imitate God. But, as we remarked then, if the motive is simply to please God, then this theory is not free from the risks of misinterpretation or of complete misunderstanding as to what would be pleasing to God.

But this, however, is only an indirect implication of some of Ramanuja's utterances. The main position of Ramanuja is that we ought to follow the moral law which is prescribed by God and which represents His intelligence. We have seen that Ramanuja and the Naiyāyikas, along with various devotional sects, are called *Paureṣeyavādins* because they believe that the moral law is prescribed by an eternally perfect being who lays down the duty for man in a code of injunctions and prohibitions. Unquestionably therefore, the moral law derives its authority from the will of God who knows what is good for us. But as in Christianity, so in Hinduism there are differences of opinion as to whether it is the pure will or the will as enlightened by His intelligence which gives the moral law its authority. In this respect, while the Naiyāyikas tend to take the position of Duns Scotus and others, Ramanuja would appear to go with St Thomas. According to the Ramanujists,

'The commands represent the Intelligence of the Lord, i.e., his *knowledge* of what is truly right and what is wrong; according to the Nyāya-Vaiśeṣikas they represent only the *will* of the Lord, i.e., his mere pleasure or fiat.'[1]

This position then is similar to the main current in Christian thinking on this issue. And there would seem to be no need for repeating what we already said in evaluating this theory.

All these explanations of the moral life discussed so far have generally been instrumental in shaping the moral attitudes of the Hindus in varying degrees. But the pride of place as the most influential and representative Hindu explanation of duty goes to the theory of *Niṣkāma Karma* or Duty for Duty's sake,

[1] Maitra, *op. cit.*, p. 161 (emphasis mine).

advocated by the Bhagavadgītā. There would hardly be any Hindu, of any denomination whatsoever, who would challenge the moral and logical excellence of this theory, even though there may be many who would stress how difficult it is to follow this theory in practice. The synthetic ingenuity of the Gītā seems to be vividly exemplified here in as much as it succeeds in preserving the lofty purity and autonomy of the moral law, spoken of by Kant, without succumbing to the rigorism or formalism of the Kantian theory of Duty for Duty's sake.

According to the Gītā, *Dharma* consists in the disinterested discharge of one's duties without being motivated by considerations of reward and punishment. Duty or the moral Imperative must not be taken to derive its authority from any extraneous source whatsoever. Duty has to be done because it is duty. The performance of duties will certainly bring its reward in due course, for this world is not a chaos but a well-ordered cosmos under the control and guidance of a perfect and all-powerful God. But this must not form part of our calculation or motivation, because this is not man's sphere but God's. Our job is to do our duty; to ensure that appropriate consequences follow our deeds is God's responsibility. So let us do what is our concern and leave the rest to God. 'To action alone hast thou a right and never at all to its fruits; let not the fruits of action be thy motive; neither let there be in thee any attachment to inaction',[1] says the Gītā.

This passage at once not only establishes the self-validating nature of the moral demand but also refutes the charge often levelled against Hinduism that its philosophy leads to inaction. One is advised to do unhesitatingly and with all his capacity the duties that are his—the duties of his class and stage, the duties of his profession, the duties to the gods and to the 'fathers'. This is, in fact, the only proper course, for man, as man, cannot live a life of impulses and instincts, like brutes do; nor can he give up action completely while he is embodied. The constituents of his body will never let him rest, for the dynamic *Prakṛti*, with its three strands, which composes man's body, is ever active. So act he must, and obviously the better man is the one who lets his duty determine his course of action rather than letting his selfish hankerings determine his course. Thus there

[1] Gītā, II, 47.

is no need to renounce the world, nor *can* one renounce action altogether; what one can renounce is the desire for reward. This is the meaning of *Nivṛtti* or renunciation according to the Gītā. '*Sarva Karma Phala Tyāga*'—the renunciation of all fruits of action is the motto.

The enlightened one who has acquired discriminative knowledge, or the privileged one, like Arjuna, to whom the Lord has revealed the whole truth, may come to know that *Dharma* is God's law and may therefore be impelled to contribute to the preservation of *Dharma* in the world. But for the average person, duty is the last word. If he cannot pierce the mystery of the world, he does not have to worry. So long as he is prepared to do his duty without any attachment to the consequences, he is already contributing to God's higher purpose and to his own salvation. For the ordinary man it is enough to know that this is God's world, and accordingly, let him dedicate to God everything that he does. There need be no other consideration except that of duty, but the believer may rest assured that the Lord who is the creator, sustainer and destroyer of the world is also the moral governor; and, therefore, if he only does what is demanded of him, the appropriate consequences will automatically follow. In this way the Gītā seems to expound the Kantian maxim of Duty for Duty's sake, and succeeds in making it morally more satisfying by relating duty to a personal God. Kant also postulates belief in a God on moral grounds, but his God is an empty logical or philosophical construction, and not the living God of the Gītā.

It should be worthwhile to examine in this connexion the comments of John Mackenzie on the ethics of the Gītā. In his book *Hindu Ethics*, he admits that this theory of the disinterested discharge of duties 'marks a great advance in ethical doctrine'. But he complains that

'no principle is provided by which the content of "right" may be discovered. For the content of morality we are pointed to *dharma*. If we ask why we should follow this strange amalgam of ethical, social and ritual principles, no answer seems to be given. Why may not a man without attachment practise other forms of conduct? No reason is given. . . .'[1]

[1] Mackenzie, *Hindu Ethics*, p. 126.

There seem to be two points involved in Mackenzie's criticism which require examination: that this theory fails to provide, first, a principle by which the content of right may be discovered and, second, an explanation of why we should follow *Dharma*.

As regards the first criticism, it can be said that the Gītā is only trying to formulate the concept of duty, and is not giving a detailed casuistry of what our duties consist of. It presupposes the time-old conception of *Dharma* as duty, and therefore merely refers to *Dharma* in answer to what we ought to do. A definition of duty and the working out of the detailed content of duty are two different tasks and it is pointless to blame for not doing the latter any system which is undertaking to do only the former. As the formulator of an independent comprehensive system Kant is justly blamed for leaving out the content of duty while fixing the connotation and implications of duty. As Lewis suggests, Kant is 'apt to give the impression of supposing that the content of duty can be derived from the idea of duty itself'.[1] But this criticism cannot apply to the Gītā, for the Gitā is not an independent system, but a link in a chain, so that it is perfectly justified in leaving the content of duty to the earlier Vedic tradition while defining our attitude to duty. This is why the Gītā refers to *Dharma* for finding out the content of duty.

To the question of why we should follow *Dharma* and not other forms of conduct, we may only say that if Mackenzie had kept in mind the wider connotation of *Dharma* as the moral order, this question should hardly have arisen. If *Dharma* is the moral law as well as the eternal law, it needs no explaining why we should follow *Dharma*. It would seem, then, that Mackenzie's criticism is centred round what he considers the arbitrary way in which the detailed content of *Dharma* is fixed. In other words, he seems to ask for an explanation as to why the content of *Dharma* should be what it is and not something else. The only answer to this is that the insight of the wiser men in the Vedic tradition happened to interpret it this way. Enlightened men may be free to depart from some details laid down by tradition, but for the average man, who lacks the intuitive power to discover the content of *Dharma* for himself,

[1] Lewis, *op. cit.*, pp. 36 *f.*

there is no alternative except to follow tradition. That *Dharma* need not always be interpreted in the traditional way, and that, therefore, it is not always necessary to follow what Mackenzie calls 'this strange amalgam of ethical, social and ritual principles', would be driven home if we carefully understand the Hindu's approach to *Dharma*. G. H. Mees very succinctly sums up this approach in these words:

'The Hindu doctrine is that all the time man has to open up all his inner faculties in order to be instrumental to Dharma. To the extent he is not able to realize Dharma intuitively, he has to perform the Dharma of his class, his family and profession, as ordained by Karman. If he has not yet any subjective realization, he must follow duty and work in society, as laid down in the scale by people wiser than himself, as a child follows a particular school and not any other, because his parents thus deem the most advisable. If later he gets the subjective realization, he ("it" in the text) may overrule the decisions and opinions of others, and change the course of his life.'[1]

We may add only that this seems to be an eminently sensible course, for the contrary would lead only to chaos.

With this consideration of the first two questions we raised at the beginning of this chapter, we must now consider very briefly the third. In fact this seems to have been demanded by our analysis of Mackenzie's objections to the ethics of the Gītā. For these objections, as we have seen, centre not so much round the conception of duty or the moral law as round the determination of the content of duty, and why one interpretation of the content of duty is to be preferred to another. We are, therefore, led to the examination of the sources of knowledge of the moral law. The determination of the content of the moral law is important and we must know which sources are to be relied on.

SOURCES OF KNOWLEDGE OF THE LAW

In the first section of this chapter we discussed the *source* of the moral law. What we meant to ask there was: Who pre-

[1] Mees, *op. cit.*, p. 23.

scribes the moral law, who is the law-giver? We are now trying to answer the question: Who or what gives us the knowledge of this law? Our answer then was that God is the source of the moral law in Christianity as well as in Hinduism generally. We shall now try to find out the various *sources of the knowledge* of this law according to Christianity and Hinduism respectively. Let us state at the outset that we do not intend here to deal with the numerous questions that will inevitably arise regarding the relative importance of the various sources. We shall merely indicate briefly what the sources, generally, are.

(*a*) *Christianity*

It can be said without fear of contradiction that Christianity recognizes at least four sources which interpret and reveal to us what the moral law means or what its contents are. These are (1) the Scriptures, (2) the Church, (3) the redeemed souls or saints, and (4) the conscience. There may be, and there actually have been, differences of opinion as to the relative priority of these sources, but it is difficult to think of any section of Christianity which would reject outright the claim of any of these to be interpreters of God's law.

In spite of the risk of stating mere generalities, we may say that the Scriptures come first as being the direct testimony of God's will. But it may be objected that Catholicism on the whole gives the pride of place to the church. This perhaps would be true up to a point. But even the Catholic church strives to judge moral issues only in conformity with the spirit of the scriptures. The church does profess to be the sole and final authority in matters of Biblical interpretation, but it can never claim to supersede the scriptures. To that extent the scriptures should be generally regarded as the first source. The church automatically comes next, for the church is the Body of Christ through which the Holy Spirit works, and accordingly, the voice of the church is claimed to be the voice of the Spirit. The saints who have undoubtedly lived a life of holiness and whose spirit, therefore, was in communion with God, could be relied upon to give guidance in matters of conduct.

These are all, however, external sources. The internal source, of course, is the conscience. If one's conscience is pure and cultivated, it is taken for granted that he will automatically know what his duty is in any situation. We have seen that Christianity believes that the natural moral law is also written in the hearts of men. St Ambrose of Milan says (and most Christian thinkers will agree with him) that

'If men had been able to follow the Natural Law which God our Creator had planted in the heart of each one, there would have been no need for the Law that was inscribed on tables of stone. That divine Law is not written; it is inborn; it is not learnt by reading anything; it finds expression through a capacity native to our minds, rising as it were like a stream whose source is in the nature of every one of us.'[1]

Actually there are many controversies on the question of conscience, for example, whether it knows through the mind or through the heart, which, though very interesting as well as important, cannot be discussed by us in the space at our disposal. We shall, therefore, content ourselves with the observation that Christianity believes in an inner faculty which has an inborn capacity to judge what is morally good. It is possible to argue that conscience is perhaps the most important source, for no Christian would be expected to advise a course of action which is contrary to his conscience. But, as we said earlier, it is not possible for us to enter into the controversy on this issue in the space at our disposal.

(b) Hinduism

Though Hinduism does not have a recognized church which could be a source of knowledge of this law, all the same it recognizes four sources. The DHARMA Shāstras lay down that the sources of our knowledge of *Dharma* are (1) Śruti or the Vedas and Upaniṣads, (2) the Smṛtis, (3) the example of the virtuous, and (4) the approval of an enlightened conscience.[2] The place of the church, thus, is taken by another group of literature, the Smṛtis, and the Vedas are taken as an independent source in themselves.

It must be admitted, however, that though the approval of the conscience (*Ātmanaḥ* or *Antaḥkaraṇa* or *Hṛdaya*) is laid

[1] Quoted by Mellone, *op. cit.*, p. 22.

[2] Manu, II, 6; II, 12.

down as a condition of action, on the whole the approach of Hinduism in matters of morals seems to be comparatively more authoritarian and uncritical. To take just one example, the writers of the Dharma Shāstras generally presupposed that 'the *Śruti* is the ultimate source of all our knowledge of Dharma'.[1] Consequently, when they discovered in the case of a particular Smṛti rule 'that no text of the *Śruti* in support of the *Smṛti* rule can be found', they took 'recourse to the fiction that a *Śruti* text must be inferred or assumed in support of the *Smṛti*'.[2] Whatever the motives in taking this attitude, there is no doubt that this has led to very unsatisfactory conclusions. Fortunately, however, this attitude is not common in later Hinduism, nor even in every section of the same group of literature. Manu, the most celebrated of the writers of Dharma Shāstras, lays equal stress on conscience. He declares, 'Perform only such actions as would satisfy your conscience. Avoid others.'[3] Similarly, '*Manah pūtaṃ Samācaret*'—act in conformity with your conscience—is the advice offered by Chanakya; and the *Bhakti* school generally stresses conscience (*Hṛdaya*) more than anything else.

[1] Aiyer, *op. cit.*, p. 19.	[2] *Ibid.*, p. 20.	[3] Manu, IV, 161.

CHAPTER V

THE CONTENT OF THE MORAL LAW: VIRTUES AND DUTIES

While examining a particular criticism of the ethics of the Gītā in the last chapter, we had occasion to note that the concept of duty, howsoever elaborately and carefully formulated, need not necessarily give any indication of the content of duty. A practical system of ethics will, therefore, be expected to pay as much attention to the content of duty as to the concept of duty. As practical systems of ethics which have helped to shape the lives of millions of human beings for hundreds of years, Christianity and Hinduism are expected to lay down a systematic and coherent pattern of duties for the guidance of their followers. And we may confidently state that they have done so in ample measure, though we cannot yet make any definite pronouncements on how successfully or how consistently this task has been carried out. As a matter of fact, this is one of the points we shall be examining in this chapter.

The discussions that we had in the last chapter on the Christian and Hindu concepts of the Moral Law could only underline our attitude to the Law, namely, that of absolute and unconditional allegiance. We shall now try to fill in the concrete details of what exactly this allegiance involves. In other words, having learnt about the concept of duty we shall now work out the detailed content of duty. Christian and Hindu teachers down the ages have made great efforts to lay down what exactly being a Christian or a Hindu means in the context of behaviour. In the first place, they have emphasized the acquirement or cultivation of certain attributes of character, traditionally called virtues. Besides, there have been innumerable exhortations either to do certain things or to refrain from certain others. These do's and don't's may be termed duties. These duties, however, are so numerous and relative that it will be palpably absurd to have a detailed discussion of them in a brief analysis like ours. We shall, therefore, be obliged to confine our discussion to virtues *generally*. We shall see, however, that in many cases the distinction between virtues and duties breaks down, for they begin to involve each other. This will be clear if we try to define virtues and their implications.

As Thomas McPherson points out, in moral philosophy these days there is hardly any discussion of virtues.[1] The reason for this, in his own words, is that

'There is, indeed, always something artificial—if useful—about the isolation of specific "virtues". A man's character is a whole; and too much concentration on separate virtues, or on separate ends or motives, however apparently necessary in the interests of order and clarity, obscures this. There is, for instance, such a thing as a Christian man, but the traditional insistence of many moral theologians on explaining him in terms of separate virtues does not always make it easier to understand this notion.'[2]

This is by and large true, but, as he himself points out, in moral theology virtues are more likely than not to be a subject of discussion. Whatever, therefore, the artificiality involved in discussing separate virtues, it seems that for a proper understanding of the ingredients of Christian or Hindu character a discussion of virtues is hardly avoidable.

To proceed with our definition of virtues, then, we may quote the words of F. J. Hall and F. H. Hallock. According to them, virtues are the 'regulative principles or habits of conduct which when fully observed produce perfect righteousness of life and character'.[3] In the words of Gilson, virtues are 'forms of habit disposing us more permanently to good actions'.[4] It appears, then, that virtues are those values or attributes of

[1] See McPherson's article on Christian Virtues in *Aristotelian Society Proceedings*, Supplementary Vol. XXXVII, 1963.

[2] McPherson, *op. cit.*, pp. 51 *f.*

[3] F. J. Hall and F. H. Hallock, *Moral Theology*, Longmans, Green, London, 1924, p. 89.

[4] Gilson, *op. cit.*, p. 248.

character which should be cultivated if we care to live a moral life. And cultivation of these almost automatically involves an unfailing practice of these virtues on every single occasion so that in due course it becomes a habit or a permanent disposition in the person concerned. Theoretically it may appear that the agent has the option not to practise a particular one of these virtues at a particular time. But this really does not square up with the notion held by Christianity as well as by Hinduism that the Moral Law must receive unconditional allegiance. If the moral law, then, consists of exhortations to certain virtues, among other injunctions, then the practice of these virtues can hardly admit of exceptions. In other words, the practice of each of the virtues prescribed on every single occasion becomes the sacred duty of every adherent of either of these religions. If, for example, Christianity prescribes justice as a virtue, then the exercise of justice under any circumstances and at any cost becomes the duty of every Christian. In fact the same moral advice can be communicated, in many cases, either by listing it as a virtue or else by giving it the form of a command or duty. To say that justice is a virtue is nothing different from saying that it is our duty to be just. This is why we said that it is extremely difficult in the context of religious ethics to maintain a sharp distinction between duty and virtue. It is perhaps because of this mutual involvement that Hinduism uses the same term, *Dharma*, for virtue as well as duty. This, as a matter of fact, is our excuse for discussing virtues and duties in the same chapter. But as we said earlier, our emphasis will be on virtues, and we shall take into account only those duties that tend to entail some kind of virtue or virtues.

We shall discuss the subject under three sections. Firstly, we shall try to enumerate in some detail the virtues and their classifications in Christianity and in Hinduism. Next, we shall try to compare the so-called Christian with the so-called Hindu virtues, notice the distinctive features, if any, of these sets of virtues, and try to indicate what kind of person the realization of these virtues is likely to produce. Finally, we shall discuss on the basis of our findings in the previous two sections in what sense, if any, can Christian virtues be called exclusively Christian and Hindu virtues Hindu.

VIRTUES AND THEIR CLASSIFICATION

(*a*) *Christianity*

McPherson is right in saying that 'there is no single Biblical source for a list of the Christian virtues'.[1] But he adds that moral theologians seem to be agreed 'that the Christian virtues are seven in number—three theological virtues, faith, hope and love, together with the four cardinal virtues, prudence, fortitude, temperance and justice'.[2] Let us add, however, that these seven are not the only virtues mentioned by Christian theologians. The belief is that though there are a host of virtues which Christians ought to cultivate, all these are reducible in the long run to these seven. The entire range of virtues that Christian literature mentions may safely be asserted to be derived from three sources primarily—the Decalogue or the Ten Commandments of the Old Testament, the teachings and ideals of Jesus as depicted in the Gospels, and the Greek canon of virtues. We shall start our analysis with a discussion of the Decalogue and its implications.

The Ten Commandments may read as follows:[3]

1. Thou shalt have none other gods but Me.
2. Thou shalt not make to thyself any graven image.
3. Thou shalt not take the Name of the Lord thy God in vain.
4. Remember the Sabbath Day to keep it holy.
5. Honour thy father and thy mother.
6. Thou shalt do no murder.
7. Thou shalt not commit adultery.
8. Thou shalt not steal.
9. Thou shalt not bear false witness.
10. Thou shalt not covet.

These Commandments, it is easy to see, are rather elementary duties, simple and direct in their presentation, originally given to the Jewish community at a very early stage of civilization. Since their adoption by Christianity, they have gradually been 'Christianized' to take account of the later revelation, and have

[1] McPherson, *op. cit.*, p. 53. [2] *Ibid.*, p. 53.
[3] See summary by W. H. Griffith Thomas, *The Catholic Faith*, Church Book Room Press, London, 1955, p. 79.

been frequently interpreted to include a more extensive and positive range of principles. In the words of Hall and Hallock,

'The provisions of the older (Old Testament) are rightly criticized as largely negative and external, regulating outward conduct; but Christianized they stand for positive principles regulating thought as well as word and act.'[1]

To give just one illustration of the extension of the scope of these Commandments as a result of their 'Christianization', the fifth Commandment is interpreted to include not only honour and obedience to one's parents but also 'obedience to all divinely sanctioned authority, whether involved in providential circumstances at large or based upon specific divine appointments. Speaking broadly, its sphere is threefold: the family, the Church and the State.'[2] Whether or not, and to what extent, the State can be regarded as a 'divinely sanctioned authority' is arguable in modern circumstances. But that is beside the point. The above opinion does serve as an instance of the reinterpretation and the consequent broadening of the scope of the Decalogue.

The Decalogue is generally divided into two tables, concerned respectively with duties to God and duties to man. Usually the first four Commandments are regarded as forming the first table. But in some divisions even the fifth is included in the first table,[3] whereas in some other divisions only the first three are included in the first table. This is, however, a question of detail which may not be relevant for our purposes. What is unquestionable is that every account regards the Decalogue as forming either the whole or part of the content of the moral law. We have seen in the previous chapter that St Thomas, after laying down the general rule for moral actions, goes on to assert that the derivatives or particular norms of morality are 'identical with the Decalogue, or Ten Commandments'.[4] Incidentally, St Thomas is one of those who draws the line between the first and second tables after the third Commandment.

It can be easily seen that the first four of these Command-

[1] Hall and Hallock, *op. cit.*, pp. 103 *f.*
[2] *Ibid.*, pp. 112 *f.*
[3] *Ibid.*, p. 104.
[4] Rommen, *op. cit.*, p. 51.

ments relate specifically to forms of belief and worship, and to that extent do not have any direct bearing on ethics, though, as we said in the Introduction, it is possible to argue that in a system of religious ethics proper worship is as much part of good conduct as anything else. The fifth Commandment, interpreted as obedience to divinely sanctioned authority, is only a special application of obedience to God as the primary obligation. The last five are prohibitions which enjoin refraining from murder, adultery, stealing, false witness and covetousness. These negative injunctions, when formulated in positive terms, lead to the virtues of respect for life, honour and property, veracity and contentment. Obviously, these are universally recognized virtues practised in every civilized society or community.

The Ten Commandments, amongst much else, formed the background against which the life and character of Jesus himself took shape. This was, however, only the outline to which Jesus added a richness of content drawn partly from the Jewish prophetic tradition but largely from his own insight and genius. The special virtues which receive pointed emphasis in the teachings of Jesus appear to be simplicity, meekness or humility, patience, forgiveness and suffering. The Sermon on the Mount, frequently hailed as the cream of Jesus' teachings, bears testimony to the new emphasis on these qualities. It is here that the 'meek' and the 'merciful', and the 'pure in heart' are declared to be 'blessed', thus giving these qualities a new sanctity. The emphasis on love, even in return for hate, and the advice to turn the other cheek receive approbation for the first time in the Judaeo-Christian tradition. St Paul is only repeating with a renewed stress this genuine teaching of Jesus when he talks of the 'fruit of the Spirit'. Enumerating these 'fruits of the Spirit', as opposed to the 'works of the flesh', St Paul says that these are 'love, joy, peace, longsuffering, gentleness, goodness, faith, meekness, temperance',[1] and adds, significantly, that 'they that are Christ's have crucified the flesh with the affections and lusts'.[2] This crucifixion of the flesh, incidentally, gives an indication of the ascetic character of early Christian teaching and the sharp opposition between the 'flesh' and the 'spirit' which is so reminiscent of the Stoic strain of thought.

[1] Galatians 5: 22, 23.

[2] Galatians 5: 24.

Stephen Neill mentions these qualities as love, joy, peace, patience, kindness, goodness, faithfulness, gentleness and self-control; he remarks that 'This is not meant to be a complete list of all the possible Christian virtues; it tells us the *kind* of people that we ought to be. In fact this may be taken as a brief sketch of what Jesus Christ was like.'[1] The last sentence makes it abundantly clear that the primary norm, of course, is *imitatio Christi*. The model is Jesus Christ, and a Christian would be expected to cultivate all the virtues that Christ demonstrated in his own life. It may be remarked that this factor that the Christian can always look to the personal life of *the one* Christ as a model and thereby derive his particular virtues gives a great theoretical advantage to the Christian over, for example, a Hindu who cannot claim a historical person as the founder of his faith. But a theoretical advantage need not always lead to a practical advantage, especially if there are counteracting factors present.

We must return from this digression, however, and continue our account of the nine qualities listed by St Paul. According to Neill,

'These nine qualities fall roughly into three groups, corresponding, but in the opposite order, to the three words, "soberly and righteously and godly" in Titus 2: 12:
in relation to God: love, joy, peace;
in relation to other men: patience, kindness, goodness;
in relation to ourselves: faithfulness, gentleness, self-control.'[2]

He goes on to add,

'It is important to note that St Paul speaks of these nine virtues as "the *fruit* of the Spirit". The Spirit is one, and I am one. I am called to be obedient to God in all things. If by His help I am obedient to Him in one respect, I shall become in all things more like Christ, and in all respects my character will begin to show that likeness.'[3]

The last sentence demonstrates unequivocally the overall emphasis on the primary virtue of obedience to God, which being there, the rest are expected to follow as necessary conse-

[1] Stephen Neill, *The Christian Character*, World Christian Books, No. 6, 1956, p. 15.
[2] Neill, *op. cit.*, p. 16.
[3] *Ibid.*, p. 16.

quences. Though we have dealt with this aspect in a previous chapter, we may once more repeat that this excessive stress on obedience only tends to detract from the value of the particular virtues referred to earlier. If all other virtues automatically issue out of obedience, there is always the risk of misinterpreting it as an exhortation to suspend practice of those virtues, and rely solely on the virtue of obedience. But we have seen that sheer obedience, even if it were a virtue, can lead to consequences of very doubtful moral quality.

A few words about the principle of classification adopted above may not be out of place. The virtues have been classified as those 'in relation to God', those 'in relation to other men', and those 'in relation to ourselves'. One may not be quite sure of what 'in relation to' exactly means, but it appears that it may signify only the direction of the virtues, that is, whether the virtues are directed primarily towards God or towards other men or towards one's own self. If this is what is meant, then love, joy and peace, for example, would be the virtues that we are to practise or demonstrate in relation to God. On this assumption it may be said that the classification does not seem to be very scientific, nor perhaps was it meant to be. What we mean is that some of the qualities listed under one head could with equal justification, if not more, be placed under another head. To take just one example, the virtue of faithfulness, it seems, could be more aptly placed under either of the first two heads instead of in the third. For this is a virtue which can be demonstrated only in relation to either God or our neighbour rather than to ourselves, unless faithfulness connotes having faith in ourselves in the sense of self-confidence. There is a sense in which we can be said to be faithful or faithless to ourselves: for example, we can be said to be faithful to our conscience or convictions. This is undoubtedly an important aspect of the meaning of this term, but we may still insist that the primary meaning of faith covers the field of our relationship with someone else.

We shall, however, leave the matter there, for volumes have been written on the exact connotation of the particular virtues and on why any of them should belong to one class of virtues rather than another. We do not intend to, nor can we afford to, let ourselves be involved in the discussion of all these details. To return to the subject of classification for a while, we find yet another principle sometimes adopted, namely, on the basis of the various faculties which are primarily involved in the exercise of these virtues or duties. According to this principle, the Ten Commandments, for example, are divided on the basis of whether any one of them is to be observed in thought or in speech or in deed or in a combination of two or more of these. Griffith Thomas, for example, adopts this principle in *The Catholic Faith*. After broadly dividing the Ten Commandments into two equal parts, viz., Duty to God and Duty to our Neighbour, he goes on to suggest that the first two Commandments are to be observed in thought, the third in word and speech, the fourth and fifth in deeds, as also the sixth, seventh and eighth, while the ninth and tenth are to be observed in both words and thoughts.[1] Even a casual examination reveals the many overlappings in this classification, but we shall not dilate on that. What we want to take note of is that so far we have come across two principles of classification of virtues and duties: (1) according to the object to which response is to be made, and (2) according to the faculties to which these duties and virtues belong generally.

We must now pass on to the consideration of the seven fundamental Christian virtues—three 'theological' and the four 'cardinal'. We have already seen that in terms of virtues it is these seven which are regarded as absolute Christian virtues, for all the rest of the virtues are considered reducible to these seven. To remind ourselves of part of our analysis in the second chapter, we have noticed that to the generally familiar and recognized virtues of love, faith and hope in the Judaeo-Christian tradition were later added the Greek virtues of wisdom, temperance, fortitude and justice. Calling them Greek virtues is only a way of saying that it was the Greeks who first formulated them and laid stress on them. In fact, however, these could be regarded as universal virtues. But we have seen that the ethic of self-achievement underlying these virtues later came into conflict with the ethic of self-surrender preached by Christianity. And since the rational appeal of these virtues was tremendous, there developed a tendency to synthesize the two canons of virtues.

[1] Griffith Thomas, *op. cit.*, p. 79.

The best known expedient devised to bring about the synthesis of the two canons of virtues was to treat all these seven virtues as Christian virtues. The seven were divided into two classes—(1) cardinal or earthly virtues pertaining to the natural order and earthly relations, and (2) theological or heavenly virtues pertaining to 'the supernatural order' and directly related to 'the attainment of the *summum bonum*'.[1] The cardinal virtues, as we know, are wisdom or prudence, temperance, fortitude or courage and justice, and the theological ones faith, hope and love. Of the four cardinal virtues, wisdom is supposed to be seated in the intellect, temperance and fortitude in the emotions, and justice in the will. The remarkable feature, however, is that the theological virtues are supposed to

> 'supplement and transfigure the cardinal virtues, giving them a pertinent relation to the attainment of the *summum bonum* which is otherwise lacking; that is, the cardinal virtues are made to serve supernatural purposes. Faith elevates wisdom, hope elevates justice, and charity elevates temperance and fortitude; but in a complex interaction and mutual dependence.'[2]

What exactly is meant by this 'transfiguration' or 'elevation' is difficult to understand, and therefore, we shall reserve our comments. We may, however, remark in passing that the model for this distinction between cardinal and theological virtues was itself probably furnished by the Greek distinction between ethical and dianoetic virtues.

St Thomas distinguishes between moral virtues and intellectual virtues. The former are the virtues leading to the rationalizing of desire or appetite itself, whereas the latter lead to the knowledge of proper means and ends. The two clearly must supplement each other. To make the distinction between moral and intellectual virtues a bit clearer, the virtues which help to *judge* properly the worth of actions and their ends as well as the right means will be called intellectual virtues. These, it may be noticed, are reminiscent of the Socratic virtue. Moral virtues, on the other hand, relate to our volition, the possession of which makes it natural for man to will what is considered good by the reason.

[1] Hall and Hallock, *op. cit.*, p. 90. [2] *Ibid.*, p. 91.

The chief intellectual virtues are intelligence, knowledge, wisdom and prudence. Of these the first three are purely intellectual and are ultimately subsumed under wisdom. Intelligence is the virtue which 'fits the intellect for the knowledge of directly evident truths or principles'[1]; knowledge is a virtue 'enabling reason to judge sanely of a certain order of knowables',[2] and admits of various degrees and kinds; wisdom, however, being the highest conclusions concerning the 'ultimate causes', must be only one. But these virtues only help to know the end. It is not, however, 'enough for man merely to think, he must also live and live rightly'.[3] Hence the need to find out the proper means as well. So we need an intellectual virtue 'which enables reason to arrive at a suitable determination of means leading to the end in view: this virtue is prudence, *recta ratio agibilium*; and this is a virtue necessary for living rightly'.[4] The purely moral virtues, of course, are justice, temperance and fortitude: 'These three moral virtues together with the one intellectual virtue of prudence, are usually described as "principal" or "cardinal" virtues, for they alone imply both the faculty of acting rightly and the performance of the good act itself, and consequently they realize by themselves perfectly the definition of virtue.'[5]

Before passing on to the consideration of Hindu virtues, we ought to draw pointed attention to the fact that in the realm of virtues Christian theologians maintain a definite gradation, some virtues being regarded as earthly (the cardinal ones) whereas others (the theological ones) are regarded as supernatural or spiritual, the latter obviously being considered primary. For, as we have seen, it is the latter which impart true significance to the former. Given faith, hope and love, the other virtues are supposed to follow automatically, for they are fruits of the spirit. St Augustine's attempt to demonstrate that all virtues are forms of love in fact makes love the primary virtue, if not the only one. The excessive stress on the duty of obedience to God, similarly, tends to imply that all the desirable virtues can issue forth from the mere will to obey. The earthly virtues, anyway, would appear to be worth cultivation only in so far as they are supposed to pave the way for the attainment of the

[1] Gilson, *op. cit.*, p. 252.
[2] *Ibid.*, p. 252.
[3] *Ibid.*, p. 253.
[4] *Ibid.*, pp. 253 *f.*
[5] *Ibid.*, p. 254.

summum bonum, that is, liberation or redemption. It would not be unfair to say that on this reading the earthly virtues do not appear to have any intrinsic worth or excellence, or at least not the same as belongs to the theological ones. This only stresses the fact that in any system of religious ethics religious piety ultimately tends to take precedence over ethical values, and Christianity is no exception to this rule.

(*b*) *Hinduism*

If we remember the remark that we just made about the relation between religious piety and ethical values, it will be infinitely easier for us to understand the fallacy underlying some ill-founded but popular misconceptions about Hindu ethics. The most widely prevalent and persistent of these is that the Hindu is so much obsessed with the desire for release or *Mokṣa* that he seldom, if at all, appreciates the need for ethical values or conduct. This criticism assumes a greater poignancy and relevance with respect to the philosophy of the Vedānta. It is argued that these schools of thought regard merger with the Absolute as the ultimate goal for human beings, hence nothing else matters to them. The state of *Mokṣa* not only transcends the truly ethical life but it in fact also denies it. But this on correct interpretation is as much true of Christianity as of Hinduism. There is no denying the fact that the ultimate religious goal does transcend earthly ethical values. We have already seen in an earlier chapter that where the ultimate religious destiny is redemption, ethical life can at best be regarded as a preparation for it. If this means that the religion in question does not have an ethics, then Christianity must be equally subject to this charge. We have seen that in Christianity there is the conception of cardinal virtues being 'made to serve supernatural purposes'. In the same way, in Hinduism *Dharma* is made to serve spiritual purposes, i.e. the attainment of *Mokṣa*.

The other misunderstanding of a similar import, but from a different angle, issues from the misinterpretation of certain scriptural passages which lend themselves to antinomian distortions. This again, is no monopoly of Hinduism, for Christianity too has suffered immeasurably from such distortions. In the words of Hopkins, a 'result of misunderstanding rather than of intelligent interpretation' is the reading of antinomian suggestions in some Hindu scriptural utterances such as: 'Sin does not cling to a wise man more than water clings to a lotus-leaf'. This 'is not to declare', he says, 'that the sage may sin and be free, but that one free from worldly attachments sheds sin, is not attached to it . . .'.[1] A perusal of some representative passages from the earliest of the scriptures will drive home how, in spite of the acceptance of *Mokṣa* as the highest destiny for man, ethical values and conduct were emphasized as the absolutely essential preparation for the former.

The Ṛg Veda declares, 'Whether in heaven or on earth, let truth be my guide'[2]; 'Mighty Lord! Prompt even a miser to practise charity, let him be kind in disposition'.[3] The Atharva Veda strikes a typically ethical note: 'We have conquered evil and gained virtue. We are then to be free from sin.'[4] The same spirit is found in some of the hymns of the Yajurveda: 'Direct our energies in the path of righteousness (*Agnenaya Supathārāyé Asmān*)'[5]; 'Good actions alone live for a hundred years. There can be no better path than this. Let your actions, however, not taint your soul (or produce attachment to the consequences).'[6] Or consider these Upaniṣadic hymns:

'The good and the pleasant approach a man, and the wise man discriminates between them, choosing the better, not the more pleasant; the fool through greed and avarice chooses the more pleasant, but well for him who chooses the better; whoso forsakes the better and chooses the more pleasant fails of his aim.[7]

'Whosoever views all beings as his own soul (*Ātmaiva*) for him there can be no delusion or misery; therefore, see all as one.'[8]

It is perhaps not necessary to add to these passages, for hundreds of them can be found scattered all through these scriptures. We shall, therefore, close this preliminary explanation and proceed with our analysis of the Hindu virtues and duties proper.

[1] E. W. Hopkins, *op. cit.*, p. 66.
[2] Ṛg Veda, X, 37, 2; VI, 53, 3.
[3] *Ibid.*
[4] Atharva Veda, XVI, 6, 1.
[5] Yajurveda, 5, 36.
[6] *Ibid.*, 40, 2.
[7] Kaṭha Upaniṣad, I, 2, 2.
[8] Īśa Upaniṣad, 7.

Not perhaps an exhaustive or systematic list of virtues or duties, but the true spirit of conduct expected of a good Hindu is reflected in the teacher's exhortation to the departing students contained in the Taittirīya Upaniṣad:

'Having taught the Veda, the teacher instructs the pupil. Speak the truth. Practise virtue. Let there be no neglect of your (daily) reading. Having brought to the teacher the wealth that is pleasing (to him), do not cut off the thread of the offspring. Let there be no neglect of truth. Let there be no neglect of virtue. Let there be no neglect of welfare. Let there be no neglect of prosperity. Let there be no neglect of study and teaching. Let there be no neglect of the duties to the gods and the fathers. Be one to whom the mother is a god. Be one to whom the father is a god. Be one to whom the teacher is a god. Be one to whom the guest is a god. Whatever deeds are blameless, they are to be practised, not others. Whatever good practices there are among us, they are to be adopted by you, not others. Whatever Brāhmaṇas there are (who are) superior to us, they should be comforted by you with a seat. (What is to be given) is to be given with *faith*, should not be given without faith, should be given in plenty, should be given with *modesty*, should be given with *fear*, should be given with *sympathy*. . . .'[1]

This exhortation to practise truth, virtue, respect for and obedience to elders, welfare of others, faith, modesty or humility, fear and sympathy provides, we may say, the background against which we can now undertake a more systematic account of Hindu virtues and duties.

Perhaps foremost amongst the lists of virtues and duties for Hindus comes what has been frequently called the Ten Commandments of Manu. Manu, like almost all other writers of Dharma Shāstras, divides the duties of men under two heads: (1) duties relative to one's station in life (the *Varṇa-Āśrama Dharma*), and (2) general or common duties (*Sādhāraṇa Dharma*) which men, as men, are to discharge irrespective of their position, station or stage in life. Naturally the former kind of duties will vary according to the *Varṇa* (class) and *Āśrama* (stage) of individuals, the former themselves depending on the

[1] Taittirīya Upaniṣad, I, 11, 1–3 (emphasis mine).

natures (*Svabhāva*) of the individuals, and therefore cannot be regarded as universal duties. Since such duties are numerous and relative, we shall be obliged to confine ourselves to the consideration of only the common duties. But it may perhaps be interesting to refer briefly to the duties and qualities of the different *Varṇas* laid down in the Gītā (Chapter XVIII). The three consecutive verses which list these run as follows:

'Security, self-control, austerity, purity, forbearance, and uprightness, wisdom, knowledge and faith in religion, these are the duties of the Brāhmin, born of his nature (*Svabhāvajam*). —XVIII, 42.

Heroism, vigour, steadiness, resourcefulness, not fleeing even in a battle, generosity and leadership, these are the duties of a Kṣatriya born of his nature.—XVIII, 43.

Agriculture, tending cattle and trade are the duties of a Vaiśya born of his nature; work of the character of service is the duty of a śūdra born of his nature.—XVIII, 44.'

To return to the common duties, however, these are ten in number according to Manu:

1. *Dhairya* or *Dhṛti* (patience or steadfastness)
2. *Kṣamā* (forgiveness)
3. *Dama* (application)
4. *Asteya* (non-appropriation or non-stealing)
5. *Śauca* (cleanliness or purity)
6. *Indriya Nigraha* (restraint of the organs of sense)
7. *Dhī* (wisdom)
8. *Vidyā* (learning or knowledge of the sacred texts)
9. *Satya* (veracity)
10. *Akrodha* (freedom from anger)

It will be seen that all these duties in fact are virtues, and this lends support to our earlier thesis about the difficulty of separating duties from virtues in the context of a religious ethics. These ten, are, however, ultimately reduced to five in their short form (*Sāmāsikaṃ Dharmam*): non-injury (*Ahiṃsā*), veracity (*Satya*), honesty or non-stealing (*Asteya*), cleanliness (*Śauca*) and restraint of senses (*Indriya Nigraha*).[1] Yajnavalkya

[1] Manu, X, 63.

substitutes celibacy (*Brahmacarya*) and non-attachment (*Aparigraha*) for *Śauca* and *Indriya Nigraha*. These five are regarded as universal injunctions with the addition of 'generosity, self-control, sympathy and patience'.[1] These five apparently negative virtues, namely, *Ahiṃsā*, *Satya*, *Asteya*, *Brahmacarya* and *Aparigraha* are perhaps the best known and most widely preached in the Indian tradition. The five *Yamas* (forms of self-restraint) of Patanjali, the *Pañca Mahāvrata* (the five great vows) of the Jainas and the *Pañca Śīla* of the Buddhists all emphasize the same qualities, though the interpretations of the content of these injunctions are quite often of a very positive nature. We shall, however, come to this point later.

Prashastapada's list of these universal or common duties, though mainly incorporating all the duties listed by Manu and Yajnavalkya, contains some new additions, so that, on the whole, his seems to be perhaps a more socially oriented account of virtues than that of Manu where the emphasis clearly seems to be on self-autonomy. The generic or *Sāmānya* duties, according to Prashastapada, are these:

1. *Śraddhā* or *Manaḥprasāda* (moral earnestness or regard for *Dharma*)
2. *Ahiṃsā* (non-injury)
3. *Bhūtahitatva* (seeking the good of creatures)
4. *Satyavacana* (veracity)
5. *Asteya* (honesty or non-stealing)
6. *Brahmacarya* (celibacy or freedom from passion)
7. *Anupadhā* (sincerity or purity of motive)
8. *Krodhavarjana* (restraint of anger)
9. *Abhisecana* etc. (personal cleanliness)
10. *Śucidravyasevana* (non-eating of impure food)
11. *Viśiṣta-Devatā-Bhakti* (devotion to the recognized deity)
12. *Upavāsa* (fasting on specified occasions)
13. *Apramāda* (moral watchfulness)[2]

It will be seen that Prashastapada adds to Manu's list of duties moral earnestness, non-injury, goodwill to creatures and moral watchfulness, while he drops from Manu's list forgiveness, application, wisdom and learning. Of the qualities that

[1] Hopkins, *op. cit.*, p. 118.

[2] Based on Maitra, *op. cit.*, p. 10.

Prashastapada adds to the list of Manu the most significant is perhaps the one of *Bhūtahitatva*, or seeking the good of creatures, which, as we said, gives his list a more social orientation. Non-injury may not be regarded as quite an addition since, as we saw, this occurs in the 'compressed' list of Manu. Moral watchfulness and moral earnestness in place of wisdom and learning are, as Maitra says, 'significant as emphasizing the ethical in place of the dianoetic virtues and thus teaching a non-intellectualistic view of morality as distinguished from the intellectualism of Sāṃkhya and Shāṃkara-Vedānta'.[1] It should also be noticed that some of the duties listed above are pure duties only, and can hardly be regarded as virtues in a proper sense, for example, the duties of fasting, cleanliness and non-eating of impure foods.

Keeping St Thomas' distinction between intellectual and moral virtues, it may be said that the only properly intellectual virtues preached by Manu are wisdom and knowledge (*Vidyā*), whereas there are hardly any strictly intellectual virtues listed by Prashastapada. The whole range of virtues occurring in the lists of all the three sources discussed so far are, therefore, a mixture of intellectual and ethical virtues (though no such distinction has been maintained by the authors of the lists themselves), with the emphasis shifting from the former to the latter as we pass from Manu to Prashastapada. Patanjali's list of *Yamas* and *Niyamas*, which has quite often been accepted as another list of Hindu virtues, not only adds the latter five but also insists on ascribing a much more positive content to the injunctions which we noticed while referring to Yajnavalkya. Thus the complete list of duties laid down by Patanjali would be these: non-injury, veracity, non-stealing, freedom from passion and non-attachment—the five *Yamas*; and cleanliness (*Śauca*), contentment (*Santoṣa*), arduous application and devotion (*Tapas*), recitation of the Scriptures (*Svādhyāya*) and meditation on the glories and perfections of the Lord (*Īśvara-pranidhāna*)—the five *Niyamas*. The *Yamas* may be called the forms ot selt-restraint and the *Niyamas* rules of self-realization. But the 'forms of self-restraint' actually become positive virtues when their connotation is enlarged, as is done by Patanjali. For example, *Ahiṃsā* not only means refraining from violence in a

[1] Maitra, *op. cit.*, p. 16.

merely negative way but also includes the positive spirit of tenderness and goodwill to all creatures irrespective of place and time. On this reading *Ahiṃsā* implies not only the resolve not to kill or harm but also the altruistic endeavour to seek the good of all creatures and may possibly be the Hindu counterpart of the virtue of love and kindness on a much extended scale in so far as it includes not only the neighbour but also all creatures as the objects of love. Thus we may say, in the words of Maitra, that Patanjali's conception may be regarded as 'an attempt to reconcile the ideal of a rigoristic autonomy of the self and freedom from desire with that of the altruistic seeking of the good of creatures through good-will and love'.[1]

It would seem from our analysis of Hindu virtues and duties so far that duties to others and to God have not been sharply distinguished from duties to oneself, nor have they been divided on the basis of faculties, though we shall have occasion to examine shortly one particular classification of virtues on the basis of the faculties that are instrumental in exercising them. The reason for mentioning *Bhūtahitatva* or the good of all creatures, for example, or the devotion to God along with other virtues which have the individual himself as their object primarily, might possibly have been that between duty to God and others and duty to oneself a distinction was perhaps considered unnecessary or artificial. But the more important reason might be that the aim of all these virtues, at least according to the sources that we have so far considered, was primarily self-autonomy, and therefore all the effort was mainly directed towards developing a certain kind of temperament for oneself which would automatically ensure the proper performance of duties to other agencies such as one's neighbour or God.

Vatsyayana, however, classifies virtues according to the faculties primarily involved in the exercise of the virtue concerned. According to him, virtues may be either relating to the body (volitional) or to speech or to thought. There are thus three kinds of virtues: (1) *Kāyika*, i.e. bodily or volitional, (2) *Vācika*, or those relating to speech, and (3) *Mānasika*, or those relating to the mind or thought. These three kinds of virtue issue from good inclinations (*Śubha Pravṛtti*) as against evil inclinations (*Pāpātmikā Pravṛtti*) which lead to *Adharma*

[1] Maitra, *op. cit.*, p. 225.

or vice. Every virtue, therefore, has a corresponding vice which is listed alongside it. These virtues and their corresponding vices are the following:[1]

	Dharma	*Adharma*
Volitional or relating to the body	1 *Paritrāṇa* (Succouring the distressed)	1 *Hiṃsā* (Cruelty
	2 *Dāna* (Charity or munificence)	2 *Steya* (Theft or appropriation)
	3 *Paricaran* (Social service)	3 *Pratisiddha Maithuna* (Sexual indulgence)
Relating to speech	1 *Satya* (Veracity)	1 *Mithyā* (Mendacity)
	2 *Priyavacana* (Agreeableness of speech)	2 *Paruṣa* (Harshness)
	3 *Hitavacana* (Beneficial speech)	3 *Sucanā* (Scandal)
	4 *Svādhyāya* (Reading of Scriptures)	4 *Asaṃbaddha* (Gossip)
Relating to mind or thought	1 *Dayā* (Kindness, benevolence)	1 *Paradroha* (Hostility)
	2 *Aspṛhā* (Indifference to material gains)	2 *Paradravyābhipsa* (Covetousness)
	3 *Śraddhā* (Reverence or piety)	3 *Nāstikya* (Irreverence or impiety)

In this classification of virtues and the corresponding vices there is only one particular virtue which does not seem to have an exact correspondence with its counterpart. It is difficult to see how sexual indulgence can be the opposite of the virtue of social service. But perhaps Maitra may be right in commenting, 'It may be said, however, that just as *paricaran* consists in doing good to society so *pratisiddha-maithuna* rends the social fabric by loosening the social bonds and weakening the stock'.[2] In any case, this correspondence is not our chief concern. Looking at the classification of virtues itself, we cannot fail to notice that just like its counterpart in Christianity, this classification suffers from overlapping, that is to say, one or the other of virtues under one particular head may be easily transferred under another head without serious difficulty. One feature

[1] Maitra, *op. cit.*, pp. 216–18.

[2] *Ibid.*, p. 218.

of this classification is remarkable, however; namely, the emphasis here seems to have shifted almost entirely to other-regarding duties. Self-autonomy is no longer the primary concern, for almost all the virtues listed here seem to have a social motivation. Virtue seems to be regarded here as qualities which must be exercised in respect of others—either the neighbour or God. The virtue which defines man's relationship with God is *Śraddhā* or piety, which may be regarded as the counterpart of the theological virtue of faith.

But it must be said that though piety is mentioned as a virtue, as are *Īśvara-Pranidhāna* and *Bhakti* in the lists of Patanjali and Prashastapada respectively, none of the lists mentioned so far could be said to have a primarily theological orientation. The virtues seem to have been derived either from the concept of self-autonomy or from the humanitarian concern for the well-being of society. Ramanuja on the other hand, as we mentioned in an earlier chapter, derives the virtues from his conception of God as the moral ideal. And since Ramanuja and the various devotional schools influenced by him undoubtedly represent the more popular form of Hinduism, we can never consider our account of Hindu virtues complete without mentioning his views on this issue. As we said, Ramanuja conceives God as the moral ideal which entails ascription of certain auspicious qualities to Him.

'God as *Bhagvāna* or Lord is conceived as *akhila-heyapratyanika*, i.e., as actively cancelling or removing all evil and imperfection of finite beings even as light cancels darkness. In this consists the life of God which is a personal life in incessant and inseparable relation to other persons.'[1]

This means that all the auspicious qualities of God must all the time be directed towards removing the obstacles from the path of His creatures: as examples, His infinite knowledge is active in dispelling the ignorance of His creatures, His might consists in enabling creatures to overcome their frailty and to have the power to eschew evil and attain the good. Now, men as finite centres of divinity can only help in the realization of the divine purpose by doing what God would do in a given context.

[1] Maitra, *op. cit.*, p. 22.

God and man are inseparable and so are their successes and failures; hence the clear and unavoidable duty of man is to imitate, as far as lies within his power, all these divine attributes. This, we remarked earlier, is very similar to the Christian doctrine of *imitatio Christi*. On this ideal the virtues that we must practise and the qualities that we must manifest in a given context become quite clear. We must give *knowledge to the ignorant* (*Jñanam Ajñānāṃ*) so that they can discriminate between good and evil; we must forgive the guilty (*Kṣamā Sāparādhānām*); the weak deserve help to overcome their moral failure (*Śakti Aśaktānām*); we must show kindness to the distressed (*Kṛpā Dukhīnām*); tenderness to the imperfect and deficient (*Vātsalyam sadoṣānām*); humility to the arrogant or uncivil (*Śilam Mandānām*); straightforwardness to the crooked (*Ārjavam Kuṭilānām*); sympathy to the wicked in heart (*Sauhārdyam Duṣṭahṛdayānām*) and gentleness to the shy and timid (*Mārdavam Viśleṣabhirunām*).[1]

Thus in this list (if we can call it a list) almost all the best qualities of the heart are laid down, and are derived from the character of the Supreme model, God. These virtues do not only lead to the well-being of man but also transform human character by bringing it more into tune with the ultimate purpose of God. It is needless to add that in this scheme the incentive to cultivate the perfections, enumerated above, comes from the sentiment of love for the Lord which is reflected in the tendency to imitate Him, faith in the intrinsic goodness of God's purpose, and hope in the ultimate possibility of achieving the good life through God's mercy. Thus the theological virtues of love, faith and hope are certainly implied, though not specifically mentioned.

COMPARISON OF CHRISTIAN AND HINDU VIRTUES

After the foregoing account of Christian and Hindu virtues, it may not sound too far fetched to say that the range of virtues and duties outlined in both systems is strikingly similar, or at least not so dissimilar as is often supposed. The language and terminology, as also quite often the emphases, are obviously and naturally different. But on the whole they compare quite

[1] Maitra, *op. cit.*, pp. 22 *f.*

favourably. In the course of our analysis in the previous section we have in places suggested how they compare in some specific details. We shall now briefly outline the overall position.

To begin with the most striking similarity, we may refer to the last five of the Commandments in the Decalogue, which are almost exactly identical with the five Hindu injunctions that recur not only in orthodox Hindu systems but also in the heterodox Indian systems such as the Jaina and the Bauddha. These are, of course, the five principles of *Ahiṃsā, Satya, Asteya, Brahmacarya* and *Aparigraha*. The correspondence of these five with the last five of the Ten Commandments may be shown by the following table:

Christian	*Hindu*
6. Thou shalt do no murder.	*Ahiṃsā* or non-injury
7. Thou shalt not commit adultery	*Brahmacarya* or celibacy
8. Thou shalt not steal	*Asteya* or non-stealing
9. Thou shalt not bear false witness	*Satya* or veracity
10. Thou shalt not covet	*Aparigraha* or non-attachment

These five, as we said earlier, come foremost amongst the principles regulating the conduct of Hindus. The Christian virtues of kindness, goodness, gentleness and faithfulness are all comprehended by the two Hindu virtues of *Dayā* and *Śraddhā*; patience and self-control are explicitly stressed in both systems; and the Greek virtues also have their counterparts. Temperance as signifying avoidance of extremes is amply covered by the injunction of self-control. The five *Yamas*, as we have seen, are literally 'forms of self-restraint'. Fortitude has its counterpart in *Dama* or even in the Yogic prescription of *Tapas*. Wisdom (*Dhī*), as distinct from mere learning (*Vidyā*), is included in the Ten Commandments of Manu, and is highly prized by every Hindu. In fact, the saving knowledge which gives one the insight into the real nature of things and helps to achieve liberation, called *Jñāna*, is not intellectual knowledge so much as wisdom in the form of realization. The virtue of justice is more than replaced by the ideal of *Bhūtahitatva*, or good of all creatures, for if one respects the Hindu teaching of treating all creatures kindly, without discrimination, justice is surely guaranteed. The Christian ideal of love or charity and universal brotherhood is covered by the three virtues of Vatsyayana, namely, *Paritrāṇa*, *Paricaraṇa* and *Dāna*. Faith, hope and love, as we said earlier, form the very basis of Ramanuja's derivation of the virtues from God's character and are the main theme of the devotional schools in Hinduism. The Gītā sets the tone for the religion of faith in these words:

'He who has faith, who is absorbed in it (i.e. wisdom) and who has subdued his senses gains wisdom and having gained wisdom he attains quickly the supreme peace.'[1]

We may approach this similarity of content between Christian and Hindu virtues from a different angle. We have noticed Stephen Neill's comment that the nine qualities listed by St Paul as 'the fruits of the Spirit' do not give a complete list of all the possible Christian virtues. They merely tell us 'the kind of persons we ought to be'. And he also adds that this may be taken to be 'a brief sketch of what Jesus Christ was like'. Jesus Christ, then, is the kind of person Christians ought to be. This would hardly be challenged even by a Hindu. Dogma apart, the Hindu would readily agree that Jesus approaches the Hindu picture of the ideal man in almost all respects. For Jesus would be viewed as the wise man who knows things in their correct perspective, is in the right kind of relationship with God, is neither elated by success nor worried by crucifixion, does always what he considers to be the good of all and has all the composure of a true *Yogin* as described in the Gītā. Extracts from a few relevant passages in the Gītā reveal the picture of a man who may appear strikingly similar to Christ:

'He whose mind is untroubled in the midst of sorrows and is free from eager desire and pleasures, he from whom passion, fear and rage have passed away, he is called a sage of settled intelligence.—II, 56.

'The holy men whose sins are destroyed, whose doubts (dualities) are cut asunder, whose minds are disciplined and

[1] Gītā, IV, 39.

who rejoice in (doing) good to all creatures, attain to the beatitude of God.—V, 25.'

Christ, in fact, would be readily accepted by the Hindu as the very familiar figure of the wise seer or sage.

THE UNIQUENESS OF CHRISTIAN OR HINDU VIRTUES

The near-identity of content between the Christian and Hindu virtues that we have noticed in the previous section obliges us to consider in what sense, if any, either Christian or Hindu virtues can be regarded as unique or exclusive. Since Hindus are not generally heard to claim any such uniqueness for their virtues, our problem, in effect, is to examine whether this Christian claim is justified. Hindus do often claim, and perhaps rightly, that their social system, by which they mean *Varṇa-Āśrama Dharma*, is unique; some of their ideas about Godhead, creation and self or *Ātman* are declared to be exclusive possessions, as also are some of their customs and practices. But when it comes to the qualities that make a good man, in other words, virtues, there seems to be no such claim. But in Christianity there is a definite tendency to regard Christian virtues as exclusively Christian and unique. Even ordinary Christians (by 'ordinary' we mean non-theologians) seem quite often to be convinced that the fact of their being 'Christian' somehow adds to the merit and the quality of the virtues. This needs examination.

Thomas McPherson, in his article referred to above, analyses at some length the grounds of uniqueness claimed for Christian virtues and comes to the conclusion that this claim is rather gratuitous. Starting with the question, 'What are "Christian virtues"?', he suggests that there can be two possible views:[1] (1) Either that 'Christian virtues' is the name of a particular list of virtues different in content from other lists (different in respect of all items or in respect of at least some items). This would mean that it contains items that one would not find in a list of, say, Greek virtues. Or, (2) that 'Christian virtues' does not signify a special list of virtues different in content from the rest, but that the virtues in question, even though common in

[1] McPherson, *op. cit.*, pp. 52 *ff.*

other lists, yet possess a special *quality* or *property* not possessed by non-Christian virtues.

In course of his examination of the first view, he takes note not only of the traditional seven Christian virtues but also of some others which are classed by Aquinas as virtues, or parts of virtue, or acts of virtue, for example, religion, vengeance, martyrdom, fasting, virginity, humility, etc. After examining the exact connotation of some of these virtues and comparing them to Greek virtues, he comes to the following conclusion:

'. . . I am suggesting that Christian virtues, considered as constituting a special class of virtues, need not be looked on as quite unique; I do not want to suggest that there is no difference at all between Christian virtues and Greek virtues.'[1]

We may only add that our examination of the content of Christian and Hindu virtues, and the near-identity that we have noticed, strengthens McPherson's argument and casts serious doubt on the claim to uniqueness of Christian virtues in the first sense.

Coming to the second view regarding the uniqueness of Christian virtues, McPherson feels that the supposed 'distinguishing mark' of Christian virtues, as claimed by theologians quite often, is the quality of being 'infused' or implanted by God as His gifts. He, therefore, feels impelled to examine this distinction between 'infused' and 'acquired' virtues; but after examining all the supposed differences between them, he finds that there is no convincing ground for maintaining a distinction between them. He feels that at least to non-theologians there appears to be no convincing proof that there are any infused virtues as distinct from merely acquired ones. Hence he concludes that there is no good evidence to show that 'Christian virtues' have any unique quality or property which non-Christian virtues lack.

And we, as non-theologians, feel inclined to accept the inescapable logic of McPherson's arguments. Thus it would seem that there is no ground to believe that being Christian could in any sense add to the merit or quality of the virtues which are listed as such. We may perhaps concede that the sense

[1] McPherson, *op. cit.*, p. 58.

of security resulting from one's belief or faith in a God may in some cases render the exercise of virtues comparatively easy. But this is something which, even if true, could apply equally well to non-Christians.

We, therefore, take the view that 'Christian virtues' is just a convenient and traditional way of describing the virtues that should be practised by Christians, without in any way suggesting that they are exclusive or unique. Similarly Hindu virtues may be only a convenient way of describing the kind of values that have been cherished by a certain community, without implying that they have been absent elsewhere. It is interesting to note in this connexion that the term 'Hindu' itself is of foreign origin. What is now known as Hinduism has actually been called by Hindus *Sanātana Dharma* or *eternal religion*. If we substitute '*Sanātana*' (eternal) for 'Hindu' in 'Hindu virtues', the term will then signify eternal virtues or universal virtues to which no claim to exclusiveness can be attributed.

CHAPTER VI

MORAL EFFORT AND HUMAN FREEDOM

We have so far examined the Christian and Hindu concepts of the Moral Law and the demand that it makes on man. We have also discussed what sort of values he must cultivate or what sort of character he must develop if he is to be in harmony with the divine law. It would, therefore, now seem appropriate to enquire whether man has the capacity or freedom to achieve what is demanded of him. On the face of it, this would hardly seem to be a problem, for we have already agreed that neither Christianity nor Hinduism have any doubts about the *potential* greatness of man and his infinite capacities. But what is potential need not be actual. In fact, both Christianity and Hinduism believe, for one reason or another, that man in his present state is far removed from his potential greatness. There lies the difficulty. Whatever his ultimate destiny, man as man is heavily encumbered by factors which clearly seem to limit seriously, if not altogether annul, his freedom of choice and action. The question that arises, then, is: Is man free to achieve what he ought to achieve? And if so, to what extent? This is the context in which we intend to make human freedom the subject of our enquiry.

Now, in view of man's consciousness of freedom of choice and action, within certain limits, this may seem a singularly idle and theoretical question. Perhaps it is; but no more so than most other problems that philosophers have racked their brains about. There is, however, the need to specify with precision the sense in which we intend to treat human freedom as a problem. For there is one very legitimate sense in which this can be called a 'pseudo-problem'. This sense is the one in which freedom is equated with indeterminism or lack of causation of any sort and is then set against determinism which is interpreted to imply lack of responsibility and freedom of conduct.

The classic argument of this kind is very succinctly stated by Moritz Schlick in his *Problems of Ethics*:

'If determinism is true, if, that is, all events obey immutable laws, then my will too is always determined, by my innate character and my motives. Hence my decisions are necessary, not free. But if so, then I am not responsible for my acts, for I would be accountable for them only if I could do something about the way my decisions went; but I can do nothing about it, since they proceed with necessity from my character and the motives. And I have made neither, and have no power over them: the motives come from without, and my character is the necessary product of the innate tendencies and the external influences which have been effective during my lifetime. Thus determinism and moral responsibility are incompatible. Moral responsibility presupposes freedom, that is, exemption from causality.'[1]

There is no denying the fact that much of the traditional discussion about the freedom of the will has been, unfortunately, on the above lines. And it is easy to see why the problem involved in this kind of reasoning has been declared by Schlick and many others to be a pseudo-problem. Freedom as meaning complete exemption from causality undermines the very foundation of morality, which it is supposed, wrongly in fact, to safeguard; and it thereby defeats its purpose. If there were no causal relation between a man's motives and his actions, and if whatever a man did were no more than a matter of chance, then indeed responsibility and, by implication, morality would become meaningless concepts. Causality, therefore, or determinism in the sense of a necessary and uniform connexion between the motives and actions, and between actions and consequences is indeed as necessary a postulate of morality as freedom of choice and conduct. Hence the genuine sense of freedom is not utter indeterminism as opposed to any kind and degree of determinism or causality but a certain amount of freedom of choice and conduct, as opposed to total and absolute compulsion and external pressure or interference. And it is in this sense of freedom that we are interested.

[1] Moritz Schlick, *Problems of Ethics*, authorized translation by David Rynin, Prentice-Hall, Inc., New Jersey, 1939, p. 146.

It is true that freedom in this—its genuine—sense can be a topic of discussion only because of its implications for another issue which is a philosopher's concern—the issue of moral responsibility. For no one can be a responsible agent if he is not a free agent. In view of this, our discussions in the present chapter are only a kind of preliminary groundwork for the next chapter wherein we intend to discuss responsibility. This division into two chapters is only for the sake of convenience, and the two are really complementary. For the present, however we shall be confining ourselves to the consideration of human freedom in Christianity and in Hinduism. In other words, we shall be asking ourselves whether the human freedom postulated by moral effort and responsibility is consistent with the religious or theological doctrines of Christianity and Hinduism.

In a very general way the crux of the problem for the religious man is touched in the following lines, quoted by Maclagan: 'Our religious convictions demand dependence on God; our ethical convictions demand freedom. . . .'[1] This is the central problem for any religious ethics—that of reconciling dependence on God, which every religion demands in varying degrees, with the freedom demanded by moral effort. Quite often this conflict is declared to be irreconcilable. This is, for example, the attitude of the author of the lines quoted above when to those lines he adds: 'The mistake that has been made has been that theologians have aimed at philosophical consistency.' It is extraordinary that he regards the attempt at philosophical consistency as a 'mistake'. Even agreeing that religion is primarily a matter of faith, it is difficult to see how we can altogether refrain from examining the philosophical consistency or otherwise of religious doctrines and their relation to non-religious facts. But this is in any case irrelevant to our present purposes. We are not interested in examining any inherent conflicts between ethics and religion in a general way, and so we must pass on to the consideration of freedom specifically in Christianity and Hinduism.

Now, human freedom may be reflected at two levels in the whole range of moral activity: at the level of choice and then at the level of execution of this choice. A particular religious

[1] *The Doctrine of Grace*, ed. Whitley, p. 20, quoted by Maclagan, *op. cit.*, p. 113.

doctrine may deny altogether the possibility that human beings can make the right choice without some supernatural aid. It may be implied that human beings by their very nature are either wholly or partially incapable of distinguishing between good and evil, and that even if they do theoretically understand what is good, it is not in their power to opt for the good because they are essentially corrupt and perverted. This would be lack of freedom at the first stage. But it may also be held that though human beings are free to choose, they do not have the power to achieve what they have chosen without divine or supernatural assistance of some sort. A typical example of this kind of incapacity is provided by Rousseau's Savoyard priest when he says: 'I have always the power to will but not always the strength to do what I will.'[1] It will be seen that freedom in the sense of capacity to undertake and achieve what is considered the right course of action is as important as in the first sense of capacity to judge what is right. For, as we shall show in the following chapter, responsibility involves not only that the agent should be a self-conscious individual who knows what he is doing and what he ought to do but also that he should not be totally incapacitated or seriously limited in his efforts by factors beyond his control. We shall accordingly consider freedom in both senses, and, to that end, single out doctrines, in Christianity and in Hinduism, which either directly or indirectly threaten to impair human freedom, and examine to what extent, if any, they do so.

CHRISTIANITY

Taking Christianity first, we suggest that there are at least two traditional doctrines which appear to curtail seriously, if not deny completely, human freedom: first, the Christian doctrine of Sin, especially the doctrines of Original Sin and Inherited Guilt; and second, the doctrine of Grace. It should be borne in mind, however, that these two doctrines are interrelated and complementary. They are in fact related as diagnosis and cure, and to that extent they may actually be different parts of a single more comprehensive doctrine. But for the purpose of greater clarity it may be desirable to examine them separately.

[1] Rousseau in *Emile*, Everyman edition, p. 243, quoted by Maclagan, *op. cit.*, p. 103.

(a) *The Doctrine of Sin and Human Freedom*

The doctrine of Sin is inextricably connected with the doctrine of the Fall to which we have had occasion to refer in a previous chapter. In its essence it relates that because of the ingratitude and disobedience of the First Man, Adam, the entire human race has become sinful and perverted. Some people consider Adam's Fall to be the cause of it; others merely regard it as symbolic of what in fact man has done and is doing. Man's sinful nature, in any case, has a twofold implication. The first and primary meaning of Sin is the leaving out of God and regarding the world as an entirely human enterprise—the attitude of defiance and disobedience which is chronic and universal. We are all creatures of God; but in our pride and self-love we tend to ignore this fact and regard ourselves as masters of our own destiny. This is, as it were, the beginning of the catastrophe. What follows as a consequence of this distorted perspective is a loss of the sense of values—a blurring or colouring of the vision, as it were. The primary and initial Sin, thus, issues forth into Sin in its secondary meaning—that of moral depravity or a general tendency towards evil. The net result is not simply a certain amount of dulling or blunting of the moral insight, but also (what is worse) a positive and inherent impulse towards evil, even where the good is somehow apprehended. As a result of Sin, then, men are *naturally* (that is, without the Grace of God) corrupt and prone to temptations of all sorts which deflect them from the path of righteousness. It is a kind of failure to place first things first.

Even if this mild version were accepted as a generally reasonable account of the Christian doctrine of Sin, it would still be difficult to miss the general pressimistic note about man's character and capacities. It is clearly implied that man, without God's grace, neither has the adequate capacity to apprehend moral values nor does he have the natural willingness to achieve them, even if his darkened conscience somehow succeeded in apprehending them. This is a gloomy view of human nature by any account, and not particularly conducive to moral freedom and effort. But this generally gloomy picture is made infinitely worse by two traditional Christian doctrines about Sin, namely, the doctrine of Inherited Guilt and that of

Total Corruption, which are both corollaries of the doctrine of Original Sin.

The doctrine of Original or Inherited Guilt implies that as descendants of Adam we are naturally guilty of his sin and that the whole human race has to suffer the consequences of this fatal and shameful ingratitude on the part of Adam. The consequences do not only include bodily death and disease but also the depravity and sinfulness that we talked of earlier. This notion of an Inherited Guilt, however, has been seriously challenged not only in modern times but even in the ancient past by thinkers like Origen, for example. Modern Christians understandably consider this an outrage. J. S. Whale illustrates this modern rejection of the doctrine when he says,

'It cannot be stated too emphatically that "Original Sin" neither implies nor means "Original Guilt". The latter expression carries with it forensic and penal implications which outrage the moral sense. No man may be judged guilty because of the misdeeds of his ancestor. Such a judgement would destroy the very meaning of morality. Therefore, such terminology which is only a stumbling-block today is better abandoned.'[1]

It should be possible to quote from other modern sources to show how much abhorred this traditional doctrine is today. And in any case this is a doctrine which has more direct implications for responsibility, which we intend to consider in the next chapter. We shall, therefore, drop this out of our account for the time being.

There is, however, still the need to explain and examine the full implications of the other strain in the doctrine of Original Sin, no less objectionable and no less damaging to morality than that of Original Guilt. This is the doctrine of Total Corruption worked out so uncompromisingly by Augustine and allowed to be an important theme in the thoughts of most of the Reformers, particularly Luther. Calvin, it must be admitted, refused to contribute to any doctrine of this kind. Total Corruption may have an advantage in the explanation of the fact of evil, but it clearly threatens to undermine the very foundations of morality, for if man's reason were *totally*

[1] Whale, *op. cit.*, p. 46.

corrupt, moral insight and judgement become meaningless expressions. And yet this has been a generally accepted doctrine in traditional orthodox Christianity. We feel like asking, with J. S. Whale,

'What are we to make of the grim and terrible doctrine of Total Corruption—found in the Holy Scripture certainly, but worked out with an unscriptural and pitiless logic by St Augustine and the Reformers? Man is "utterly leprous and unclean". If this is not blasphemous pessimism, what is? What did it mean?'[1]

Answering the question himself, Whale goes on to tell us in what sense the doctrine of Total Corruption could be acceptable. He writes:

'If total Corruption meant that every man is as bad as he can be, it would be totally absurd, simply because the conception is self-destroying, as Professor John Baillie has reminded us. "A totally corrupt being would be as incapable of sin as would a totally illogical being of fallacious argument". But in spite of the deplorable extravagance of the language of some Reformers here, notably, Luther, this doctrine of Total Corruption was really insisting that the depravity which sin has produced in human nature *extends to the whole of it,* permeates human life and experience *in all its ranges*; that there is no part of man's nature, *not even his virtue,* which is unaffected by it.'[2]

It is not difficult to see that even on this interpretation the doctrine of Total Corruption connotes only marginally less than total corruption and, therefore, fails to alter significantly the essential view of human nature, its freedom and capacity.

Reinhold Niebuhr, giving his reasons for why the doctrine of 'total depravity' must be given up, says that 'the orthodox doctrine of a "total depravity", resulting from a complete corruption of the "image of God" in man, is equally destructive of the very insight which it seeks to perfect'.[3] The word 'equally' refers to the other destructive doctrine, namely, that of inherited corruption. Niebuhr is undoubtedly right in this

[1] Whale, *op. cit.*, p. 39. [2] *Ibid.*, pp. 39*f.*

[3] Niebuhr, *An Interpretation of Christian Ethics*, p. 101.

opinion. But the question is: Is it possible to give up this theory or to decry it as completely un-Christian? Perhaps Augustine and Luther and others were wrong in deducing a doctrine of Total Corruption from the doctrine of Sin. But from all evidence, it does not appear that Christianity, in its insistence on the doctrine of Sin, has actually been saying nothing more than the truism that man is liable sometimes to sin. And classical Christianity certainly does not seem to encourage the view that man is self-sufficient and free and capable of achieving his moral end. A passage from Niebuhr himself will prove the point. Commenting on the 'moral realism' and pessimism implied in the Christian doctrine of Sin, he says:

'In liberal Christianity there is an implicit assumption that human nature has the resources to fulfil what the gospel demands. The Kantian axiom, "I ought, therefore, I can", is accepted as basic to all analyses of the moral situation. In classical Christianity the perfectionism of the gospel stands in a much more difficult relation to the estimate of human resources. The love Commandment stands in juxtaposition to the fact of sin.'[1]

It becomes clear on this evidence, then, that if the deduction of total corruption from the classical Christian doctrine of Sin is rather extremist, the interpretation of complete freedom and unlimited capacity which the liberal Christians put on this doctrine is no less so. Even on the mildest and most modest account, therefore, sin, because of the perversion of values that it engenders and the natural temptation to evil that it fosters, does to that extent curtail human freedom and capacity, and is, therefore, detrimental to the pursuit of a moral end.

(*b*) *The Doctrine of Grace and Human Freedom*

The deterministic and pessimistic implications of the doctrine of Sin become clearer when we relate it to the doctrine of Grace. For it is not difficult to see that if Christianity believed in the self-sufficiency of man, there would hardly be any need for God's grace. It is precisely because man is naturally perverted and limited by his sin that there arises the need for God's

[1] Niebuhr, *op. cit.*, p. 75.

forgiveness and active help in order to redeem mankind from the shackles of sin. As we have seen earlier, it is primarily this lack of realization of man's utter incapacity and complete dependence on God which constitutes sin. This fact of man's 'utter need of God' and his complete dependence on God in everything he does, however, is itself felt to give rise to problems. If man is so utterly dependent, how can he be free at the same time? This is why we must examine the meaning of Grace and find out whether it leaves man the minimum of freedom demanded by morality.

We ought to make it clear at this point that what we are examining here is not the familiar, age-old problem of God's omnipotence and man's freedom. For we are assuming that in any system of religious ethics like Christianity, or Hinduism for that matter, man can be expected to enjoy only a limited amount of freedom delegated to him by the omnipotent God. Ultimately, of course, all the power must belong to God. This must be accepted if the theory of Grace is to make any sense. But it is possible to interpret grace in such a way that it may not leave to man any significant degree of even this delegated freedom. It is from this angle that we propose to consider the Christian theory of Grace.

Let us formulate precisely the question that we shall try to answer in this section. We have seen that sin primarily results in a darkening of conscience and perversion of will which prevents man from knowing what is good as well as from opting for the good naturally. We are now asking: Assuming that somehow, either as a result of sudden insight or effective instruction, man, in spite of his sinfulness, is able to know what is right and is also prepared to follow the right course, how far can his own moral efforts (that is, without the mercy or grace of God) secure the end he aspires after? The doctrine of Grace seems to imply that it is within man's power to make the necessary effort toward righteousness, but whether he will attain the desired state is something that depends on the will of God. This is a bit disturbing, for it leaves at least one end loose. There seems to be no guarantee that the right kind of effort in adequate measure is sure to take one to the desired goal. It becomes clear that unaided man or 'natural man', that is, man without the grace of God, is incapable of reaching the goal of holiness by himself. This kind of belief, particularly in some of its more dogmatic and literal interpretations, deprives moral effort of its entire purpose and meaning. But whatever we have said so far is only by way of anticipation. Let us first have some of the traditional views regarding the doctrine of Grace.

The Report of the Commission on Christian Doctrine (1922) gives the primary and essential meaning of grace in Christian theology as 'the will of God (which is also His love) regarded as active on behalf of and in man'.[1] Another committee—the Theological Committee of the Faith and Order Movement—recommends the drawing of a distinction between 'Grace' and the 'work of the Spirit', 'Grace being restricted "to its original meaning as an attribute of God" and "the work of the Spirit" signifying "His activity in man".'[2] It is easy to see that the meaning of grace as laid down in the first of our definitions is equivalent to that of 'the work of the Spirit' in the second definition. But the conclusion in any case is that the 'Spirit' is always active 'on behalf of and in man' so that on any particular occasion when we think that we have been able to do our duty, it is not quite *we* so much as the Spirit in us which has in fact achieved this, albeit, through the instrumentality of our own will. Now since the Spirit is supposed to be working through our will, the Doctrine in the Church of England, for example, claims that 'the operation of grace is not opposed to the freedom of the human will, since grace acts through the will and not externally to it'.[3] But further reflection does not appear to support the claim.

Professor Maclagan's criticism of this claim deserves respectful consideration. According to him, to suppose that apart from our own will there is another unobserved and unobservable factor (grace) working when we set ourselves to face a 'moral challenge', is not only an unverifiable phenomenon, but even 'in contradiction with the idea of a free willing'.[4] It may be possible to drop Professor Maclagan's criticism regarding verifiability on the ground that we cannot always take recourse to empirical verification in matters of faith. But all the same, his second charge—that the involvement of God's grace in all our willing is contradictory to our idea of free willing—is too

[1] Maclagan, *op. cit.*, p. 100.
[2] *Ibid.*, p. 108.
[3] *Ibid.*, p. 111.
[4] *Ibid.*, p. 111.

serious and sensible to be ignored. Grace as constitutive of human will does really seem to make human freedom a mere illusion. We seem to come to the unsatisfactory conclusion that man, as man, is certainly not free; only man aided by the Spirit, or more precisely, only the Spirit in man (which is certainly not man) is free. Instead of human freedom, then, we are asserting the freedom of the Spirit which, however, has never been in question. Thus even if we ignore the Augustinian or Pelagian theories of grace 'that set "God's grace and man's resolution" in opposition, assigning "so much to God and so much to man",'[1] we do not yet seem to have a way out of the difficulty created by grace. We are obliged to agree with Professor Maclagan that grace as a kind of '*environmental*' help does not seriously interfere with the idea of willing, but if it is interpreted as in any way '*constitutive*' of human will, it takes the essence out of our moral response, and makes the idea of free willing a farce.[2]

It is needless to point out that if this comparatively moderate and liberal interpretation of grace cannot find room for human freedom in the fullest sense of the term, more extremist, and perhaps even more popular, continental theories of grace can only reduce human freedom to an illusion. An example of the theologians' conviction that moral achievement is impossible without the grace of God is provided by the following passage quoted by H. D. Lewis from Brunner's *The Divine Imperative*:

'Duty and genuine goodness are mutually exclusive. Obedience due to a sense of unwilling constraint is bondage, and indeed the bondage of Sin. If I feel I *ought* to do right, it is a sign that I cannot do it. If I could really do it, there would be no question of "ought" about it at all. The sense of "ought" shows me the good at an infinite impassable distance from my will. Willing obedience is never the fruit of a sense of "ought" but only of love. This is the paradox: that the sense of "ought", through which alone I learn at all what freedom is in this sense of "ought", unveils to me my formal freedom—announces to me that I am in bondage to sin.'[3]

[1] Maclagan, *op. cit.*, pp. 116 *ff.*
[2] *Ibid.*, p. 113.
[3] Emil Brunner, *The Divine Imperative*, p. 74, quoted by H. B. Lewis, *op. cit.*, p. 30.

It is easy to see that the above passage, apart from coming to a most extraordinary conclusion from the analysis of *ought*, clearly denies man's capacities for moral achievement without the grace of God. The argument is based primarily on the supposition that since the moral demand is rooted in the will of God, our capacity to respond to this demand must also come from the same source. In the words of H. D. Lewis,

'For the ascription of the alien categorical character of ethical demands directly to their origin in the will of God carries with it also, as a rule, the curious but very persistent belief that these demands are so foreign to our nature that we cannot in any measure yield them of our own volition, but only in so far as the power to obey is also given us by God. Indeed it is frankly asserted that obligation is not obligation proper unless it is alien in *both* these senses.'[1]

The passage quoted from Brunner, 'who is considered a good example of the more moderate of the Continental theologians',[2] lends ample support to what Lewis seems to be saying. It will be agreed that when the power to respond to the moral demand is made subject to the grace of God, we are no more expecting from God the mere delegated freedom, which is understandable, but are making morality itself depend on the will of God, and thus deprive morality of the human significance and context.

Grace as such, then, it would appear, is not particularly conducive to human freedom and hence to moral effort. What makes it outrageous, however, is the arbitrariness implied in another doctrine, quite frequently associated with the traditional doctrine of Grace, namely, the doctrine of divine Election. This doctrine amounts to saying that no matter what men do to be saved or redeemed, whether they will really be redeemed depends not on their effort but on the discretion of God. 'Not all who are called are chosen' reflects the arbitrary mode in which divine Election works, and which at one stroke makes human effort and the moral freedom to achieve one's end a chimera. It was this completely irrational doctrine which elicited the following expression of bitter abhorence from J. S. Mill:

[1] Lewis, *op. cit.*, p. 29.

[2] *Ibid.*, p. 30.

'But there is one moral contradiction inseparable from every form of Christianity, which no ingenuity can resolve, and no sophistry explain away. It is, that so precious a gift (grace), bestowed on a few, should have been withheld from the many; that countless millions of human beings should have been allowed to live and die, to sin and suffer, without the one thing needful, the divine remedy for sin and suffering, which it would have cost the Divine Giver as little to have vouchsafed to all, as to have bestowed by special grace upon a favoured minority.'[1]

This passage is as much an indictment of divine injustice as of the irrationality of the theory of grace and divine election, so clearly detrimental to moral effort and human freedom.

HINDUISM

We now turn to the consideration of human freedom in the context of Hinduism. Let us state at the outset that much of the difficulty caused by the concepts of sin and grace are not exclusive to Christianity. In so far as Hinduism, or sections of Hinduism, subscribe to these beliefs, they expose themselves to the same charges, though not necessarily to the same extent. For sin and grace, though forming significant elements in the devotional cults of Hinduism, which, as we have seen, may be regarded as the more influential and popular form of this faith, do not have quite the same connotation in Hinduism nor the same implications.

Sin, for example, is as much an obsession with some of the modern poet-saints of Hinduism as it is with Christian theologians. A perusal of some lines from poet-saints like Dadu, Suradas or Tukaram will convince us of this. Dadu, in one of his many moments of agonizing self-appraisal, exclaims:

'I have neglected God's service: a sinful servant am I;
There is no other so foul as I am.
I offend in every act, I fail in every duty,
I sin against Thee every moment. Pardon my transgressions.'[2]

[1] J. S. Mill, *Three Essays on Religion*, Longmans, Green, Reader and Dyer, London, 1874, p. 115.

[2] Quoted by John Mackenzie, *Two Religions*, Lutterworth Press, London, 1950, pp. 107 *f*.

Tukaram, the Maharashtrian saint and poet, similarly declares:

'Fallen of fallen, thrice fallen am I;
But do Thou raise me by Thy power.
I have neither purity of heart, nor a faith firmly set at Thy feet;
I am created out of sin, how oft shall I repeat it? says Tuka.'[1]

Innumerable passages can be quoted from Suradas or Tulsidas or any of the other *Bhakti*-poets which dwell on the theme of sin and guilt in relation to God.

But let this not blind us to the fact that in the tradition of the Hindus there is no belief corresponding to either Original Sin or Total Corruption. On the metaphysical plane, in fact, sin is conceived as moral evil which is a force to be reckoned with. This evil is opposed to good, but the victory of good in the long run is assured. Individual men can either promote or frustrate this ultimate victory of good by opting for good or for evil. The stories of the battles between the gods and the demons (*Devas* and *Asuras*) are only symbolic representations of the conflict between good and evil. Hinduism, then, does admit the tremendous fact of sin and moral evil, but does not suggest that every man is necessarily overpowered by sin, except in so far as his previous life and actions have created in him a natural temptation for evil. But this need not be universal. Sin in the form of wickedness, selfishness and pride, the tendency to do evil, is certainly recognized to be ingrained in the human constitution, but no more so than the tendency to do good. The *Citta*, the faculty of volition, is a store-house of good as well as bad impulses, and whether a man will direct his *Citta* to one or the other of these is entirely his own responsibility. Hence the traditional Yogic emphasis on the control of these impulses (*Citta-Vṛtti-Nirodha*), which leads to purification of the self (*Ātmaśuddhi*), and thus, in spite of the presence of evil as a force in the very constitution of man, whether a man will actually become a sinner or a saint is a result of his own discretion. This explains the anguish in the utterances of the poet-saints. They feel guilty in their own eyes and guilty in the presence of God because of their realization that they could

[1] Quoted by John Mackenzie, *Two Religions*, Lutterworth Press, London, 1950, pp. 107 *f*.

have directed all their energies to the love of God and to moral betterment, but have unfortunately allowed their *Citta* to be swayed by selfish hankerings.

Similarly, the Hindu doctrine of Grace, though a very dominant and almost universal feature, stands in juxtaposition to another equally influential belief which has been held since the earliest days and which runs contrary to the determinism implied in the theory of Grace (*Prasāda* or *Anugraha*). This other belief is the one that either by extreme penance or devotion the deity can be made to bestow lovingly his grace on the devotee or seeker. We have had occasions to refer to the belief in grace in the earliest literature of the Hindus which has continued to be an important feature of Hinduism. The passages quoted above from two of the *Bhakti*-poets well illustrate the general Hindu attitude. In fact, Ramanuja's followers are divided into two schools holding two different views of the operation of grace. These two views are regarding *Prapatti*, that is, how communion with God comes about. One school holds the view that God, in His mercy, picks the sinner as the cat picks its kitten (*Mārjāra Nyāya*); the other believes that God carries the sinner to be sure, but only when the sinner or devotee has done what is expected of him, or, in other words, actively cooperates with God, just as the monkey carries its young baby only while the baby is holding fast to its mother (*Markaṭa Nyāya*).[1] This is strikingly similar to the differences in the Christian church between Synergists and Monergists. It must be added, however, that Ramanuja himself does not approve of *Mārjāra Nyāya*, for in his view this gives rise to the dangerous doctrine of *Doṣabhogya*, that God enjoys sin since it gives a larger scope for the display of His grace.[2]

It should be clear that grace has been as much a part of the dominant section of Hinduism as it has been of Christianity, and therefore, the former should normally be subject to the same charges as the latter. But it must be stated, however, that the insistence on preparation to receive grace, as in Ramanuja and the school of *Markaṭa Nyāya* generally, restores to moral effort the significance which is belittled by the school of *Mārjāra Nyāya*. Grace, on Ramanuja's account, then, is not as damaging to moral effort and freedom as it could have been.

[1] Eliot, *op. cit.*, II, 236. [2] *Ibid.*, p. 236.

On this view, grace is no more the gift of a capricious God but the reward of devotion and moral effort. God does aid the devotee after a certain stage, but does not interfere with his normal activity or with his freedom to decide for himself what course he is going to take.

Moreover, as we mentioned earlier, the doctrine of grace and its deterministic note is tempered by the other belief that the deity can be persuaded or even compelled by one means or another. This rather unusual doctrine, which forms the basic theme of *Haṭha Yoga*, has its roots in the Vedic idea of *Tapas* which signified that by spiritual penance, self-abnegation and self-discipline it was possible to compel the gods to bow down to the will of the aspirant. It is as a consequence of this belief, again, that Hindu devotees in their exuberance sometimes take recourse to the alternative of compelling the deity by genuine devotion and self-denial in its extreme form. It is true that such techniques have often degenerated into queer aberrations and indiscretions, but that is another matter. As far as human freedom is concerned, one can only complain of excess of it rather than lack of it. God's grace is neither denied nor underrated; but it is primarily the human power to invoke this grace that is underlined by these beliefs. It appears, then, that the Hindu concept of grace sheds off much of its unsavoury colour as a result of the impact of the concepts of *Tapas* and Yogic self-discipline.

But the above account need not be taken to imply that there is nothing in Hindu doctrine to undermine human freedom. There are two concepts universally accepted in Hinduism (also Buddhism and Jainism) which threaten to jeopardize the Hindu's belief in self-autonomy and human freedom. These two are the doctrines of *Avidyā* or *Ajñāna* (ignorance) and the Law of *Karma*. These two are interrelated to such an extent that a discussion of one would always involve that of the other. But in spite of this difficulty, we intend to consider the implications of the doctrine of *Avidyā*, or ignorance, first.

Ignorance, in the broadest sense, means the lack of knowledge or realization of the true nature of things, more specifically of the self, which is especially reflected in man's identification of his *Ātman* with the body–mind organism and the consequent perversion of values. Freedom from such ignorance, negatively, and the acquirement of genuine discriminatory knowledge or wisdom (*Viveka Jñāna*), positively, is the most important condition of freedom from bondage, or of liberation. Though there are many differences of opinion amongst various schools of Hindu thought as to the exact nature, status and the extent of its consequences, it may be unanimously accepted that *Avidyā* is a kind of primordial element in the very constitution of the universe which may, and in fact does, lead a man to a confusion between the essence and the appearance of things, and thereby create a distortion of the goal of human life. In a sense it is possible to compare *Avidyā* with Original Sin, as Professor Smart appears to do,[1] in so far as both ('Original') *Avidyā* and Original Sin refer to a transcendent state to which it is man's duty to return. But this comparison cannot go very far. *Avidyā*, as we said earlier, is a cosmic principle which does not come into being as a result of human indiscretion as does sin in the Biblical account. *Avidyā* is prior to man. Moreover, it neither implies total and inescapable corruption nor inherited corruption, for we can pierce through the veil of *Avidyā* and attain liberation. Besides, whereas in the case of *Avidyā* knowledge is the antidote (although this is not *primarily* the knowledge of good and evil), in the case of Original Sin it is the very cause of the ailment. Man's knowledge of good and evil or his attempt to have it is, as we have seen, the cause of the Fall. It seems, then, that the comparison between *Avidyā* and Original Sin cannot go beyond a certain limit.

In any case, this conception of *Avidyā* or *Ajñāna* as an ultimate cosmic principle is more philosophical than popular. There is another, more popular, sense of *Ajñāna* in which it is treated as an empirical phenomenon, that is, as resulting from man's own carelessness and sloth. As we have seen, Hinduism regards the soul or *Ātman* to be an essentially spiritual principle distinct from the body, the mind and the sense organs. The body is merely a vehicle of the soul. Though this distinction between the self and the not-self is blurred by *Avidyā* in its primary sense, *Avidyā* in its secondary sense makes the distinction even hazier and infinitely more difficult to grasp. Since the soul is always perceived to live and act through the body, the unsuspecting, inalert man further confuses the two.

[1] Ninian Smart, *A Dialogue of Religions*, SCM Press, London, 1960, p. 32.

Not only is the distinction itself but even the will to acquire knowledge of the distinction lost. Once this happens, we become subject to the passions and desires of the body to an extent which makes us completely oblivious of the real nature of the *Ātman*, and we are deluded by false values. We then go on living a life of egotism, selfishness and pride, and worst of all, have an unhealthy craving for the pleasures of the world. Through such selfish and lustful living we become subject to the inexorable Law of *Karma* which, without our being aware of it, gradually determines and moulds our future existence in tune with our present dispositions.

But let us not forget that *Avidyā*, though beginningless (*anādi*), has an end. It is true that once we have fallen a victim to ignorance, it will definitely have a momentum of its own whereby we may continue to be under delusion for a time. But it is always, at least theoretically, within our power to put an end to this process. Indeed even while the process is in operation, we are never altogether incapable of seeing through this pernicious self-deception, because the soul, however concealed, never actually deserts us. At any point of time we can reassert our will and acquire knowledge or wisdom which will restore the proper perspective. Thus the soul is free in all other respects and at all times except in its descent into the world-process (*Saṃsāra*).

But it may be asked with ample justification: What about the wrong or evil we did while we were under the spell of ignorance? Can we undo the evil that was generated by our wrong judgement and actions? This question brings us to the consideration of the Law of *Karma*. This Law, we have seen, is the counterpart in the moral field of the Law of Conservation of Energy. This implies that whatever actions we perform—good or bad—generate certain potencies, primarily in the form of dispositions, so that it is impossible for us to escape the consequences of our actions. The actions, therefore, that a man performed while under the spell of ignorance will definitely lead him to reap the consequences either in the present life or in the life hereafter. It is these that will determine what the circumstances of his next life are going to be. The fact that he has now been able to realize the true nature of the *Ātman* will prevent him from further selfish and interested conduct, but it cannot annul the consequences of what he has already done. By this transformed perspective, he may prevent the accumulation of fresh *Karmas* (*Saṇcīyamāna Karmas*), and he may also stop the operation of the *Karmas* which have been accumulated already but have not yet started operating (*Saṇcita Karmas*), but the *Karmas* that are already in operation (*Prārabdha Karmas*) will compel him to undergo a certain kind of life—for better or for worse—depending on what his past actions have been like.

Now this has sometimes been interpreted as implying determinism. The argument advanced is very similar to the one summarized by us earlier in the words of Moritz Schlick. Since our present nature and dispositions, it is argued, as well as the conditions of our existence, have already been determined by our previous birth, do we really have any choice between good and evil? Are we not being driven by our nature to do whatever we do? We are, the argument runs, slaves to our dispositions and circumstances, which are completely beyond our control. This apparently does sound deterministic, but careful reflection does not sustain this notion. There are two considerations that go against a deterministic interpretation of the Law of *Karma*. In the first place, we have to recognize that precisely because of this law is introduced into the moral field the element of causation which, we have agreed, is a must for assigning responsibility for actions. In the words of Dr Radhakrishnan,

'It (the Law of Karma) is the principle of science which displaces belief in magic or the theory that we can manipulate the forces of the world at our pleasure. The course of nature is determined not by the passions and prejudices of personal spirits lurking behind it but by the operation of immutable laws.'[1]

The Law of *Karma*, in fact, guarantees that we shall get what we have deserved, and thus rules out the element of chance. It is not the freedom of conduct that this law denies but the freedom from causation.

It seems, then, that determinism in the sense of compulsion can be read into this law only on a very distorted interpretation

[1] Radhakrishnan, *Hindu View of Life*, p. 52.

of the working of this law. If we have led a generally bad life in the past, it is certain that we shall have a generally evil disposition as also other circumstances appropriate to such a disposition. But unless one has been the devil himself, his character will never be quite so depraved and perverse as to make it impossible for him to see at any stage whatever what the good life was. This leaves the possibility of a change of heart altogether open. If at any time, either due to a sudden flash of insight or due to revelation or instruction, one came to realize the evil character of his life, it would always be within his power to strive for the better. In short, it is always possible for the bad man to transform his conduct and thereby to create better conditions for himself in any future existence. If this transformed man takes up the good life in right earnest, it will be only a matter of time before he will be ready for final liberation. For the Law of *Karma*, in the ultimate analysis, is not quite so unsparing. For this is not a blind law. It is governed and administered by a living and personal God. To quote Dr Radhakrishnan again, '*Karma* is not a mechanical principle but a spiritual necessity. It is the embodiment of the mind and will of God. God is its *supervisor* (*Karmādhyakṣaḥ*).'[1]

Sometimes the objection against the Law of *Karma* is presented in a slightly modified language. It is argued that since (due to the operation of *Karma*) every action performed—even good ones—must generate potencies which involve us in the cycle of births and deaths (*Saṃsāra*) and thereby at least delay our liberation, a person who is anxious for liberation will in effect find this law rather obstructing and to that extent limiting his freedom. The best thing, therefore, that a seeker of liberation would be advised to do would be to give up action altogether. Unfortunately, such an interpretation of this law seems to be implied in the school of Shamkara Vedānta, which prescribes a life of *Nivṛtti* for the seeker of liberation. But we have seen that *Nivṛtti* need not mean inactivity, but only disinterested discharge of duties as prescribed by the Gītā. For it is not action that binds but only attachment to results. 'He who works, having given up attachment, resigning his actions to God, is not touched by sin, even as lotus leaf (is untouched) by water.'[2]

[1] Radhakrishnan, *op. cit.*, p. 53.

[2] Gītā, V, 10.

CHAPTER VII

MORAL FAILURE AND RESPONSIBILITY

In the last chapter we stated that our discussion of freedom was only a preliminary to our consideration of the various problems raised by the concept of responsibility. For only a responsible agent can be regarded as a properly moral agent, and freedom is a vital, if not the sole, condition of responsibility. In the present chapter, then, we shall merely be carrying forward the discussion we undertook in the previous one with, of course, specific reference to responsibility. This would involve an analysis of the concept of responsibility in order to find out precisely the conditions of moral responsibility, and then the examination of whether, how and to what extent the concept of responsibility is consistent with the theological presuppositions of Christianity and Hinduism.

That both Christianity and Hinduism generally subscribe to human responsibility for moral failure can hardly be questioned. We have already seen that in both these systems there is the belief in an order of values and in a Moral Law which demands unconditional allegiance. Any deflection from the path of duty gives rise to what in religious terminology is called sin. There may be, and in fact there are, some minor differences in the Christian and Hindu conceptions of sin. But despite these differences, sin is generally regarded as identical with moral failure ('moral' being used in the widest sense, including religious and sacramental duties) and is supposed to be the responsibility of man. If this were not so, the system of rewards and punishments—of which the best known are heaven and hell respectively—which both Christianity and Hinduism lay down will hardly make sense. The question, then, is not whether in fact Christian and Hindu ethics hold men responsible for moral failure but whether they can really do so in consistency with their religious doctrines, and if so, to what extent.

This question, however, cannot be answered unless we know what responsibility in the context of morality means. William Frankena mentions 'at least three kinds of cases' in which we 'attribute moral responsibility to certain agents':[1]

'(1) We sometimes say, in recommending *X*, that he is responsible or is a responsible person, meaning to say something morally favourable about his character. (2) We also say, where *Y* is a past action or crime, that *X* was and is responsible for it. (3) Finally, we say that *X* is responsible for *Y*, where *Y* is sometimes still to be done, meaning that he has the responsibility for doing it.'[2]

Commenting on these three senses of the word 'responsibility', he goes on to say that when we state that *X* is responsible in the first sense, we simply mean to say that *X* can be counted on to carry out his responsibilities. Responsibility in this sense is a 'second-order trait' which we ought to cultivate. Saying that *X* has certain responsibilities, in the third sense, is simply to say that he has obligations, 'either because of his office or because of his previous commitments to do certain things, and hence is a straight normative judgement of obligation'.[3] The particular meaning of responsibility which raises problems of an interesting and controversial kind is the second one of the three senses mentioned above. For here the question that immediately arises is: 'Under what conditions is it correct or right to judge or say that *X* was responsible for *Y*?'

It is this—the second of the three senses of responsibility mentioned above—which is of special interest to us, and accordingly we intend to confine our discussion to this sense only. About this particular sense Frankena rightly asserts that

'To say that *X* is responsible for *Y* is not merely to make a causal statement of a special kind. Neither is it simply a statement that *X* was *able* to do *Y*, as the "ible" ending suggests. Suffixes like "ible" and "able" do not always indicate ability. They may have a normative meaning.'[4]

[1] Frankena, *Ethics*, p. 55.
[2] *Ibid.*, p. 55.
[3] *Ibid.*, pp. 55 *f.*
[4] *Ibid.*, p. 56.

The real meaning of a statement like *X* was responsible for *Y*, he says, is something like 'It would be right to hold *X* responsible for *Y* and *to blame or otherwise punish him*'.[1] This accords with the views of most contemporary thinkers. Moritz Schlick, for example, is of the opinion that the question regarding responsibility is the question: 'Who, in a given case, is to be punished? Who is to be considered the true wrongdoer?'[2] Similarly, H. D. Lewis asserts that 'the etymology of this word suggests that it means "liability to answer", this being, of course, liability to answer to a charge, with the implication that if the answer is not satisfactory a penalty will be incurred'.[3] Thus it is clear that responsibility is meaningful only in the context of punishment. The punishment, however, need not always be in the form of legal or social sanctions, as, for example, imprisonment or ostracism; quite often it may be only an expression of disapproval or a judgement blaming the agent for his failure.

In other words, the determination of responsibility is the same as the act of apportioning praise or blame to whoever we consider to be the real agent or doer of a certain act. It should not be difficult to see that responsibility, then, has an essentially human context. It would be plainly ridiculous to blame animals for any of their (what we might call) misdeeds. Similarly, there would be no point in taking to task for their failures insanes, idiots or infants. The first condition, then, of responsibility is self-consciousness. Only those persons can be held responsible who know what they are doing so that even a normal human being can hardly be blamed for what he has been doing, say, in a hypnotic trance. Similarly, if a person has been forced to commit an offence at the point of a gun, we would rather sympathize with this unfortunate victim than censure him. Thus the two conditions of being responsible would seem to be: firstly, that the agent had the capacity to do it; and secondly that he in fact did it without any external pressure or compulsion, that is, he did it voluntarily, knowingly or intentionally.

Aristotle's observations in this respect are still eminently acceptable. According to him an individual is responsible for his act only when

[1] Frankena, *op. cit.*, p. 56 (emphasis mine). [2] Schlick, *op. cit.*, p. 152.

[3] H. D. Lewis, *Morals and Revelation*, George Allen and Unwin, London, 1951, p. 108.

'(1) its cause is internal to him, i.e. he is not compelled to act by someone or something external to him, and (2) his doing it is not a result of any ignorance which he has not brought about by his own previous choices.'[1]

It seems, then, that the two conditions of responsibility are (1) a conscious motive to perform a certain act, and (2) the freedom of choice and capacity to perform it. This question of freedom, we pointed out in the previous chapter, has given rise to the problems of determinism or indeterminism versus responsibility. There have been those who believe that determinism is opposed to the very concept of responsibility, whereas there have been others who have asserted equally emphatically that it is indeterminism which is destructive of responsibility. In the history of philosophy so much has been written for and against either of the views in this controversy that it is clearly impossible for us to analyse the merits of the respective cases in any detail. Nor, fortunately, is it necessary for us to do so. We have stated in the chapter on freedom that much of this problem has been grounded on misconceptions and confusions in the use of terms. We have made our own position clear. Determinism as external compulsion, we said, is certainly antithetical to freedom; but determinism in the sense of causation or causal connexion between motive and action and between one's character and his motives is not only not opposed to freedom but is the absolute condition of freedom. On this—the latter meaning of determinism—it is not determinism but indeterminism which destroys responsibility by denying any necessary connexion between character, motive and action.

With this preliminary examination of the meaning of responsibility and its conditions, it should now be possible for us to examine the main question of this chapter, namely how far the theological presuppositions of Christianity and Hinduism allow responsibility to be a meaningful concept. Part of the answer to this question has already been provided by our discussion in the previous chapter. Freedom in the sense of lack of compulsion, and not of indeterminism, being a condition of responsi-

[1] Aristotle, Nicomachean Ethics, III, 1, summarized by Frankena, *op. cit.*, p. 56.

bility, those doctrines of Christianity and Hinduism which interfere with human freedom in this genuine sense are to that extent detrimental to the concept of responsibility. Thus our task in this chapter will mainly consist in relating our observations in the previous chapter specifically to the problem of responsibility. This, however, will be supplemented by consideration of some other issues which arise in connexion with responsibility and to which we had no occasion to refer in the previous chapter.

ORIGINAL SIN AND RESPONSIBILITY

In the light of what we said about sin earlier on there can be no question, at least on the face of things, that sin involves human responsibility. If sin means moral failure—albeit in the wider sense which includes ingratitude to God—then man can hardly disown responsibility for it. But the position is not quite as simple as it may at first sound. Complications begin to arise as soon as the connotation of sin is extended beyond empirical and actual moral failure to include what sounds more like constitutional defect and incapacity. And Original Sin is certainly of the latter order. Let us, therefore, work out the implications of Original Sin for responsibility.

(*a*) *Christianity*

We have seen that of the manifold corollaries of the doctrine of Original Sin two traditionally important ones are those of Total Corruption and Inherited Guilt or Inherited Corruption. Leaving Inherited Guilt aside for the time being, it does not take much effort to realize, especially in the light of our detailed discussion in the previous chapter that Total Corruption, if accepted, makes a mockery of human responsibility. For it denies both conditions of responsibility. If man is naturally totally corrupt, he does not only lack the power or freedom to opt for the good but also the basic minimum of the awareness of good. In other words, he is no better than the brute or the insane whose capacity to apprehend the good is as limited as his capacity to achieve it. This tragic implication of this doctrine has been realized in modern times sufficiently well to encourage milder versions of this doctrine, if not always the absolute rejection of it. We have seen that most modern scholars and theologians of Christianity refuse to read any doctrine of Total Corruption in Original Sin. One very cogent argument for rejecting this belief is put forward by Niebuhr, whose opinion in this context we have quoted elsewhere. He argues that 'It is human freedom, in other words, created by the transcendence of reason over impulse, which makes sin possible. Therefore, if man is totally corrupt he is not sinful at all.'[1] That is to say that there seems to be a contradiction involved between total corruption and sinfulness. Sinful, as an adjective of moral disapproval, implies responsibility for a certain course of action, and it would to that extent be misapplied to men if, by nature, they were totally corrupt.

But the fact remains that this belief has been an important refrain in much of traditional Christian thinking. Moreover, we have also seen that even the modern interpretations of Original Sin, especially undertaken to rule out total corruption, do not entirely succeed in substantially improving the position. We have examined in the previous chapter the attempts of Niebuhr and Whale, for example, and have found that howsoever anxious they have been to rule out total corruption, they have been somehow prevented from doing so by the immense weight and emphasis that traditional Christianity has attached to the fact of sin. Original Sin might not mean total corruption, but neither can it mean the simple fact of man's occasional temptation or inclination to sin. In fact it must mean much more than that if the place of Sin in Christian thinking is to be adequately accounted for. Thus Original Sin, it seems, cannot imply anything far short of total corruption. And the room left for moral responsibility can only be inversely proportional to the degree of corruption this doctrine implies.

(*b*) *Hinduism*

The Hindu conception of sin, especially the Vedic, has been very often misunderstood. It has been frequently argued by some Western scholars that Hinduism in fact does not have the same awareness of sin, and, even when there is some awareness, sin is understood in a 'quasi-physical' way, that is it is regarded as a kind of substance floating in the atmosphere, as it were,

[1] Niebuhr, *An Interpretation of Christian Ethics*, p. 101.

which just attaches itself to individuals and therefore need not signify any responsibility. Moreover, it is said, the Hindu considers sin in the material context, that is, he is averse to sin only because he feels that wrong-doing leads to material adversity. Most of this criticism seems to display such an ignorance of the facts that it can hardly deserve any reasoned answer. We have seen elsewhere that the leading medieval and modern poet-saints of India show an awareness, in fact an obsession, with sin which is hardly any different from the Christian awareness of sin. As far as the Vedic idea of sin is concerned, the acute and painstaking analysis of Henry Lefever, in his book *The Vedic Idea of Sin*, systematically refutes almost all the misinformed criticism we have noted above.

Examining Hopkins' opinion that 'the translators have injected into Ṛg Veda more consciousness of sin than really attaches to it', Lefever has this to say: 'To regard adversity as the inevitable consequence of sin is to display, not a weak, but an exceedingly vivid, consciousness of the gravity of sin.'[1] And again, 'So vividly is the gravity and power of sin realized, that evil is regarded as an objective force in the world, capable of leading men astray (Ṛg Veda, I, 189, 1; X, 37, 12), or of rebounding upon the wicked to his own hurt (Ṛg Veda, I, 147, 4; VI, 51, 7)'.[2] This last observation about evil being an objective force in the world is quite in consonance with our remark in the earlier chapter that Hinduism juxtaposes evil as a force as opposed to good in which, of course, the ultimate victory of good is assured. Whether a man will help the victory of good by acting rightly or will delay and obstruct it by turning wicked is entirely his own choice, and, therefore, his own responsibility. This should help to put the Hindu view of sin in the correct perspective.

There is, however, one respect in which the Vedic idea of sin may justly be regarded as different from the Biblical one. Commenting on a verse quoted from the Ṛg Veda (Ref. I, 25, 1–3), Lefever says:

'There is in this passage a full consciousness of guilt and a realization of its consequences unless God's mercy is obtained.

[1] Lefever, *op. cit.*, p. 18. [2] *Ibid.*, p. 19.

But there is no personal sense of *shame* before a God who is himself wronged by the sin. It is the confession of guilt made by a criminal before a king or judge who is the custodian of the law which has been infringed. The attitude expressed in the words, "Against thee, thee only, have I sinned and done this evil in thy sight", is lacking.'[1]

Perhaps this is correct. And the explanation why this is, or should be, so is offered by Lefever himself in a later passage. The explanation for this is that according to the Vedic conception, the Gods

'are "charioteers of *ṛta*", guarding the transcendent cosmic Law by means of their statutes. These statutes have thus their origin, not so much in the pure will of the Gods, as in the transcendent *ṛta*. Therefore, the breach of such statutes is not so much a personal offence against the Gods as a violation of the *ṛta*, which the Gods protect. The sole duty of the Gods, as guardians of *ṛta*, is to punish the violation or to reward the keeping of *ṛta*. It is in relation to this office that the attitude of the sinner towards the Gods must be understood.'[2]

This insight into the basic fact prevents Lefever from the mistake of judging the Hindu conception of sin from the Christian standpoint, which generally characterizes some other writers' views. Every conception of sin need not be modelled on the Christian pattern. The important thing to look for is whether sin has a moral context and whether men can be held responsible for it. It seems that this condition is entirely satisfied. *Ṛta* is the moral law and infringement of this law is sinful, and since man is free to either obey this law or to infringe upon it, he is obviously answerable.

Moreover, this Vedic conception of sin does to an extent undergo modifications in the *Bhakti* schools. The passages that we quoted from the poet-saints in the last chapter unmistakably manifest the same sense of anguish and guilt in the presence of the Deity which generally characterizes the Christian conception of sin. But let us not forget that even when the Hindu conception of sin comes so close to the Christian, it is never

[1] Lefever, *op. cit.*, p. 20.

[2] *Ibid.*, p. 20.

really identical with it. The intimacy and the confidence that the Hindu devotee experiences in his relationship with the Deity makes the dependence on God less than crippling, and to that extent more conducive to human responsibility.

In any case, as we have seen earlier, there is no conception in Hinduism resembling Original Sin or Total Corruption. The suggested parallel between Original Sin and *Avidyā* (ignorance), as we pointed out in the last chapter, cannot really go very far. *Avidyā* is certainly an objective force which temporarily clouds the nature of reality, thereby causing the soul to get involved in *Saṃsāra*. But it is primarily of the nature of an intellectual error. It is only *Avidyā* in its secondary sense that relates to the will proper. It would, therefore, be absurd to deduce anything like total corruption from *Avidyā*, especially since it operates in the context of knowledge rather than of the will. It can conceal and distort the real nature of things, thereby indirectly and in a secondary sense, engendering false values; but it does not directly imply any inevitable corruption of the will. By application and self-control it is possible to escape the delusion caused by *Avidyā*; and the acquirement of the right kind of knowledge destroys all its direct and indirect consequences. The general Hindu position, then, would seem to be that sin is the violation of the divinely-ordained Law (*Dharma*) which springs from man's selfishness and pride and his failure to control his impulses (*Citta*); and since it is possible, as it has been for many, to tread the path of *Dharma* alone, all responsibility for sin must be assigned to man himself. The soul's 'descent' into the world may not be of its own choosing, but its choice between good and evil is entirely its own.

But this, however, is the general position which is unfortunately complicated by the implications of inherited sinfulness in the shape of inherited *Karmas*. And since Christianity also—at least orthodox Christianity—contributes to a doctrine of inherited corruption, it seems desirable at this stage to examine the problem of responsibility as against the notion of inherited guilt or sin.

INHERITED GUILT AND RESPONSIBILITY

The problem here involved is one of reconciling responsibility with the belief that at least part of our moral failure or sin is not the result of our own conscious choice but is inherited either from our own previous life, as in Hinduism, or from the First Man, as in much of orthodox Christianity. This is, therefore, one of those situations in which both Christianity and Hinduism are faced with the same kind of problem, though, of course, for entirely different reasons.

(*a*) *Christianity*

We have seen that one of the traditional doctrines of Christianity is that of Inherited Corruption or Guilt. It will not be necessary to explain the details of this doctrine, for we have done so earlier. The nut-shell of the doctrine, however, is that we, as descendants of the First Man, Adam, have inherited the burden of his sin, which is why every human being is naturally corrupt and sinful. God's grace or mercy is the only means of redemption from this sin. There seem to be two undercurrents in this doctrine. One is that we are responsible for Adam's sin and that we have to carry the burden of guilt for *his* sin. This implication, however, seems to have a more direct bearing on what is called Collective Responsibility, and would, accordingly, be examined under that section. The other implication—and this is the one we are concerned with at the moment—is, as we said, that the corruption of human nature, i.e. our inclination toward evil as well as our actual sins, are largely the inevitable consequences of this first act of defiance and ingratitude on the part of Adam. In other words, much, if not all, the evil in the world is a kind of divine punishment, not for our own actual crimes, but this crime committed by the First Man. It is not at all difficult to see that this is a highly unsatisfactory position which is not only damaging to responsibility but to morality itself.

To quote Niebuhr again,

'If original sin is an inherited corruption, its inheritance destroys the freedom and therefore the responsibility which is basic to the conception of sin. The orthodox doctrine is therefore self-destructive.'[1]

What is particularly offensive and singularly irrational about this doctrine is that the whole of humanity is put in the docks,

[1] Niebuhr, *An Interpretation of Christian Ethics*, p. 100.

as it were, for the indiscretion of one man with whom we may have only the remotest possible connexion. It is not uncommon to hear of a family being blamed, though not punished, for the crime of one of its members. But to hold the whole of mankind responsible for the sin of Adam sounds incredibly absurd. And the modern outcry against this orthodox doctrine is fully understandable, for this makes a mockery of human moral effort, merit and responsibility.

It would be interesting to analyse at this stage Origen's effort to introduce another version of inherited sin. We have seen that according to Origen, every individual is born with an inherited burden of failures and sins, not inherited from Adam but from his own previous life. Origen's thinking on this issue, however, cannot be regarded as representative of Christianity, for Christianity does not accept the belief in transmigration or rebirth, which is the essential presupposition of his theory. But strangely enough, or perhaps not so strangely after all, this explanation of man's character and his moral failures or sins is surprisingly close, in fact identical in its main import, to the Hindu explanation. We shall, therefore, pass on now to Hinduism.

(*b*) *Hinduism*

The twin Hindu doctrines of *Karma* and *Saṃsāra*, we have stated elsewhere, signify that each of man's actions in this life leads to consequences which he personally must enjoy or suffer either in this life or in the life hereafter. It is in fact one's actions in this life that determine what kind of life in the future he is going to have. To borrow a couple of lines from Rhys Davids,

> Our deeds follow us from afar,
> And what we have been makes us what we are.[1]

In other words, if one has been a sinner in his previous life, he starts this life with the natural disadvantage of this burden of inherited *Karmas*. This clearly implies some kind of doctrine of inherited sin, though not at all in the Christian sense of the term. The inheritance here does not come down from a remote ancestor but from one's own previous life.

[1] Quoted by Sivaswamy Aiyer, *op. cit.*, p. 139.

This belief, we said earlier in another context, seems in a sense to be particularly conducive to moral effort by encouraging confidence in the efficacy of the moral law in the sense that one can be sure that his moral effort will never be wasted. But whatever the advantage of the Law of *Karma* in this respect, it must be frankly stated that it creates an ethical paradox in assuming that part, at least, of the hardships and sufferings of this life are a disciplinary expiation for sins committed in a previous life of which the individual has no recollection. This lack of recollection does raise a problem as to man's responsibility. It certainly appears morally unsatisfying that a man should be made to suffer for something which he did in his previous life and of which he is not even remotely aware. Awareness or self-consciousness, we have seen, is as important a condition of responsibility as freedom is. It is true that we do not absolve a person of responsibility for a crime which he actually committed so long ago that he might possibly have forgotten almost entirely about his part in the crime. Clear evidence from a criminal that he really does not remember having committed a certain crime will surely not lead to his acquittal if there is conclusive evidence otherwise that he did actually commit it. Thus lack of recollection in itself may not be enough to absolve a man of responsibility, if it is otherwise possible to relate the criminal act to the person under judgement. The real difficulty with the Law of *Karma*, it seems, is that it introduces unverifiable phenomena into the whole issue so that responsibility for crimes of a previous life can rest only on an unquestioning belief in the validity of the doctrine that all the various births and deaths that a man is supposed to undergo according to this doctrine are only links in a larger chain or stages in one continuous life.

The main objection, then, to the above view of responsibility is not that an individual does not as a matter of fact *recollect* his past crimes—for this, we have seen, need not absolve one of his responsibility—but that *it is ex hypothesi impossible for him to do so*. This is a serious enough objection. But without dissociating ourselves from this criticism, we might suggest how the Hindu answers it. He may argue that recollection or no recollection, our present life is a continuation of a previous life, and we cannot disown responsibility for the crimes of the previous life, just as we cannot disown responsibility for a proved crime which we might have committed at a time so long past that we cannot reasonably be expected to remember it. It seems, then, that the whole problem hinges on the acceptance or rejection of the belief in personal identity carried through a whole series of lives and deaths. The acceptance of this Hindu dogma entails acceptance of responsibility for all crimes of a previous life whether or not we recollect them. But if this underlying belief is rejected, and responsibility is confined to crimes or sins of the present life only, then naturally the Hindu belief in punishment for sins of an earlier life falls down as well. And whether or not this central belief or dogma should be accepted would involve us in metaphysics which is beyond the sphere of our interest at the moment. We shall, therefore, leave this question here and pass on to the consideration of another aspect of the problem of responsibility.

UNINTENTIONAL SIN AND RESPONSIBILITY

Before we consider the question of collective responsibility, it may be interesting to compare the Christian and Hindu positions on responsibility in the case of sin that is unintentional. Where there is a clear intention to do what is known to be a sin, it is undoubtedly not only desirable but also necessary to hold the person responsible and to punish him. This is very plain. But when we come to unintentional sins, the position appears to be a bit complicated. It would seem that since motive or intention is part of the condition of responsibility, wherever there is no intention to commit a crime, the agent cannot be held responsible. As Lewis remarks, 'Nothing can be put into the reckoning that we do not intend.'[1] But howsoever fair this position might sound and however simple, it is actually very difficult. We are not referring to the empirical difficulty of finding out whether a person did really intend to commit a crime. What we are suggesting is that in spite of the general position about intention and responsibility, we are quite often blamed for unintentional offences or moral failures as well. We are blamed for carelessness, for example, which might have led to the offence even though we did not intend it. Similarly, we

[1] Lewis, *Morals and the New Theology*, p. 48.

are blamed for not being aware that a certain act was in fact a crime or sin. It is, therefore, important to note how Christian and Hindu thinking proceed on this issue.

(*a*) *Christianity*

Consideration of the Christian view on this issue brings us to the examination of the distinction between formal and material sin. A formal sin is an act committed which the agent was aware he ought not to have committed, whereas a material sin is the committing of an act which *is in fact wrong* but which the agent did not believe or know to be wrong. It is clear then that the committing of an act which is only a material sin cannot be described as an intentionally committed sin. Now, the Christian position about responsibility for material and formal sin may be stated in the following passage from R. C. Mortimer's *Christian Ethics*:

'Thus a formal sin is always blameworthy: it is what we generally mean by sin. A material sin is not blameworthy: it is not an action which can be approved, because it is in fact wrong, yet no stigma attaches to the agent who has only done what he honestly believed right.'[1]

To this position, however, is added the following caution or explanation:

'This distinction between formal and material sin, and the attachment of blame only to those actions which are done in violation of conscience, or in obedience to a conscience which is wrong because of the negligence or wilfulness of the agent, is a necessary corollary of the principle that conscience is the guide and norm of moral conduct. *Yet it must not be taken to mean that it does not matter much what one does provided that one meant well in doing it. It must always be remembered that actions done in obedience to a conscience which ought to have known better, are formal sins and so blameworthy.*'[2]

The statement entailed in the last but one sentence above gives the real clue to our attitude to unintentional sins. Having

[1] R. G. Mortimer, *Christian Ethics*, Hutchinson, London, 1950, p. 56.
[2] Mortimer, *op. cit.*, pp. 36*f.* (emphasis mine).

meant well is not enough; the acts must be good by objective standards as well. In other words, unintended sins or offences are blameworthy too, though not to the same degree as intended ones. And what makes such acts blameworthy is the suggestion of negligence or 'wilfulness' implied by their performance. And this applies also to what we may call 'accidental' crimes or offences. Thus the conclusion would seem to be that unintentional sins, though not subject to censure in the same degree as intentional ones, are not altogether free from blame.

(*b*) *Hinduism*

On the question of intention versus responsibility there are two main views in Hinduism.[1] One of these considers the subjective intention or motive to be an important part of the act. Hence where a definite motive to achieve a certain end is not there, the agent will not be regarded as responsible for the act. An unintended *Brahmahatyā* (murder of a *Brāhmaṇā*), for example, will incur only half the normal punishment. It would seem that here the emphasis is on motive; not overt acts but motive and intention is the object of moral judgement.

But there are others who regard certain acts as evil in themselves. In whatever circumstances and from whatever motives certain acts are committed, they will lead to sin and hence deserve punishment. Even accidental *Brahmahatyā* is to be punished in the usual way. This, it must be said, is a rather extreme position. To make the actual overt act the sole condition of responsibility without taking into account the motive of the agent is morally unsatisfactory. To say that sin committed in any form, even unintentionally, is sin and therefore punishable is one thing; but to say that unintentionally committed sin is punishable in the same way as intentional sin is to deny the significance of intention and therefore of conscience. If degrees of moral failure are allowed, then clearly intentional sins must be distinguished from unintentional ones.

What Professor Maclagan says in the context of Christian ethics is equally applicable here. Sin may normally mean ' "actual" sin in the "formal" mode', i.e. an immoral act wilfully committed. But sometimes this is also taken to include 'perverse' action resulting from ignorance which cannot really be

[1] Maitra, *op. cit.*, pp. 188 *f.*

subject to censure in the same sense as the former. And these two, again, must be distinguished from what he calls a mere 'infancy of value-consciousness'[1] which is, strictly speaking, not an object of moral judgement at all. And the difference between these various kinds of 'sinful' action lies precisely in the kind of conscience the agent has and the degree to which his conscience has been involved in the act. Of the two kinds of sins for which, we said, the agent may in some degree be held responsible, the first would be an instance of acting against conscience whereas the second is a case of having a 'darkened' or perverted conscience itself. It is the will, therefore, that is held responsible rather than the overt act or physical movement of the agent.

This is why both Christianity and Hinduism emphasize the participation of the mind and the heart along with the body (*Manasā Vācā Karmanā*) in any moral resolution. The same point seems to underlie Shridhara's belief that all unintentional failures are subject to reproach, for they all imply carelessness (*Pramāda*) on the part of their agents,[2] and, consequently, either a failure to train and inform their consciences or else a failure to control their impulses. The general Christian as well as Hindu position, then, would seem to be that though unintentional sins are not subject to censure in the same degree that intentional ones are, one is not all the same absolved of responsibility for the former because they may imply carelessness, wilfulness or ignorance, which are themselves evil attributes.

COLLECTIVE RESPONSIBILITY

We have so far considered the various aspects of individual responsibility in the Christian and Hindu traditions. We shall now turn our attention to what is called collective responsibility. When, for example, we speak of a whole group or society to be 'sinful'—and Christianity certainly does so—we seem to hold the whole group or society as such responsible for a certain evil state of affairs. In what sense, if any, and to what extent is the concept of collective responsibility meaningful?

[1] Maclagan, *op. cit.*, p. 36. [2] Maitra, *op. cit.*, p. 190.

(a) *Christianity*

This problem of collective versus individual responsibility is undoubtedly a very pertinent one in the context of Christian ethics, for it is in Christianity, if anywhere, that the concept of collective responsibility has formed an important part of the traditional creed. The concept of 'Universal Sin', quite often expressed in terms like 'man's solidarity in sin' or 'the collective guilt of man' or 'each man's share in the sin of his society or his race', implies that we are all equally sinners in the eyes of God and therefore we all share the responsibility for the sinful state of affairs in the world. It seems that this concept is more or less a direct corollary of the Christian concept of inherited guilt. It has been part of the Christian dogma that Christ's crucifixion was a sacrifice that he knowingly made as an expiation for the sins of mankind which initially entered into the human world with the disobedience of Adam. Adam's sin was in need of expiation, and it was and is the duty of every man to feel himself responsible for the sin and to do everything he could to undo the effects of this shameful conduct on Adam's part. This rupture of the relationship between God and man that was brought about by the ingratitude of Adam could only be repaired by the sacrifice of a Second Adam, Christ. This latter was a great event which laid the foundation of a fresh beginning of relations between God and His creatures. This could give us hope; but all the same we must forever bow our heads in shame for the sin of Adam and for the sins of all men for which we are jointly responsible.

We feel tempted to quote a rather lengthy passage from Lewis' *Morals and Revelation* which not only summarizes the Christian position but also includes his own criticism of the concept of collective responsibility.

'. . . I should like to insist that the belief in "individual", as against any form of "collective", responsibility is quite fundamental to our ordinary ethical attitudes. For if we believe that responsibility is literally shared, it becomes very hard to maintain that there are any properly moral distinctions to be drawn between one course of action and another. All will be equally good, or equally evil, as the case may be. For we shall be directly implicated in one another's actions, and the praise or blame for them must fall upon us all without discrimination. This, in fact, is what many persons do believe, and it is very hard to uphold any form of traditionalist theology on any other basis. Of late this has been very openly affirmed by noted theologians who, if they seem to do very great violence to common sense, have, at any rate, the courage and consistency to acknowledge the implications of their view, and do not seek to disguise them by half-hearted and confused formulations. We have thus witnessed recently some very uncompromising affirmations of the belief in "universal sin" or "the collective guilt of man". This does not imply that there are no ethical distinctions of any kind which we may draw. Judgements may be passed upon the outward course of our conduct without prejudice to the view that guilt itself is "universal", and this is why Reinhold Niebuhr, whose influence on religious thinking today is very pronounced, is able to combine with his assertion of the doctrine of universal sin on account of the "relative moral achievements of history". One action may be much more regrettable than another, it may be uglier in some ways or it may do much more harm to our fellows, and thus we have "the less and more" of our day-to-day judgements, but where proper moral estimation is concerned there is not "a big sinner and a little sinner". We are all involved in the sins of all.'[1]

Niebuhr, we have had occasion to see, is one of those modern theologians who does not hesitate to reject what he considers to be an irrational doctrine, even if it has been traditionally accepted in Christianity. So when even he seems to uphold the above view of collective responsibility, it leaves no room for doubt about the position of Christianity with regard to this issue. What has been said above, then, may be accepted as representing a typical Christian opinion. Now the main objection to any kind of collective responsibility is already contained in the above passage from Lewis: that it is contrary to our ordinary ethical attitudes. The conditions of knowledge, capacity and freedom that make responsibility meaningful have clearly an individual context. In other words, it is only an individual who can fulfil these conditions, and therefore, it

[1] Lewis, *Morals and Revelation*, pp. 102 *f.*

must be only an individual who can properly be called responsible. A whole society or the whole of mankind can bear the consequences of one person's misdeeds, but to say that the whole society is morally responsible for the crime is plainly absurd and meaningless. In the words of Lewis, again,

'. . . to incur certain consequences for what another person has done, is one thing, to be morally accountable is another; and in this last regard we cannot answer for one another or share each other's guilt (or merit), for that would imply that we could become directly worse (or better) persons morally by what others elect to do—and that seems plainly preposterous.'[1]

It is true that we often use loose expressions in which a whole society or group is implicated in the crime of one of its members, for example, when an aggressor nation is supposed to be responsible for what actually its government decided to do. But this in fact is a kind of metaphorical way of indicating the general area of responsibility. Germans who actually participated in the crimes of the Hitler regime against the Jews are justly punished for their part in the brutality, but reasonable persons would not like to hold the German nation as such guilty, even though we may sometimes be using expressions like 'the guilt of Germany in the murder of the Jews'. One would easily agree with Maclagan that when we speak of a certain society or group as being 'sinful', it involves a conscious misapplication of the term: 'That is to say, we may be speaking of the society *as though* it were an individual while recognizing that in fact it is not. . . .'[2]

If we retain this individual context necessarily suggested by moral responsibility, it is not difficult to see that collective responsibility in the sense in which theologians generally use it is not, and cannot be, a meaningful concept. Professor Maclagan rightly insists that responsibility can be meaningful only when the action involves conscious choice, and since the concept of collective responsibility 'disjoins' the concepts of choice and responsibility, 'the attempt to saddle mankind with *responsibility* for their supposed universal sinfulness fails accordingly'.[3] One may perhaps also feel inclinded to agree

[1] Lewis, *op. cit.*, p. 113. [2] Maclagan, *op. cit.*, p. 40. [3] *Ibid.*, p. 47.

with his view that collective responsibility may be admitted in the only sense suggested by Scheler, namely, that

'Every one of us has been an active participant in an uncountable number of good and bad things of which he does not have, and indeed can not have, any knowledge, and for which he is none the less co-responsible before God.'[1]

(*b*) *Hinduism*

In Hinduism there does not seem to be any counterpart of the concept of 'man's solidarity in sin' and hence no question of collective responsibility. But nonetheless in Hindu tradition certain acts are considered so sinful—*Mahāpātaka*—that they pollute not only the sinner but also other members of his family, even his village or society. This should not, however, be taken to denote collective responsibility. It might imply co-responsibility of some sort, but in its proper import it is intended to be more a sanction than anything else. Successful burglary, for example, by one member of a family and prosperity based on this is likely to induce other innocent members of the family or of society at large to attempt something similar. Hence the need to emphasize the polluting effect of sins. The underlying belief seems to be that, like some kind of poisonous gas which, once emitted from a certain source, gradually infects larger and larger areas, some kinds of sins have a polluting effect, chiefly in the sense that they serve as bad examples for other members of the society. This is probably what forms the basis of the charge, noted earlier on, that the Hindu conception of sin is 'quasi-physical'. Popular expressions about sin and its effects may give rise to this impression, but actually this is neither quasi-physical nor does it imply collective responsibility in its usual sense. These expressions about 'pollution' may be regarded simply as a rather crude, but effective, way of discouraging people from actions that are regarded as dangerously evil and sinful.

[1] Maclagan, *op. cit.*, p. 41.

CHAPTER VIII

CONCLUSION

We do not claim to have examined *all* the questions that may arise in connexion with Hindu and Christian ethics. But perhaps some of the more fundamental ones have been discussed. It would be tempting to go ahead with our enquiries and to add some more to the problems we have discussed so far. But considerations of time and space would not seem to allow this. Leaving, therefore, the many more problems, some of which might have been suggested in course of our own effort in the preceding pages, to more competent scholars, it seems to be time to examine the upshot of our arguments. Going back to the introductory chapter in which we specified the nature of our enquiry, we suggested that our purpose was not to establish or reject the alleged superiority of one of these two systems over the other. What was proposed was to place one by the side of the other in order to find out whether, and to what extent, Hindu and Christian ethics resembled each other. In other words, this was intended to be an objective and scientific enquiry; and, as is well known, in such enquiries collection of the data or facts of the case may often be more important than the conclusions themselves. But since all such collection of data generally presupposes a provisional hypothesis, we cannot deny that some such hypothesis has given the direction to our search for facts. Our hypothesis in this case was a modest one. We had only affirmed that though Hinduism and Christianity are very different in many respects, especially in matters of metaphysical and theological beliefs, 'the gap becomes considerably narrower' when it comes to the ethical implications of these metaphysical beliefs. In other words, whatever their differences as religions, as systems of ethics they are remarkably similar, or, at least, not so far apart as is often imagined. The question now is: Is our provisional hypothesis supported by facts? The answer, it seems, cannot but be in the affirmative.

We do not wish to reiterate our arguments in the preceding pages, but it may be desirable to make pointed references to our observations in order to justify our affirmative answer to the above question. To start with, we noticed that the two systems of ethics are characterized by remarkable catholicity and comprehensiveness, though there may be differences of degrees. Both are committed to a high notion of the potential greatness of man; both believe in a transcendental and spiritual destiny for man which, though not entirely ethical ends in themselves, make ethics an indispensable step in the realization of this final destiny. Morality in each system derives its significance and authority from the belief in a divinely implanted moral law which is revealed to man by similar sources. With some differences of emphasis, the range of virtues is by and large the same. Absolute freedom of choice and actions is neither asserted nor implied. Freedom is only delegated or conditional, and each system believes that there is enough freedom to make morality possible, though, as we saw, there is room for controversy in this respect. And, finally, human responsibility for moral failure is an important tenet of belief, though appearances to the contrary sometimes occur in either system.

These similarities of approach and content are surely impressive. But let us not for a moment imagine that the two systems are identical, and, therefore, interchangeable. This notion would be as ridiculous as the one we have tried to refute, namely, that they have nothing in common. Our reflections in these pages should, it is hoped, have also shown that, in spite of the similarities, the two remain distinct and independent systems, and it would be vain and pretentious for either to claim to take the other's place. Neither of these are temporary and evanescent phenomena. Hinduism has a history of over three thousand years and Christianity of about two. In the course of their histories they have proved their vitality as systems, and have given rise to distinct cultural traditions which it would be impossible for any power to wipe out of existence. In fact it is this total accumulated pattern of behaviour and attitude, generated by centuries of repetition and assimilation, which gives distinctiveness to the character of each system, and which also sometimes obscures the fundamental similarity or unity in basic principles that the two display on closer inspection.

Without sounding didactic, therefore, we may say that if our arguments show anything at all, it is that Hinduism and Christianity, or, more specifically, Hindu and Christian ethics, should both recognize and face the fact that each has in the other a competent and powerful adversary; and that any tendency on the part of one to dismiss the other lightly is not only naïve but extremely dangerous. It seems to be worth quoting the remark of Hopkins in this context. Concluding his observations on Indian ethics, he says,

'And when we of the West visit India hoping to instil into the Hindus the "higher spirituality" of which we vaunt ourselves the proud possessors, it will be well to remember that, as a goal of living, strict morality and high spirituality will not seem to the Hindus a sudden revelation from abroad, but that they have had that goal before them for many centuries.'[1]

These words were written in 1924, but it is doubtful that many have still learnt the lesson conveyed through them. Nor is this attitude exclusive to the Christian West. The Hindu who takes excessive pride in his 'spiritualism' and hopes to 'teach' his spiritualism to the 'materialistic' West will profit no less from the lesson referred to above.

With the change in the pattern of political power, and each nation or culture restored to its rightful place of equality in the comity of nations, no world view or ethical system can hope to win in the competition of equals except on the strength of its ideas and ideals. And, as in any competition, the only healthy and realistic attitude is one of respect and humility toward all the competitors. An excessive pride in one's own heritage, with the natural tendency to belittle the other point of view, is born of ignorance and bigotry. And bigotry is always abominable, whether it is Hindu or Christian. Love of one's own religion and heritage is natural and perhaps necessary; but when it degenerates into uncritical and exclusive adulation, it can never do anything but harm. In the words of Dr Radhakrishnan, 'Those who love their sects more than truth end by loving themselves more than their sects.'[2]

[1] Hopkins, *op. cit.*, pp. 257 *f*.
[2] Radhakrishnan, *The Hindu View of Life*, p. 37.

We have thus far generally dwelt on the basic similarities between Hindu and Christian ethics, and remarked on the proper attitudes that Hindus and Christians may be well advised to cultivate toward each other's faith and morals. It would be interesting to pick out, next, for closer examination and special emphasis some outstanding features of either of these systems of ethics and find out how and whether they compare.

OUTSTANDING FEATURES OF HINDU AND CHRISTIAN ETHICS

It is possible to mention more than one feature in either Christian or Hindu ethics which can justifiably be claimed to be exclusive to only one of these systems, at least in emphasis. But if we were to single out from each the most outstanding, there can be hardly any doubt that in Christian ethics it would be the philosophy of love or '*agape*', and in Hindu ethics the philosophy of non-violence, '*Ahiṃsā*'. While examining the catholicity of Hindu and Christian ethics in Chapter II, we did observe that each of these systems is liable to various interpretations, with various degrees of emphasis on one or the other feature from among the whole range of ideas and ideals that permeate them. But we must add, as a corrective against any misunderstanding that might have been caused by our deliberate emphasis on the differences within each system, that, irrespective of whatever else also happens to be the case, the following basic fact must never be lost sight of. And that is that *no shade of Christian ethics is properly Christian unless the philosophy of love is central to it*. Similarly, in tune with the whole religious tradition of India, including Buddhism and Jainism, *no shade of Hindu ethics can be called properly Hindu unless the philosophy of non-violence is fundamental to it.*

The above unqualified statements are perhaps in need of some explanation. For Hindus may object that after all it has been the Christian world which has fought the largest number of devastating wars, which certainly has done nothing to demonstrate that the philosophy of love is central to Christianity. It may also be that the Christian world has on the whole been as much, if not more, susceptible to the impulse of hatred. But those who emphasize these facts in order to refute that the philosophy of love is central to Christian ethics have unfortunately missed the whole point of our argument. They are falling a prey to the same misconception against which we tried to warn them, namely, that occasional deviations from a certain principle, though unfortunate, do not prove the lack of the principle itself; they only emphasize human frailty which is always responsible for man's fall from high and edifying ideals. Moreover, we stated at the very outset that we are concerned with the principles rather than with the practice, with the fundamental rules that ought to govern conduct rather than with the degree of conformity to the rules. Hence conduct to the contrary, even if conclusively demonstrated, will not be taken to imply that the principle itself is missing.

If we keep these facts in mind, it will not be difficult to see that if anything is central to all forms of Christianity, it is the philosophy of love. Christ's exhortation in the Sermon on the Mount—

> 'Ye have heard that it hath been said, Thou shalt love thy neighbour and hate thine enemy.
>
> But I say unto you, Love your enemies, bless them that curse you, do good to them that hate you, and pray for them which despitefully use you, and persecute you. . . .'[1]

—has, in spite of all the strain that such lofty principles expose themselves to, always remained in Christian society the goal to strive for. For this reason the frequent characterization of Christian ethics as the 'ethics of love' must be deemed justified, though not completely adequate.

The principle of non-violence must be considered equally characteristic of all forms of Hinduism. Non-violence has been frequently misunderstood as a merely negative concept which enjoins refraining from killing but does not imply a positive attitude of love to the sentient beings. But if we remember Patanjali's explanation of *Ahiṃsā*, as given in Chapter V, it should not be difficult to see that it is meant to be much more than a mere negative virtue of non-killing or non-injury. Patanjali defines *Ahiṃsā* as '*Sarvathā Sarvadā Sarvabhūtānām*

[1] Matthew 5: 43, 44.

Anabhidroha',[1] that is, a complete absence of ill will to all sentient creatures irrespective of time or place. Even if 'complete absence of ill will' does not *literally* mean a positive attitude of good will and love, it comes very close to the latter. This, it will be seen, brings the essential presupposition of *Ahiṃsā*, in spite of the use of a grammatically negative term, very much closer to a positive philosophy of love. It may not be out of place to mention here that in propounding his philosophy of love and non-violence, Gandhi might have appeared to Christians to be propounding a philosophy which they would think was exclusively Christian; but as far as Gandhi was concerned, he was merely drawing on the full meaning of the age-old Hindu philosophy of non-violence. That his teaching appeared to Christians as Christian and to Hindus as Hindu only proves the similarity of approach that Hinduism and Christianity have in this respect.

The other equally common misunderstanding about the Hindu ideal of *Ahiṃsā* is that the Hindu refrains from killing animals not because of any lofty principle of love but from his fear, following from his belief in the transmigration of souls, that in killing a certain animal he might unwittingly be killing one of his ancestors whose weary soul has been condemned into this form of existence by some of his past immoral conduct. This is not only a complete misinterpretation of the essential idea of non-violence and a complete travesty of fact, but perhaps, and above all, a typical example of the colonials' sense of humour which often infected and misled even the better-knowing scholar. Sir Charles Eliot puts the perspective right in this context when he says,

'. . . the beautiful precept of *Ahiṃsā* or not injuring living things is not, as Europeans imagine, founded on the fear of eating one's grand parents but rather on the humane and enlightening feeling that all life is one and that men who devour beasts are not much above the level of the beasts who devour one another.'[2]

We may add that the Hindu emphasis on vegetarianism is not only based on the principle of *Ahiṃsā*, but also on the equally

[1] Maitra, *op. cit.*, p. 220.

[2] Eliot, *Hinduism and Buddhism*, I, lvi.

important conviction that animal flesh has undesirable effects on the body and mind. It impedes the development of the *Sattva* element and the purification of the *Citta* which is indispensable for *Mokṣa*. But there can be no doubt that the principle of *Ahiṃsā* is involved too. The essential philosophy underlying the precept of *Ahiṃsā* might, in the words of Albert Schweitzer (even though Schweitzer denies the presence of this ethic in Indian thought), be called 'the Ethic of Reverence for Life'.[1] A verse from Manu underlines the reason as well as the reward of non-violence. It says:

'That knower of the Self who perceives the Self in all sentient beings (*Sarva bhuteṣu ca ātmānam*) and all sentient beings as equal to his own Self (*Sarva bhūtāni ca ātmani*), attains to his sphere (liberation).'[2]

It is true that man's baser instinct to kill, which afflicts the Hindu as much as it does the Christian, has frequently found support in statements like, '*Vaidic Hiṃsā Hiṃsā na bhavati*', i.e. killing of animals for sacrifices in accordance with Vedic injunctions does not amount to violence, or '*yagyārthe pasavaḥ sṛṣṭāḥ*', i.e. animals have been created to be offered at sacrifice. It should be remembered, however, that even these statements justify only the killing of animals for sacrificial purposes, not otherwise. So in spite of these, the fact remains that *Ahiṃsā* is one of the central pillars of the Hindu's moral superstructure.

When we say that *Ahiṃsā* is a central concept in Hindu ethics, we do not mean to suggest that it is so to the same extent or in the same sense as it is, say, in Buddhism or Jainism. These latter, particularly Jainism, make a fetish of this concept and take it to absurd extremes. Hinduism does not. For Hinduism has been more pragmatic in its treatment of *Ahiṃsā*, as in so many other respects. It accepts *Ahiṃsā* as the ideal, but it is prepared to make compromises in exceptional circumstances or special contexts. That is why the killing of animals for Vedic sacrifices is not considered contrary to the precept of *Ahiṃsā*. Similarly, Krishna's exhortation to Arjuna to fight is justified on the ground that the latter was a member

[1] This is the title of Chapter XXI of Schweitzer's *Civilisation and Ethics*, George Allen and Unwin, London, 1961.

[2] Manu, XII, 91.

of the *Kṣatriya Varṇa*, whose duty it was to protect *Dharma* and the rule of Law. If this involved violence, as it naturally would, it was unfortunate but it could not be helped. The preservation of *Dharma* must come first. Or again, in more recent days, when Gandhi ordered the killing of an ailing calf in his *Āśrama*, it was not considered an infringement of the rule of non-violence, for the motive in this killing was to relieve the poor calf of its terrible suffering caused by its incurable ailment. But whatever the nature of these exceptions, *Ahiṃsā* as a rule of conduct and as ideal has been accepted by all sections of Hinduism.

It is possible to prove that Hindu society has not always been able to live up to the ideal of *Ahiṃsā* just as Christian society has not always lived up to the ideal of love and forgiveness. Just as many Hindus understand by *Ahiṃsā* nothing more than a mechanical refraining from killing, without much feeling of reverence or sympathy for the living beings, so also to many Christians, 'love' does not mean much more than dropping some silver into the collection box at the church or donating some money to Oxfam after persistent visits by its indefatigable workers. But these facts do not prove anything like what some people intend to read in them. If they prove anything, it is that a scrupulous and consistent practice of *Ahiṃsā*, with the reverence for life that it connotes, is as difficult as a consistent and unfailing adherence to the philosophy of love and forgiveness. Both are ideals too difficult to be consistently and effectively practised by ordinary mortals. It needs a Gandhi or a Buddha to incorporate into life all that *Ahiṃsā* stands for, and it takes a Christ or a St Francis to adhere to the ideal of 'offering the other cheek'.

Ahiṃsā and love, though distinctive enough of Hindu and Christian ethics respectively, are not, however, the features that set them apart; they in fact bring them closer still, for they are different sides of the same coin. What does set Hinduism apart from Christianity, and both from every other religion, is the institution of the *church* in Christianity and that of *Varṇa* and *Āśrama* or class and stages in Hinduism. It is not enough for a Christian to subscribe to ideals laid down in the Christian scriptures; and it is not enough for a Hindu to adhere to what is preached by the Hindu scriptures. Apart from everything else, the Christian must belong to one of the numerous churches, and the Hindu must be a member of one of the four classes or of subsections of the latter, now known as castes. This is where the differences between Christians and Christians and those between Hindus and Hindus begin to raise their heads. The principles of Christian or Hindu ethics, as outlined by us, give only the rough outline of what being a Christian or a Hindu involves in the realm of morals. The specific details in the outline must be filled by the church in the case of the Christian and by his place in the class and stage structure in the case of the Hindu. From a wider angle, a Christian is a Christian first and a member of his particular church later. Similarly, a Hindu is a Hindu first and then anything else. But from the narrower angle, the whole picture is reversed. A Christian is a Christian by virtue of his affiliation to a church, and, naturally therefore, his first allegiance is to his own church; his specific duties and obligations follow from his membership of this church. Likewise, the specific duties and obligations of the Hindu follow from his membership of a particular class in the Hindu social structure and from the particular stage that happens to be his.

It is very difficult to substantiate in this brief analysis what specific differences in terms of duties result from one's membership of one or another of the various Christian churches. But it is evident that if these denominational differences are not to be regarded as merely superfluous and meaningless, some differences in belief, and consequently in practice, must inevitably follow from the former. On the Hindu side, it is comparatively easy to settle, within certain limits, what the membership of one rather than the other class entails in terms of specific duties. The Hindu classification of *Varṇas* or classes presupposes, to start with, temperamental and vocational differences among individuals as its basis. The *Brāhmaṇa* is the intellectual, moral and spiritual leader of the community who must personify scholarship, enlightenment and understanding. The *Kṣatriya* is the ruler or administrator and soldier who must be prepared to defend, by all means, the integrity and interests of the society. The *Vaiśya* must show that clever grasp of practical matters and the industry that would ensure the community's self-dependence in respect of trade and welfare.

And finally, the *Śūdra*, who by temperament is only fitted to serve unquestioningly the leaders of the community, must above all demonstrate obedience and readiness to serve. It is easy to see that a certain quality which it is good for the member of one class to have may be absolutely undesirable in a member of another class. For example, the subservience and readiness to obey that is essential for the *Śūdra* may be suicidal if found in a *Brāhmaṇa* because the latter is the intellectual leader of the community whose function is not submission to the general will of the community, even when this will was misinformed and misdirected, but to resist and reshape it in the light of his better judgement. Similarly, as a military man, it is not wrong for the *Kṣatriya* to resort to arms for a just cause, but it is abominable if found in either a *Brāhmaṇa* or a *Vaiśya*. This is why in the Hindu classification of duties and virtues it is customary to find not only the list of universal or common duties and virtues but also the specific ones prescribed for members of the different classes.

Lest our discussion of the differences in training and temperament underlying the Hindu institution of *Varṇa* may be mistaken to be suggestive of any such distinctions fundamental or even accidental to the Christian institution of church, we must hasten to add that nothing of the kind is implied. The reason for talking of the church and the *Varṇa-Āśrama* in the same context is solely this: that these are the institutions that create differences between one Christian and another and between one Hindu and another respectively, and also between Christians and non-Christians and Hindus and non-Hindus. For a Hindu may in most matters of ethics be like a Christian and a Christian, likewise, may be close to a Hindu or a Buddhist in these respects. But the Hindu will still be a Hindu primarily because of his membership of this institution of *Varṇa-Āśrama*, and the Christian remain a Christian because of his membership in the church. It is, therefore, not at all unreasonable to say that the proper 'differentia' of Christian ethics, as of the Christian faith itself, is its unique institution of the church; and that of Hindu ethics, and of Hinduism in general, its institution of *Varṇa-Āśrama*.

While talking of these two institutions, it may be interesting to note another incidental similarity between the Hindu and the Christian approach in this context. This is that both these institutions claim divine origin and sanctity and command unconditional allegiance on that account. Just as the Christian church is 'the body of Christ', so the Hindu institution of *Varṇa* is, in a way, literally the 'body of God'. The famous *Puruṣa Sūkta* of the Ṛg Veda states that the Divine Man, *Puruṣa*, the soul and original source of the universe, created the universe by 'immolating' his own embodied spirit. It then goes on to say that 'the *Brāhmaṇa* was his mouth, of both his arms was the *Rājanya* (*Kṣatriya*) made, his thighs became the *Vaiśya*, [and] from his feet the *Śūdra* was produced'.[1] Thus the four main *Varṇas* represent the various limbs of the divine *Puruṣa*. Hence this institution symbolizes the body of God. The least that follows from this figure is that neither the Christian church nor the Hindu system of *Varṇas* can be regarded merely as artificial organizations to promote certain ends, as is quite often argued. They have an authority and sanctity of their own which cannot be seriously tampered with without doing violence to the structure of the faiths themselves.

There are thus important similarities between the Christian and Hindu institutions of church and *Varṇa-Āśrama* respectively[2] which should not be ignored. These are the institutions which have been responsible for the preservation and continuation of the respective world-views; these, again, have provided the background for the social and community life of the two societies, and have thus been the instruments of harmonizing individual and social interests; and they have given to the respective ethical systems their unique appearances. And since these are what have been at least partly responsible for creating differences within the systems themselves, there may, within a certain limit, be eminent sense in suggesting that the concern of some Christians to restore the unity of the churches is not basically different from that of those Hindus who have unceasingly tried to abolish the innumerable caste distinctions to which the original institution of *Varṇa* has now degenerated. But we have qualified our statement of this similarity by the clause 'within a certain limit'. And it is important not to misread too much in this similarity.

[1] Ṛg Veda, X, 90, 12.

[2] It is difficult to determine exactly when the theory of *Āśrama* was first related to that of *Varṇa*, but they are now usually conjoined.

For the church, though encouraging differences, does not perpetrate what in Hinduism has now become hereditary caste distinctions. Whatever the advantages of the original theory of 'natural classes' on the basis of essential temperamental and vocational differences, it has to be realized by every Hindu that the modern form of this Platonic Utopia is monstrously perverted. The Christian church has not created different orders of citizenship within the same society; the Hindu *Varṇa-Āśrama* has. By making a creed of the natural differences among human beings and by continuously playing on these differences, the custodians of Hindu ethics and religion have unwittingly undermined the ideal of the basic equality of human beings. And this result is not at all surprising. The equality of all men, as men, is *not* a compelling *fact* of the same order as the differences among individual men. The former tends to be an ideal in need of careful and constant support from enlightened institutions. The differences, on the contrary, are so glaring and irresistible that *they* do not have to be nurtured; they will assert themselves naturally. And Hindu ethics and religion has to restore the proper perspective by turning its attention away from *differences* and by stressing the ideal of equality.

BIBLIOGRAPHY

I. ON CHRISTIANITY AND CHRISTIAN ETHICS

Books

Barth, Karl. *Evangelical Theology: An Introduction*, trans. G. Foley. Weidenfeld and Nicolson, London, 1963.

Bell, Bernard Iddings. *Religion for Living: A Book for Postmodernists*. John Gifford, London, 1939.

Bonhoeffer, Dietrich. *Ethics*. The Library of Philosophy and Theology. SCM Press, London, 1955.

Bouquet, A. C. *Is Christianity the Final Religion?* Macmillan, London, 1921.

Brunner, Emil. *The Divine Imperative: A Study in Christian Ethics*, trans. Olive Wyon. The Lutterworth Press, London, 1937.

Burnaby, John. *The Belief of Christendom:* A Commentary on the Nicene Creed. National Society: S.P.C.K., London, 1960.

Butler, F. W. *Christianity and History*. S.P.C.K., London, 1925.

Butler, Joseph (Bishop). *Fifteen Sermons and A Dissertation upon the Nature of Virtue*. Bell, London, 1914.

Cairns, D. S. *The Reasonableness of the Christian Faith*. Hodder and Stoughton, London, 1924.

Carpenter, S. C. *Christianity*. Penguin Books, London, 1953.

Cullman, Oscar. *Immortality of the Soul or Resurrection of the Dead?* The Epworth Press, London, 1958.

Fison, J. E. *The Faith of the Bible*. Penguin Books, London, 1957.

Gilson, Étienne. *Moral Values and the Moral Life: The Ethical Theory of St Thomas Aquinas*, trans. Leo Richard Ward. The Shoe String Press Inc., 1961.

—— *The Philosophy of St Thomas Aquinas*, authorized translation by Edward Bullough. W. Heffer and Sons, Cambridge, 1929.

—— *The Spirit of Mediaeval Philosophy*, Gifford Lectures, 1931–2, trans. A. H. C. Downes. Sheed and Ward, London, 1936.

Hall, F. J. and F. H. Hallock. *Moral Theology*. Longmans Green and Co., London, 1924.

Henson, H. H. *Christian Morality* (Natural, Developing, Final), Gifford Lectures, 1935–6. Clarendon Press, Oxford, 1936.

Hogg, A. G. *Redemption From This World*, or The Supernatural in Christianity, Cunningham Lectures, 1921. T. and T. Clark, Edinburgh, 1922.

Holy Bible, The, Two-Version Edition, Oxford University Press, London and New York, 1899.

Kirk, Kenneth E. (ed.). *The Study of Theology*. Hodder and Stoughton, London, 1939.

Lecky, W. E. H. *History of European Morals from Augustus to Charlemagne*. 2 vols. Longman, Green and Co., London, 1884.

Lehman, Paul L. *Ethics in a Christian Context*. The Library of Philosophy and Theology. SCM Press, London, 1963.

Luther, Martin. *The Bondage of the Will:* Reply to Erasmus, trans. J. I. Packer and O. R. Johnston. James Clarke and Co., London, 1957.

Mellone, S. H. *Leaders of Early Christian Thought*. The Lindsey Press, London, 1954.

Mercier, Cardinal and others. *A Manual of Modern Scholastic Philosophy*, authorized translation by T. L. Parker and S. A. Parker, Vol. II. Routledge and Kegan Paul, 1950.

Mortimer, R. C. *Christian Ethics*. Hutchinson, London, 1950.

Neill, Stephen. *The Christian Character*. World Christian Books No. 6. United Society for Christian Literature. Lutterworth Press, London, 1956.

Niebuhr, Reinhold. *An Interpretation of Christian Ethics*. SCM Press, London, 1936.

—— *The Nature and Destiny of Man: A Christian Interpretation*. 2 vols. Nisbet and Co., London, 1941–3.

Paton, William. *Jesus Christ and the World's Religions*. The Cargate Press, London, 1928.

Quick, O. C. *Christianity and Justice*. Sheldon Press, London, 1940.

Ramsey, Paul. *Basic Christian Ethics*. SCM Press, London, 1953.

Rickaby, Joseph. *Moral Philosophy* (or Ethics and Natural Law). Manuals of Catholic Philosophy, Stonyhurst Series. Longmans, Green and Co., London, 1892.

Rommen, H. A. *The Natural Law*, trans. Thomas R. Hanley. B. Herder Book Co., St Louis and London, 1949.

Salmond, S. D. F. *The Christian Doctrine of Immortality*. T. and T. Clark, Edinburgh, 1913.

Santayana, George. *The Idea of Christ in the Gospels or God in Man*. Charles Scribner's Sons, New York, 1946.

Thomas, W. H. Griffith. *The Catholic Faith* (A Manual of Instruction for Members of the Church of England). Church Book Room Press, London, 1955.

Trench, Richard Chenevix (Archbishop). *Notes on the Parables of Our Lord*. Routledge and Kegan Paul, London, 1910.

Whale, J. S. *Christian Doctrine*. Fontana Books, London, 1963.

Articles and Essays

Mackenzie, D. 'Christian Ethics and Morality', *Encyclopaedia of Religion and Ethics*, Vol. V, ed. James Hastings. T. and T. Clark, Edinburgh, 1912.

McPherson, Thomas. 'Christian Virtues', *Aristotelian Society Proceedings*, Supplementary Volume, 1963.

Taubes, Jacob. 'Virtue and Faith', *Philosophy East and West*, Vol. VII, April–July 1957.

II. ON HINDUISM AND HINDU ETHICS

Sanskrit Texts and Translations

Atharva Veda Saṃhitā, ed. D. Satvalekar. Swādhyāya Mandal, Paradi, 1957.

The Bhagavadgītā, with an Introductory Essay, Sanskrit Text, English Translation and Notes by S. Radhakrishnan. George Allen and Unwin, London, 1960.

The Mahābhārata, edited under the auspices of the Committee of Public Instruction, Govt. of Bengal, and the Asiatic Society of Bengal. Education Committee Press, and Baptist Mission Press, Calcutta, 1834–9.

The Manusmṛti, ed. Nārāyaṇ Rām Āchārya 'Kāvyatīrtha'. Nirṇaya Sāgar Press, Bombay, 1946: G. Bühler, trans., *The Laws of Manu*, Clarendon Press, Oxford, 1886.

Rig-Veda-Samhitā, ed. F. Max Müller. 4 vols. Henry Frowde: Oxford University Press, London, 1890; R. T. H. Griffith, trans., *The Hymns of the Rigveda*, 2 vols., E. J. Lazarus & Co., Benares, 1920–6.

Śukla Yajurveda Saṃhitā, ed. Wāsudeva Laxmaṇ Shāstrī Pansīkar. Nirṇaya Sāgar Press, Bombay, 1912.

The Upaniṣads: A Compilation of Well-Known 120 Upaniṣads, ed. Nārāyaṇ Rām Āchārya 'Kāvyatīrtha'. Nirṇaya Sāgar Press, Bombay, 1948: R. E. Hume, trans., *The Thirteen Principal Upanishads*, Oxford University Press, London, 1921.

Other Sources—Books

Aiyer, Sivaswamy P. S. *Evolution of Hindu Moral Ideals*. Kamala Lectures. Calcutta University Press, 1935.

Benton, A. H. *Indian Moral Reconstruction and Caste Problems*. Longmans, Green and Co., London, 1917.

Dasgupta, S. N. *A History of Indian Philosophy*, Vols. I–V. Cambridge University Press, 1922–55.

Deussen, Paul. *The Philosophy of the Upanishads*, authorized English translation by Rev. A. S. Geden. T. and T. Clark, Edinburgh, 1906.

Eliot, (Sir) Charles. *Hinduism and Buddhism*. 3 vols. Routledge and Kegan Paul, London, 1954.

George, S. K. *Gandhi's Challenge to Christianity*. Navajivan Publishing House, Ahmedabad, 1947.

Hopkins, E. W. *Ethics of India*. Yale University Press, New Haven; Humphrey Milford: Oxford University Press, London, 1924.

Lefever, Henry. *The Vedic Idea of Sin*. London Mission Press, Nagercoil, Travancore, India, 1935.

Mackenzie, John. *Hindu Ethics.* The Religious Quest of India Series. Humphrey Milford: Oxford University Press, 1922.
Maitra, S. K. *The Ethics of the Hindus.* Calcutta University Press, 1925.
Mangalvedkar, V. *The Philosophy of Action of Lokmanya B. G. Tilak's Githarahasya.* Indian Literature Publishers, Madras, 1919.
Mees, G. H. *Dharma and Society.* Luzac and Co., London, 1935.
Nikhilananda, Swamy. *Hinduism.* (World Perspectives). George Allen and Unwin, London, 1959.
Radhakrishnan, S. *The Hindu View of Life.* George Allen and Unwin, London, 1963.
—— *The Philosophy of the Upaniṣads.* George Allen and Unwin, London, 1924.
Ray, Benoy Gopel. *Gandhian Ethics.* Navajivan Publishing House, Ahmedabad, 1950.
Schweitzer, Albert. *Indian Thought and Its Development,* trans. Mrs C. E. B. Russell. Adam and Charles Black, London, 1951.
Scott, E. W. *Social Ethics in Modern Hinduism.* Y.M.C.A. Publishing House, Calcutta, 1953.
Thadani, N. V. (trans.). *Mimamsa: The Secret of the Sacred Books of the Hindus.* Bharati Research Institute, Delhi, 1952.
Zaehner, R. C. *Hinduism.* Oxford University Press, 1962.

Articles and Essays

Gauchwal, Balbir Singh. 'The Sphere and Significance of Ethics, Morality and Religion in Hindu Tradition', *Philosophy East and West,* Vol. XIII, No. 4, January 1964.
Ingalla, Daniel H. H. 'Dharma and Mokṣa', *Philosophy East and West,* Vol. VII, April–July 1957.
Jolly, J. 'Hindu Ethics and Morality', *Encyclopaedia of Religion and Ethics,* ed. James Hastings, Vol. V., T. and T. Clark, Edinburgh, 1912.
Van Buitenen, J. A. B. 'Dharma and Mokṣa', *Philosophy East and West,* Vol. VII, April–July 1957.

III. GENERAL, PHILOSOPHICAL AND COMPARATIVE WORKS

Books

Aristotle. *The Works of Aristotle,* ed. W. D. Ross. Vol. IX. Oxford University Press, 1940.
Armstrong, Arthur Hilary and R. A. Markus. *Christian Faith and Greek Philosophy.* Darton, Longman and Todd, London, 1960.
Bouquet, A. C. *Comparative Religion.* Penguin Books, London, 1962.
Brandon, S. G. F. *Man and His Destiny in the Great Religions.* Wilde Lectures, 1954– . Manchester University Press, 1962.
Cave, Sydney. *Redemption: Hindu and Christian.* The Religious Quest of India Series. Oxford University Press, 1919.

Flew, Antony and Alasdaire McIntyre (eds.). *New Essays in Philosophical Theology*. SCM Press, London, 1963.

Frankena, William K. *Ethics*. Prentice Hall Inc., N.J., 1963.

Hirst, E. W. *Jesus and the Moralists:* A Comparative Study of the Christian Ethic. The Epworth Press, London, 1935.

James, William. *Varieties of Religious Experience*. Longmans Green and Co., London, 1929.

Jones, Henry. *A Faith that Inquires*. Gifford Lectures, 1920–1. Macmillan, London, 1922.

Lewis, H. D. *Morals and the New Theology*. Victor Gollancz, London, 1947.

—— *Morals and Revelation*. George Allen and Unwin, London, 1951.

Mackenzie, John. *Two Religions*. (A Comparative Study of Some Distinctive Ideas and Ideals in Hinduism and Christianity, being the Croall Lectures for 1948.) Lutterworth Press, London, 1950.

Maclagan, W. G. *The Theological Frontier of Ethics*. An essay based on the Edward Cadbury Lectures at the University of Birmingham (1955–6). George Allen and Unwin, London, 1961.

Mill, John Stuart. *Three Essays on Religion*. (2nd ed.). Longmans, Green, Reader and Dyer, London, 1874.

Mitchell, Basil (ed.). *Faith and Logic*. George Allen and Unwin, London, 1958.

Nowell-Smith, P. H. *Ethics*. Basil Blackwell, Oxford, 1957.

Radhakrishnan, S. *Eastern Religions and Western Thought*. Oxford University Press, London, 1940.

Reid, L. A. *Creative Morality*. George Allen and Unwin, London, 1936.

Schlick, Moritz. *Problems of Ethics*, authorized translation by David Rynin. Prentice Hall, Inc., New York, 1939.

Schweitzer, Albert. *Civilization and Ethics*. George Allen and Unwin, London, 1961.

Smart, Ninian. *A Dialogue of Religions*. The Library of Philosophy and Theology. SCM Press, London, 1960.

Smith, Huston. *The Religions of Man*. Harper and Row, New York, 1964.

Sneath, E. Hershey (ed.). *The Evolution of Ethics*. As revealed in the great Religions. Yale University Press, New Haven, 1927.

Article

Verdenius, W. J. 'Plato and Christianity', *Ratio*, Vol. V, No. 1, June 1963.

INDEX

Note: Names of Authors and details of works quoted in this book will be found in the Bibliography on pages 209–13.

Adam 94, 186, 187; fall of 161; sin of 193
Adharma 62, 112
Agapism 119
Ahiṃsā 203, 204
All-soul, the 69
Ambrose, St 129
Antinomianism 104
Aquinas, St Thomas 48, 49, 110, 114, 155; influence of 49
Aristotle on responsibility 179
Artha 122
Atharva Veda 56, 60
Ātman 88, 89, 97, 98, 100, 172, 173, 174
Augustine, St 46, 107, 161, 164; and virtues 141
Austerity 60
Avidya 98, 185

Bhagavadgītā 124. *See also* Gītā
Bible, the 29
Brahman 59, 69, 80, 81, 100
Brahman-Ātman, doctrine of 68
Buddhism 172; pessimism of 101

Categorical Imperative 50, 106
Catholicism and fellowship with God, 104
Christian 26; attitude to Hinduism 14; belief in Man 87; and destiny 103; doctrine of man 84; doctrine of Grace 160, 164 ff.; doctrine of Sin 160, 161, 164; and Hindu virtues 151 ff.; meaning of 20, 24; and moral values 71; morality and sex 48; and sin 190; tradition and creation myth 76 f.; view of Man 93 f.; view of virtue 134–41; West, the 13. *See also* Christian ethics *and* Christianity
Christian Divine Imperative 50, 51
Christian ethics 30, 39, 51, 71 f.; background of 32; exponents of 51; later history 48; and love 200; nature of 31 ff.; outstanding features 200 ff.; sources of 32, 33. *See also* Christian *and* Christianity
Christianity 13, 19, 28, 71, 73, 83; authentic doctrine of 77; and collective responsibility 193–6; doctrine of Original Sin 181 f.; features of 204–5; Greek belief 43; history of 198; and Inherited Corruption and Guilt 186; and moral law 107 f., 114 ff., 128; and transcendence 102–3. *See also* Christian *and* Christian ethics
Christians 13, 15, 21
Church, the 128
Church of England, doctrine of 166
Class, institution of 52
Collective guilt 194
Collective responsibility 192
Commission on Christian Doctrine, Report on 166
Conservation of Energy, Law of 174
Corruption, total 162–4
Creation 82, 83, 101; myths 76 ff.

Decalogue 36, 110, 134 f.
Defiance, greatest sin 94 f.
Destiny 105; of man 75 ff.
Dharma 21, 22, 24, 55 ff., 62, 64, 65, 68, 111, 112, 113, 114, 122, 124, 125, 126, 133, 142, 144, 185, 204
Dharma Shastras 130
Divine Law 36
Divine punishment 186
Duty and duties 106, 117, 122, 123, 124, 126, 131, 145, 147; discharge of 125

East, the 13
Ego 99
End, the 75
Epics, ethics of 65
Eroticism 74
Eternal Law 113
Eternal life 22
Ethical fruitfulness 102
Ethics 18 f., 22 ff.; Christian and Hindu resemblance 197; and love 201; meaning of 20
Eudaemonia 43, 50

Fall, the 93, 161, 193; effect of 98
Four desirable ends 22
Freedom 180; absolute 198

Gandhi 17, 204; and non-violence 202
Gītā 29, 61, 68, 80, 82, 88, 90, 97, 99, 124, 125, 126, 127, 176; ethics of 131; on duties 145

Index

God, creation of 76; and disobedience 98–9; and goodness 78; love of 119; need of 84; obligation to obey 118; responsibility of 124; and universe 79; verdict of 86; Will of 50, 102, 109, 115, 118
Godhead 115
Grace, Christian doctrine of 160, 164 ff.; Hindu doctrine of 171, 172; theories of 167
Graeco-Roman influence 46, 48
Greek influences 43
Guilt, inherited and original 161–4

Hindu belief 80; classifications 205–6; concept of collective responsibility 196; concept of sin 182 f.; cosmology 80; doctrines 171, 172, 187–9; history 198; institutions 207; literature 53; meaning of 20, 26 f.; objection to Christian wars 200; philosophy of non-violence 200; scriptures 14, 29; tradition and man 88; tradition, creation myths in 79 ff.; view of destiny of man 97 ff.; view of man 87–92; virtues 147. *See also* Hindu ethics *and* Hinduism
Hindu ethics 16, 30, 32, 33, 69, 71 f., 205; growth of 53; nature of 31 ff.; outstanding features of 200 ff.; sources and development of 52 ff.
Hinduism 13, 14 f., 19, 28, 71, 83; features of 204–5; and human freedom 169 ff.; and the individual 52; and moral law 111–14; and moral life 120; pessimism of 101; and sin 170, 191; and transcendence 102–3; and virtues 142–51. *See also* Hindu *and* Hindu ethics
Hindus 13, 15, 21; beliefs of 80; and Christian ideas 17; and destiny 103; and *Dharma* 55; and the killing of animals 202–3; and knowledge of moral law 129 ff.; and moral values 71; and political power 14; and spiritualism 199; and vegetarianism 57. *See also* Hindu *and* Hinduism
Holy Father 57
Human freedom 157 ff.; Christian doctrine of 161, 164 ff.; Hindu doctrine of 169

Ignorance 98, 99, 172, 185
India 13, 200; ethics of 199; Christians in 14; and human material 73; poet-saints of 81, 92; Western colonization of 14
Inherited Corruption 181; and Guilt 186
Inherited Guilt 181; and responsibility 185
Īsa Upaniṣad 81–2
Islam 71

Jainism 172, 203
Jesus Christ 17, 32, 34, 96, 136, 204; catholicity of 72, 73; life and teaching of 38 ff.; as model 137; and rewards 116; and Sermon on the Mount 201
Jews 35 ff.; ethics of 36; morality of 35
Judaeo-Christian tradition 136
Judaic inheritance 34
Judaism 34, 107
Justice, exercise of 133

Kāma 22
Kāmanā 120
Kant, Immanuel, 106, 119, 120, 124; ethics of 50 f.
Karma 27, 62, 80, 99, 172, 174, 175, 176, 177, 187; Law of 55 ff., 62, 63, 83, 90, 99, 185, 188
Kaṭha Upaniṣad 62
Kingdom of God 96, 97, 101, 103
Knowledge of moral law 127 ff.
Krishna, Śri 81; advice to Arjuna 100, 203

Law, allegiance to 131
Law of Conservation and energy 56
Law of *Karma*. See *Karma*
Liberation 62 f., 90, 91, 92 f., 142
Love 199; and gratitude 73; philosophy of 200

Mahānārāyaṇa Upaniṣad 111
Mahésa 81
Man: Christian belief 84; final destiny of 92–104; and God, differences between 84; Hindu view of 88–92; likeness to God 84, 85; nature and status 83–88; potential greatness of 157; responsibility of 92; and sin 94 f.; status of 91, 92
Manu 144, 147; and conscience 130; list of duties 145–6
Māyā (Cosmic Ignorance) 63, 69
Mīmamṣā 80, 114, 121
Mokṣa 22, 23, 62, 68, 69, 70, 90, 91, 100, 103, 105, 142, 143, 203; meaning of 63
Moral effort 102–4, 157 ff.
Moral failure 177 ff.
Moral Imperative 120
Moral Law 59, 60, 105–30; authority of 114 ff.; contents of 131–56; knowledge of 127 ff.; nature and source 107; and Order 54; and Will of God 123

Moral Order 59, 60
Moral responsibility 177 ff., 159
Morality 19, 54, 75, 198
Muslims 25

Naiyāyikas 120, 122, 123
Nature, Law of 111
Nature of man 75 ff.
Nicene Creed 25, 29, 31
Nīmāmṣā system 27 n.
Nivṛtti Mārta 68
Non-dualism 24, 68, 69
Non-violence and Hindus 201
Nyāya-Vaiséṣeka 83; theory of creation 80

Original Guilt 182
Original Sin 162, 173; Christian doctrine of 181–2; Hindu doctrine of 182 f.; and responsibility 181 ff.

Pāramārthika Sattā 69
Paramātman 80
Passion Mysticism 49, 50
Paul, St 32, 86, 89, 108, 136, 137; and Stoics 46
Perfect Being 109
Plato 76
Platonic Utopia 208
Prabhahara and Dharma 121–2
Prakṛti 80, 100, 124
Prashastapada's list of duties 146–7
Prasthānatrayī 70
Pre-existence 87, 90
Primal Being 60
Protestant view of redemption 97
Puraṇās 65
Purisārthas, theory 27
Purusa 80

Rabbinical casuistry 36, 37
Radhakrishnan, Dr S. 26, 68, 70, 72, 89, 91, 175, 176, 199
Ramanuja 80, 100, 122–3, 171; ethics of 70; influence of 69
Redemption 92 ff., 103
Religion 18 f.
Renunciation 125
Responsibility, collective 192; condition of 180; determination of 179; and unintentional sin 189
Resurrection, Christian doctrine 87; St Paul's doctrine 86
Right and reason, law of 112
Righteousness 103
Roman influences 43

Sāṃkhya 68, 80, 114, 147; system 27
Saṃsāra 62, 63, 89, 90, 98, 100, 187
Sanātama Dharma 113
Scribes 37
Scriptural Imperative 120–2
Scriptures 128
Self-mortification 60
Sermon on the Mount 136
Shaṃkara 16, 24, 69, 70 f., 100; and *Ātman* 81
Shāṃkara-Vedañta 147, 176
Shridhara's belief 192
Sin 94 f., 143, 177, 181 ff., 195, 196; Christian doctrine of 160 ff.; Hindu belief 170; unintentional 189 ff.
Smṛtis 129, 130
Soul, the 63; Hindu view 90; immortal 89
Spirit 80
Spiritual freedom 70
Status of man 91, 92
Stoic: concept of World-Reason 107, 108; philosophy 46
Supreme, the 68; God 27; Reason 80, 100; Self 81

Tapas concept of 60
Teittirīya Upaniṣad 144
Ten Commandments 134 f. *See also* Decalogue
Ten Commandments of Manu 144
Theological Committee of the Faith and Order Movement 166
Thomas, St 77, 78, 86, 109, 110, 118, 119, 123, 135, 147; and virtues 140. *See also* Aquinas, St Thomas
Thomas, St (à Kempis) 49
Torah 36, 56, 108
Total Corruption 181–2
Transmigration 90

Ultimate Good 23
Universal sin 193
Upaniṣads 16, 29, 57, 63, 65, 69, 129; ethics of 61 ff., 70

Vaisnavism 73
Varna, institution of 207
Varṇa-Āśrama 206, 207, 208
Varṇa-Āśram Dharma 52, 113
Vedānta 142
Vedas 27, 29, 53 f., 60, 61, 65, 129
Vedic: animal sacrifices 203–4; Hindus 59, 60; idea of sin 183–4; injunction on sacrifice 120; literature 52
Vices 149
Virtues, classification of 134 ff., definition of 132 f.; and duties 131 ff.; intellectual 141; seven fundamental 139 f.; and vices 139 f.
Viśṇu 81

World, creation of 79
World-Reason 107

Yoga 27, 68, 80

For Product Safety Concerns and Information please contact our EU
representative GPSR@taylorandfrancis.com
Taylor & Francis Verlag GmbH, Kaufingerstraße 24, 80331 München, Germany

www.ingramcontent.com/pod-product-compliance
Lightning Source LLC
Chambersburg PA
CBHW052112300426
44116CB00010B/1642
* 9 7 8 0 3 6 7 1 4 3 6 6 4 *